Wiley Study Guide for
2015 Level I CFA Exam

Volume 3: Financial Reporting & Analysis

Thousands of candidates from more than 100 countries have relied on these Study Guides to pass the CFA® Exam. Covering every Learning Outcome Statement (LOS) on the exam, these review materials are an invaluable tool for anyone who wants a deep-dive review of all the concepts, formulas and topics required to pass.

Originally published by Elan Guides, this study material was produced by CFA® Charterholders, CFA® Institute members, and investment professionals. In 2014 John Wiley & Sons, Inc. purchased the rights to Elan Guides content, and now this material is part of the Wiley Efficient Learning suite of exam review products. For more information, contact us at info@efficientlearning.com.

Wiley Study Guide for 2015 Level I CFA Exam

Volume 3: Financial Reporting & Analysis

WILEY

Contents

STUDY SESSION 7: FINANCIAL REPORTING AND ANALYSIS: AN INTRODUCTION

READING 22: FINANCIAL STATEMENT ANALYSIS: AN INTRODUCTION

LESSON 1: FINANCIAL STATEMENT ANALYSIS: AN INTRODUCTION

LOS 22a: Describe the roles of financial reporting and financial statement analysis. Vol 3, pp 6–11

Role of financial statement reporting: To provide information about a company's financial performance, financial position, and changes in financial position.

Role of financial statement analysis: To assess a company's past performance and evaluate its future prospects using financial reports along with other relevant company information. Assessments are performed prior to making an investing decision, offering any credit facilities, or making other economic decisions related to the company.

A company's performance can be examined through profitability (ability to generate profits from core business activities) and cash flow (ability to generate cash receipts in excess of cash payments) measures. A forecast of the expected amount of future cash flows is important in determining the company's ability to meet its obligations.
- Liquidity refers to a company's ability to meet its short-term obligations.
- Solvency refers to a company's ability to meet its long-term obligations.

LOS 22b: Describe the roles of the key financial statements (statement of financial position, statement of comprehensive income, statement of changes in equity, and statement of cash flows) in evaluating a company's performance and financial position. Vol 3, pp 11–24

Companies prepare financial statements to report their operating performance to investors and creditors.

Statement of Comprehensive Income (or Income Statement plus Statement of Other Comprehensive Income)

The income statement is also known as the statement of operations or profit and loss statement. It provides operating information relating to a company's business activities over a period of time (the accounting period). The income statement presents revenues earned by a company and corresponding costs. The difference between a company's total revenue and total costs equals net income.

> Income statements and other comprehensive income (and the statement of comprehensive income) are discussed in more detail in Reading 25.

$$\text{Net income} = \text{Revenue} - \text{Expenses}$$

Income statements are useful in evaluating a company's profitability and therefore are an important source of information for financial statement analysis.

Balance Sheet

Balance sheets, also known as statements of financial position, present a company's assets, liabilities, and equity at a point in time. The interrelationships between these three components of the balance sheet is presented in the basic accounting equation:

$$\text{Assets} = \text{Liabilities} + \text{Owners' equity}$$

Assets are the productive resources that a company owns. Liabilities are amounts that the company owes other entities. Owners' equity represents shareholders' residual claim on the company's assets after deducting liabilities.

$$\text{Owners' equity} = \text{Assets} - \text{Liabilities}$$

The information contained in balance sheets is used to assess a company's financial position and to evaluate its ability to meet short-term and long-term obligations. We will learn more about balance sheets in Reading 26.

Cash Flow Statement

A cash flow statement reports the various sources of cash receipts and cash payments. The statement classifies the sources and uses of cash into operating, investing, and financing activities.

- Operating activities refer to the day-to-day core business activities of a company.
- Investing activities relate to the acquisition or disposal of long-term assets.
- Financing activities relate to the injection or repayment of capital.

Cash flow statements reflect a company's ability to generate cash from its core business activities. It is desirable that a company generates most of its cash from operating activities, as opposed to investing and financing activities. A company's sources and uses of cash provide valuable insight into its liquidity and solvency levels and its financial flexibility (ability to react and adapt to financial adversities and investment opportunities). We will learn more about cash flow statements in Reading 27.

Statement of Changes in Owners' Equity

This statement reports any changes in owners' investment in the business. It is useful in understanding changes in the financial position of a company. We will learn more about this statement in Reading 26.

LOS 22c: Describe the importance of financial statement notes and supplementary information—including disclosures of accounting policies, methods, and estimates—and management's commentary. **Vol 3, pp 24–27**

Financial Notes and Supplementary Information

Financial notes are an important part of financial statements because they provide detailed explanatory information about the following:

- Accounting policies, methods, and estimates
- Business acquisitions and disposals
- Commitments and contingencies
- Legal proceedings
- Subsequent events
- Related-party transactions
- Business and geographic segments
- Financial instruments and risks arising from them

Footnotes contain important details about the accounting methods, estimates, and assumptions that have been used by the company in preparing its financial statements. For example, information about the choice of revenue recognition method used and assumptions made to calculate depreciation expense are typically found in the footnotes. The availability of such information facilitates comparisons between companies that prepare their financial statements in accordance with different accounting standards (**IFRS** vs. **U.S. GAAP**). Note that financial statement footnotes are also audited.

Management's Discussion and Analysis (MD&A)

The management discussion and analysis section (required under **U.S. GAAP**) highlights important trends and events that affect a company's liquidity, capital resources, and operations. Management also discusses prospects for the upcoming year with respect to inflation, future goals, material events, and uncertainties. The section must also discuss critical accounting policies that require management to make subjective judgments and have a material impact on the financial statements. Although it contains important information, analysts should bear in mind that the MD&A section is not audited.

IFRS is in the process of finalizing a framework to provide guidance relating to items that should be discussed in management commentary. These items include:
- The nature of the business
- Management objectives and strategies
- The company's significant resources, risks, and relationships
- Results of operations
- Critical performance measures

LOS 22d: Describe the objective of audits of financial statements, the types of audit reports, and the importance of effective internal controls. Vol 3, pp 27–30

The financial statements presented in a company's annual report must be audited. They must be examined by an independent accounting firm (or audit practitioner) which then states its opinion on the financial statements. Audits are required by contractual arrangement, law, or regulation.

Objective of audits: Under International Standards for Auditing, objectives of an auditor are:

1. To obtain reasonable assurance about whether the financial statements as a whole are free from material misstatement, whether due to fraud or error, thereby enabling the auditor to express an opinion on whether the financial statements are prepared, in all material respects, in accordance with an applicable financial reporting frame-work; and
2. To report on the financial statements, and communicate as required by the ISAs, in accordance with the auditor's findings.[1]

Types of Audit Opinions

- An unqualified opinion states that the financial statements have been presented *fairly* in accordance with applicable accounting standards.
- A qualified opinion states that the financial statements have been presented fairly, but do contain exception(s) to the accounting standards. The audit report provides further details and explanations relating to the exception(s).
- An adverse opinion states that the financial statements have *not* been presented fairly and significantly deviate from acceptable accounting standards.
- A disclaimer of opinion is issued when the auditor, for whatever reason, is not able to issue an opinion on the financial statements.

Internal controls: The internal control system of a company seeks to ensure the reliability of processes used by the company in preparing its financial statements. In the United States, management is responsible for the effectiveness of internal control, to evaluate the effectiveness of internal control, to support the evaluation, and to provide a report on internal control.

LOS 22e: Identify and describe information sources that analysts use in financial statement analysis besides annual financial statements and supplementary information. Vol 3, pp 31–32

- Interim reports are prepared either semiannually or quarterly. They contain the four financial statements and footnotes, but are not audited.

- Proxy statements are distributed to shareholders when there are matters that require a shareholder vote. They provide information about management and director compensation, company stock performance, and potential conflicts of interest between management, the board of directors, and shareholders.

---

1 - See the International Auditing and Assurance Standards Board (IAASB) *Handbook of International Quality Control, Auditing, Review, Other Assurance, and Related Services Pronouncements.*

- Press releases, in addition to a company's website and conference calls, provide current information about the company.

- External sources provide information about the economy, the industry that the company operates in, and the company's competitors. Such information is useful as it allows the analyst to place the company's performance in perspective. Examples of external sources include trade journals and government agencies.

LOS 22f: Describe the steps in the financial statement analysis framework. Vol 3, pp 31–32

A generic framework for financial statement analysis involves the following steps:

1. Define the purpose and context of the analysis

   In cases where the task is well-defined, the purpose is governed by institutional norms. However, there are also analytical tasks that require the analyst's discretion in defining the purpose. The definition of the purpose determines the approach, tools, data sources, and the format used to present results. In this preliminary stage, the analyst is also required to define the context of the analysis, which requires understanding the audience, the time frame, and the resources available for completion of the task.

2. Collect data

   The analyst acquires the necessary information to answer the questions that were defined in the previous stage. For instance, a task with the purpose of analyzing the historical performance of a company could be carried out by understanding the financial statements alone. However, a more thorough analysis that requires understanding a company's financial performance and position relative to the industry would require collecting industry data as well.

3. Process data

   The financial information collected is converted into ratios, growth rates, common-size financial statements, charts, and regressions.

4. Analyze/interpret the processed data

   The data is interpreted and a recommendation is reached.

5. Develop and communicate conclusions

   An appropriate format for the presentation of analysis is determined. The presentation format is sometimes determined by regulatory authorities or professional standards.

6. Follow up

   Financial statement analysis does not end with the preparation of a recommendation report. When equity analysis is performed or a credit rating is assigned, periodic reviews are required to determine whether previously drawn conclusions remain valid.

See Table 1-1.

Table 1-1: Financial Statement Analysis Framework[2]

Phase	Sources of Information	Output
1. Articulate the purpose and context of the analysis	• The nature of the analyst's function, such as evaluating an equity or debt investment or issuing a credit rating • Communication with client or supervisor on needs and concerns • Institutional guidelines related to developing specific work product	• Statement of the purpose or objective of analysis • A list (written or unwritten) of specific questions to be answered by the analyst • Nature and content of report to be provided • Timetable and budgeted resources for completion
2. Collect data	• Financial statements, other financial data, questionnaires, and industry/economic data • Discussions with management, suppliers, customers, and competitors • Company site visits (e.g., to production facilities or retail stores)	• Organized financial statements • Financial data tables • Completed questionnaires, if applicable
3. Process data	• Data from the previous phase	• Adjusted financial statements • Common-size statements • Ratios and graphs • Forecasts
4. Analyze/interpret the processed data	• Input data as well as processed data	• Analytical results
5. Develop and communicate conclusions and recommendations (e.g., with an analysis report)	• Analytical results and previous reports • Institutional guidelines for published reports	• Analytical report answering questions posed in phase 1 • Recommendation regarding the purpose of the analysis, such as whether to make an investment or grant credit
6. Follow up	• Information gathered by periodically repeating above steps as necessary to determine whether changes to holdings or recommendations are necessary	• Updated reports and recommendations

---

2 - Components of this framework have been adapted from van Greuning and Bratanovic (2003, p. 300) and from Benninga and Sarig (1997, pp. 134–156).

READING 23: FINANCIAL REPORTING MECHANICS

LESSON 1: CLASSIFICATION OF BUSINESS ACTIVITIES AND FINANCIAL STATEMENT ELEMENTS AND ACCOUNTS

Business activities are classified into three categories for financial reporting purposes:

Operating Activities

These are related to the day-to-day business activities of a company. Typical activities that fall in this category are:

- Sales of goods and services to customers.
- Costs associated with the provision of goods and services.
- Income tax expenses.
- Investments in working capital to support the firm's ordinary business.

Investing Activities

These are related to the acquisition and disposal of long-term assets. Examples of transactions that fall in this category include:

- Acquisition or disposal of fixed assets like property, plant, and equipment (PP&E).
- Purchase or sale of other corporations' equity and debt securities.

Financing Activities

These are related to raising and repaying capital. Examples of financing activities include:

- Issuance or repurchase of common or preferred stock.
- Issuance or redemption of debt.
- Dividend payments on common and preferred stock.

The nature of a firm's operations dictates where certain transactions fall within these classifications. For example, interest received on an investment in a debt instrument by a music store is classified as an investing activity, but interest received by a bank is classified as an operating activity. The sale of an oven by an oven manufacturer is an operating activity, while the sale of an oven by a restaurant is an investing activity.

Table 1-1: Typical Business Activities and Financial Statement Elements Affected[1]

Type	Business Activity	Elements Affected
Operating activities	• Sale of goods and services to customers • Cost of providing the goods and services • Income tax expense • Holding short-term assets or incurring short-term liabilities directly related to operating activities	Revenue Expenses Expenses Assets, liabilities
Investing activities	• Purchase or sale of assets such as property, plant, and equipment • Purchase or sale of other entities' equity and debt securities	Assets Assets
Financing activities	• Issuance or repurchase of the company's own preferred or common stock • Issuance or repayment of debt • Payment of distributions (i.e., dividends to preferred or common stock holders)	Owners' equity Liabilities Owners' equity

1 - Exhibit 1, Volume 3, CFA Program Curriculum 2014

LOS 23a: Explain the relationship of financial statement elements and accounts, and classify accounts into the financial statement elements. **Vol 3, pp 43–46**

There are five financial statement elements:
- Assets
- Liabilities
- Owners' equity or shareholders' equity
- Revenues
- Expenses

An increase or a decrease in any of these elements is recorded in a specific account. For example, accounts receivable is an account that falls under the financial element of assets.

Financial statements present condensed information regarding financial statement elements and accounts. The actual accounts used in a company's accounting system are listed in a chart of accounts.

Classification of Accounts into Financial Statement Elements

Assets are a company's economic resources. They include:

Current assets:
- Cash and cash equivalents.
- Accounts receivable, trade receivables.
- Prepaid expenses.
- Inventory.

Noncurrent assets:
- Property, plant, and equipment.
- Investment property.
- Intangible assets (patents, trademarks, licenses, copyrights, and goodwill).
- Financial assets, trading securities, and investment securities.
- Investments accounted for by the equity method.

Sometimes contra accounts are used to reduce the balance of certain assets. Common contra asset accounts include allowance for bad debts (offset against accounts receivable) and accumulated depreciation (offset against PP&E).

Liabilities are creditors' claims on a company's economic resources. They include:
- Accounts payable and trade payables.
- Financial liabilities such as notes payable.
- Deferred tax liabilities.
- Long-term debt.
- Unearned revenue.

Owners' equity represents owners' residual claim on a company's resources. It includes:
- Capital in the form of common and preferred stock.
- Additional paid-in capital.
- Retained earnings.
- Other comprehensive income.

Each of the items that comprise the elements of the balance sheet (assets, liabilities, and owners' equity) are discussed in detail in Reading 26.

Revenues represent the flow of economic resources into the company and include:
- Sales.
- Gains.
- Investment income.

Expenses represent the flow of economic resources out of the company, and include:
- Cost of goods sold.
- Selling, general, and administrative expenses.
- Depreciation and amortization expenses.
- Interest expense.
- Tax expense.
- Losses.

> Each of the items that comprise the elements of the income statement (revenues and expenses) are discussed in detail in Reading 25.

For presentation purposes, assets are categorized as current and noncurrent assets.

Noncurrent assets are expected to benefit the company over an extended period of time (usually over one year).

Current assets are expected to be used by the company or converted into cash in the short term (less than one year). Current assets include:
- Inventories: Unsold products on hand (also called inventory stock).
- Trade receivables: Amounts customers owe the company for products that have been sold.
- Cash on hand and at the bank.

LESSON 2: ACCOUNTING EQUATIONS

LOS 23b: Explain the accounting equation in its basic and expanded forms. Vol 3, pp 46–51

The basic accounting equation is:

$$\text{Assets} = \text{Liabilities} + \text{Owners' equity}$$

Owners' equity is the residual claim of the owners on a company's assets after all liabilities have been paid off.

$$\text{Owners' equity} = \text{Assets} - \text{Liabilities}$$

Owners' equity can be further divided into its two components:

$$\text{Owners' equity} = \text{Contributed capital} + \text{Ending retained earnings}$$

Ending retained earnings are calculated as:

Ending retained earnings = Beginning retained earnings + Net income – Dividends declared

The equation for ending retained earnings can also be stated as:

$$\text{Ending retained earnings} = \text{Beginning retained earnings} + \text{Revenue} - \text{Expenses}$$
$$- \text{Dividends declared}$$

Therefore, the basic accounting equation can be expanded into the following forms:

$$\text{Assets} = \text{Liabilities} + \text{Contributed capital} + \text{Ending retained earnings}$$

and:

$$\text{Assets} = \text{Liabilities} + \text{Contributed capital} + \text{Beginning retained earnings}$$
$$+ \text{Revenue} - \text{Expenses} - \text{Dividends declared}$$

Example 2-1

An analyst has the following information regarding XYZ Company:

	(Amounts in millions)
Net income	$225
Beginning retained earnings	$1,250
Dividends declared	$75

Calculate ending retained earnings for 2008.

Solution

$$\text{Ending retained earnings} = \text{Beginning retained earnings} + \text{Net income}$$
$$- \text{Dividends declared}$$

$$\text{Ending retained earnings} = \$1,250 + \$225 - \$75 = \$1,400 \text{ million}$$

Example 2-2

An analyst has the following information regarding ROB Company:

	(Amounts in million)
Revenue earned during the year	$350
Beginning retained earnings	$90
Expenses incurred during the year	$280
Dividends declared for the year	$25
Liabilities	$120
Contributed capital	$75

Calculate ROB's total assets at the end of 2008.

Solution

Step 1:

$$\text{Ending retained earnings} = \text{Beginning retained earnings} + \text{Revenues} - \text{Expenses}$$
$$- \text{Dividends declared}$$

$$\text{Ending retained earnings} = \$90 + \$350 - \$280 - \$25 = \$135 \text{ million}$$

Step 2:

$$\text{Assets} = \text{Liabilities} + \text{Contributed capital} + \text{Ending retained earnings}$$

$$\text{Assets} = \$120 + \$75 + \$135 = \$330 \text{ million}$$

LESSON 3: THE ACCOUNTING PROCESS

LOS 23c: Explain the process of recording business transactions using an accounting system based on the accounting equation. Vol 3, pp 51–65

LOS 23e: Explain the relationships among the income statement, balance sheet, statement of cash flows, and statement of owners' equity. Vol 3, pp 65–68

Remembering the basic accounting equation and understanding which direction the financial elements will move given a certain transaction is EXTREMELY important to do well on the exam.

The process of recording business transactions is based on double-entry accounting (i.e., every transaction affects at least two accounts). If an asset account increases, either a liability or an equity/capital account will also increase, or another asset account will decrease to keep the accounting equation in balance.

Example 3-1 illustrates the process of recording business transactions in an accounting system.

Example 3-1: Recording Transactions in an Accounting System

Sunshine Inc. operates a shoe store. It purchases each pair of shoes for $100 and sells each pair for $150. Sunshine's activities for the month of June are listed below.

No.	Date	Business Activity
1	June 1	Sunshine Inc. started business by depositing $100,000 in its bank account.
2	June 3	Purchased a shop for $55,000 in cash.
3	June 7	Purchased stock of 25 pairs of shoes for $2,500 on credit from suppliers.
4	June 10	Purchased 230 more pairs of shoes on credit for $23,000.
5	June 13	Sold 50 pairs of shoes for $7,500. Received $3,000 in cash and the rest was treated as a receivable.
6	June 15	Sold 20 pairs of shoes for $3,000 cash.
7	June 18	Received $2,500 cash for shoes sold on June 13.
8	June 23	Paid $2,000 cash for shoes bought on June 7. Paid $16,500 cash for shoes bought on June 10. The balance amount is payable after a month.
9	June 30	Received $2,000 for shoes that were sold on credit on June 13.
10	June 30	Paid utility bills amounting to $950. Wages amounting to $2,000 were also paid.

Analysis of Transactions

1. Cash and owners' equity increase by $100,000. (Assets and owners' equity increase.)

2. Premises asset account increases by $55,000 and cash decreases by $55,000. (Noncurrent assets increase and current assets decrease.)

3. Inventory increases by $2,500 and accounts payable increase by $2,500. (Current assets and current liabilities increase.)

4. Inventory and accounts payable increase by $23,000. (Current assets and current liabilities increase.)

5. Cash increases by $3,000 and accounts receivable increase by $4,500. Inventory decreases by the cost of 50 units, $5,000. (Net current assets increase by $2,500.)

   Revenue increases by $7,500 and cost of goods sold (COGS) increases by $5,000. The excess of revenues over COGS contributes to net income and increases owners' equity through retained earnings. (Owners' equity increases by $2,500.)

6. Cash increases by $3,000 while inventory decreases by $2,000. (Net assets increase by $1,000.)

   Sales revenue increases by $3,000 and COGS increase by $2,000. (Owners' equity increases by $1,000.)

7. Cash increases by $2,500, and accounts receivable fall by $2,500. (Total current assets stay at the same level.)

8. Cash and accounts payable fall by $18,500. (Current assets and current liabilities decrease.)

9. Cash increases by $2,000 and accounts receivable decrease by $2,000. (Total current assets stay at the same level.)

10. Cash falls and expenses (utilities) increase by the same amount ($950).
    Cash falls and expenses (wages) increase by the same amount ($2,000).
    (Owners' equity falls by $2,950.)

An increase in expenses reduces net income, retained earnings, and owners' equity.

The following worksheet presents the effects of each transaction.

		Assets			=	Liabilities	Owners' Equity		
Date	Cash	Accounts Receivable	Inventory	Shop Premises	=	Accounts Payable	Owners's Capital	Revenue	Expenses
June 1	100,000				=		100,000		
June 3	(55,000)			55,000	=				
June 7			2,500		=	2,500			
June 10			23,000		=	23,000			
June 13	3,000	4,500	(5,000)		=			7,500	5,000
June 15	3,000		(2,000)		=			3,000	2,000
June 18	2,500	(2,500)			=				
June 23	(2,000)				=	(2,000)			
	(16,500)					(16,500)			
June 30	2,000	(2,000)			=				
June 30	(2,950)				=				2,950
Total	34,050 +	0	+ 18,500 +	55,000	=	7,000	+ 100,000 +	10,500	− 9,950

A final income statement, balance sheet, cash flow statement, and statement of changes in owners' equity can now be prepared reflecting all transactions and adjustments.

Sunshine Inc.
Income Statement
For the month ended June 30, 2008

Notice that income statements are prepared for a period.

	$
Sales revenue	10,500
COGS	(7,000)
Gross Profit	3,500
Expenses	
Wages	2,000
Utility expenses	950
Total Expenses	2,950
Net Income	**550**

Sunshine Inc.
Balance Sheet
As of June 30, 2008

	$
Assets	
Cash	34,050
Accounts receivable	0
Inventory	18,500
Shop premises	55,000
Total Assets	**107,550**
Liabilities and Owners' Equity	
Liabilities	
Accounts payable	7,000
Total liabilities	**7,000**
Owners' Equity	
Contributed capital	100,000
Retained earnings (net income of June 2008)	550
	100,550
Total Liabilities and Owners' Equity	**107,550**

Sunshine Inc.
Statement of Cash Flows
For the month ended June 30, 2008

	$
Cash Flow from Operating Activities	
Cash received from customers	10,500
Cash paid to suppliers	(18,500)
Cash paid for operating expenses	(2,950)
Net Operating Cash Flow	**(10,950)**
Cash Flow from Investing Activities	
Purchase of shop premises	(55,000)
Net Investing Cash Flow	**(55,000)**
Cash Flow from Financing Activities	
Capital contributed by owner	100,000
Net Financing Cash Flow	**100,000**
Net Increase in Cash	**34,050**
Cash balance at June 1, 2008	0
Cash Balance at June 30, 2008	**34,050**

Sunshine Inc.
Statement of Changes in Owners' Equity
For the month ended June 30, 2008

	Contributed Capital $	Retained Earnings $	Total $
Balance at June 1, 2007	100,000	0	100,000
Net income (loss)		550	550
Balance at June 30, 2008	100,000	550	**100,550**

Financial statements are prepared from the data provided by the accounting system. Accounts that fall under revenues and expenses become a part of the income statement. Accounts that fall under assets, liabilities, and owners' equity are used to construct the balance sheet.

Now we will use the example of Sunshine Inc. to illustrate the relationships between different financial statements.

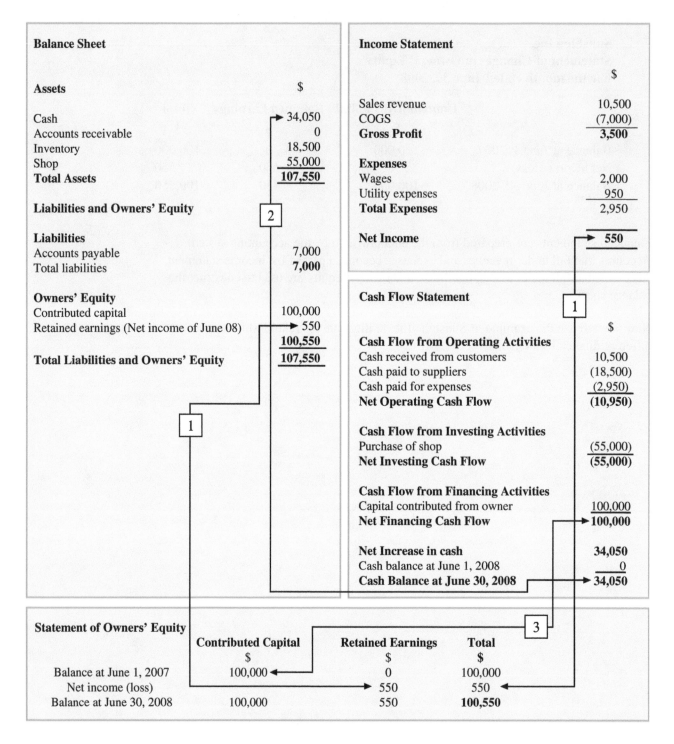

Balance Sheet

Assets	$
Cash	34,050
Accounts receivable	0
Inventory	18,500
Shop	55,000
Total Assets	**107,550**

Liabilities and Owners' Equity

Liabilities	
Accounts payable	7,000
Total liabilities	**7,000**

Owners' Equity	
Contributed capital	100,000
Retained earnings (Net income of June 08)	550
	100,550
Total Liabilities and Owners' Equity	**107,550**

Income Statement

	$
Sales revenue	10,500
COGS	(7,000)
Gross Profit	**3,500**
Expenses	
Wages	2,000
Utility expenses	950
Total Expenses	2,950
Net Income	**550**

Cash Flow Statement

	$
Cash Flow from Operating Activities	
Cash received from customers	10,500
Cash paid to suppliers	(18,500)
Cash paid for expenses	(2,950)
Net Operating Cash Flow	**(10,950)**
Cash Flow from Investing Activities	
Purchase of shop	(55,000)
Net Investing Cash Flow	**(55,000)**
Cash Flow from Financing Activities	
Capital contributed from owner	100,000
Net Financing Cash Flow	**100,000**
Net Increase in cash	34,050
Cash balance at June 1, 2008	0
Cash Balance at June 30, 2008	**34,050**

Statement of Owners' Equity

	Contributed Capital $	Retained Earnings $	Total $
Balance at June 1, 2007	100,000	0	100,000
Net income (loss)		550	550
Balance at June 30, 2008	100,000	550	**100,550**

1) The income statement shows a net income of $550 for June 2008, which, in the absence of dividends, increases retained earnings by $550. This increase is reflected on the statement of shareholders' equity and on the balance sheet under owners' equity.

2) The cash flow statement shows that cash increases by $34,050 over the period. The increase in cash is also seen on the balance sheet under current assets.

3) The owners' capital contribution of $100,000 is listed under cash flow from financing activities. The balance sheet shows this contribution under owners' equity.

LOS 23d: Describe the need for accruals and other adjustments in preparing financial statements. Vol 3, pp 69–72

Accrual Entries

Accrual accounting is based on the principle that revenues should be recognized when earned and expenses should be recognized when incurred, irrespective of when the actual exchange of cash occurs. The timing difference between cash movements and recognition of revenues or expenses explains the need for accrual entries. When cash is transferred in the period that the related revenue/expense is recognized, there is no need for accrual entries. There are four types of accrual entries:

1. Unearned (or deferred) revenue arises when a company receives a cash payment before it provides a good or a service to the customer. Because the company still has to provide the good/service, unearned revenue is recognized as a *liability*. Unearned revenue is subsequently earned once the good is sold or the service is provided.

Example 4-1: Unearned Revenue

On September 30, Nicky receives $1,000 from a tenant as rent for October.

Originating Entry
September 30: Cash (asset) ↑ $1,000
　　　　　　　Unearned rental income (liability) ↑ $1,000

Assets ↑= Liabilities ↑+ Owners' equity

Adjusting Entry
October 31: Unearned rental income (liability) ↓ $1,000
　　　　　　　Rent revenue (income/equity) ↑ $1,000

Assets = Liabilities ↓+ Owners' equity ↑

> Rental income increases net income, retained earnings, and owners' equity.

---

2. Unbilled or accrued revenue arises when a company provides a good or service before receiving the cash payment. Because the company is owed money, accrued revenue is recognized as an *asset*.

Example 4-2: Accrued Revenue

Jelena Inc. provides services worth $5,500 to another company during the month of May. The payment will be received a month later.

Originating Entry
May 31: Accounts receivable (asset) ↑ $5,500
      Revenue (income) ↑ $5,500

Assets ↑ = Liabilities + Owners' equity ↑

Adjusting Entry
June 30 (when payment is received): Cash (asset) ↑ $5,500
                    Accounts receivable (asset) ↓ $5,500

Assets ↑↓ = Liabilities + Owners' equity

3. Prepaid expenses arise when a company makes a cash payment before recognizing the expense. Expenses that have been paid in advance are an *asset* of the company.

Example 4-3: Prepaid Expenses

Aztec Inc. purchased an insurance policy for $1,200 for the year 2008. It made the entire payment on January 1, 2008.

Originating Entry
Jan. 1: Insurance prepaid (asset) ↑ $1,200
      Cash (asset) ↓ $1,200

Assets ↑↓ = Liabilities + Owners' equity

Every month, the company will recognize insurance expense of $100 and reduce the prepaid asset by the same amount. By the end of the year, the entire insurance prepaid asset will be written off and a total insurance expense of $1,200 would have been recognized.

Insurance expense reduces net income, retained earnings, and owners' equity.

Adjusting Entry
Every month: Insurance expense ↑ $100 (owners' equity ↓)
             Insurance prepaid (asset) ↓ $ 100

Assets ↓ = Liabilities + Owners' equity ↓

4. Accrued expenses arise when a company recognizes an expense in its books before actually making a payment for it. Because the company owes a payment, the accrued expense is treated as a *liability*.

Example 4-4: Accrued Expenses

Prudent Inc. owes its employees $2,250 for work performed during the month of March. Wages are actually paid in May.

Originating Entry
March: Wages expense ↑ $2,500 (owners' equity ↓)
　　　　Wages payable (liability) ↑ $2,500

> Assets = Liabilities ↑ + Owners' equity ↓

Adjusting Entry
May: Wages payable (liability) ↓ $2,500
　　　　Cash (asset) ↓ $2,500

> Assets ↓ = Liabilities ↓ + Owners' equity

Exhibit 4-1: Accruals[2]

Cash movement in the same period as accounting recognition

Cash Movement prior to Accounting Recognition

Cash Movement after Accounting Recognition

Settled transaction- no accrual entry needed

Unearned (deferred) Revenue

Originating Entry
Record cash receipt and establish a liability
Adjusting Entry
Reduce the liability and recognize revenue

Unbilled (accrued) Revenue

Originating Entry
Record revenue and establish an asset
Adjusting Entry
When billing occurs, reduce unbilled revenue and increase accounts receivable. When cash is collected, eliminate the receivable

Prepaid Expense

Originating Entry
Record cash payment and establish an asset
Adjusting Entry
Reduce the asset and recognize the expense

Accrued Expenses

Originating Entry
Establish a liability and record an expense
Adjusting Entry
Reduce the liability as cash is paid

---

2 - Exhibit 10, Volume 3, CFA Program Curriculum 2014

Valuation Adjustments

Most assets and liabilities are recorded on the balance sheet at their historical cost. However, accounting standards require certain items to be shown on the balance sheet at their current market values. The upward or downward adjustments to the values of these assets and liabilities are known as valuation adjustments. For example, if there is a decline in the value of an asset, the new decreased value is recorded on the balance sheet and the amount of the decrease in value is recognized as a loss either on the income statement or in other comprehensive income.

LOS 23f: Describe the flow of information in an accounting system. Vol 3, p 72

> Accountants use the terms debit and credit to describe changes in accounts resulting from a transaction. For the purposes of the CFA exam, you do not need to be able to classify accounting entries in terms of debits and credits. In case you are still interested in understanding the system you may want to refer to Appendix 23 on page 77 in Volume 3 of the CFA Program Curriculum 2014.

In an accounting system, information flows through four stages:

- Journal entries: The amount and relevant accounts affected by transactions are chronologically recorded in journals. At the end of the accounting period, adjusting entries are made to journal entries to account for accruals that had not been recorded earlier.

- General ledger: The general ledger sorts all the entries posted in journals into accounts. For example, the general ledger contains an inventory account where all inventory-related journal entries are listed.

- Trial balance: An initial trial balance lists all the ending balances of general ledger accounts. Adjustments to record accruals and prepayments that had not been considered in constructing the initial trial balance are made in the adjusted trail balance.

- Financial statements: The account balances in the adjusted trial balance are used to construct financial statements.

LOS 23g: Describe the use of the results of the accounting process in security analysis. Vol 3, pp 73–74

Financial statements provide the basis for equity and credit analysis. However, analysts must make adjustments to reflect the effects of items not reported in the statements. Analysts must also evaluate management's assumptions regarding accruals and valuations. Information related to most of these assumptions can be found in the significant accounting policies footnote and in the management discussion and analysis (MD&A) section of the annual report.

Since assumptions within the accounting process are, to an extent, in the hands of management, financial statements can be manipulated to misrepresent a company's true financial performance. Companies can recognize fictitious assets and liabilities on the financial statements in an attempt to cover aggressive accounting practices or even fraud. For example, if management wanted to inflate reported revenue, it would also recognize a fictitious asset (a receivable) to balance the accounting equation. On the other hand, if the company has received cash but management does not want to recognize the related revenue, it could create a fictitious liability to keep the accounting equation in balance. We will study incentives for accounting manipulation and keys to detecting such fraudulent practices in later readings.

READING 24: FINANCIAL REPORTING STANDARDS

LESSON 1: FINANCIAL REPORTING STANDARDS

LOS 24a: Describe the objective of financial statements and the importance of financial reporting standards in security analysis and valuation. **Vol 3, pp 100–102**

The International Accounting Standards Board's (IASB's) objective of general purpose financial reporting, as stated in its Conceptual Framework for Financial Reporting 2010 (Conceptual Framework 2010), is to "provide financial information about the reporting entity that is useful to existing and potential investors, lenders, and other creditors in making decisions about providing resources to the entity. Those decisions involve buying, selling, or holding equity and debt instruments, and providing or settling loans and other forms of credit."[1]

The process of developing financial reporting standards is quite complicated. Some transactions do not necessarily have one correct treatment, so standards are set with the aim of achieving some degree of consistency in the treatment of these transactions. Therefore, the IASB and U.S. Financial Accounting Standards Board (FASB) have developed similar frameworks for financial reporting.

Financial statements are not designed only to facilitate asset valuation; they provide information to a host of users (e.g., creditors, employees, and customers). At the same time, they do provide important inputs for the asset-valuation process. For analysts, it is extremely important to understand how and when judgments and subjective estimates affect the financial statements. Such an understanding is important to evaluate the wisdom of business decisions, and to make comparisons between companies.

LOS 24b: Describe roles and desirable attributes of financial reporting standard-setting bodies and regulatory authorities in establishing and enforcing reporting standards, and describe the role of the International Organization of Securities Commissions. **Vol 3, pp 103–111**

The Role of Standard-Setting Bodies and Regulatory Authorities

Standard-setting bodies, such as the IASB and FASB, are private sector organizations of accountants and auditors that *develop* financial reporting rules, regulations, and accounting standards. Regulatory authorities, like the Securities and Exchange Commission (SEC) in the United States, and Financial Standards Authority (FSA) in the United Kingdom have legal authority to *enforce* financial reporting requirements, and can overrule private sector standard-setting bodies. Standard-setting bodies have no authority unless their standards are recognized by regulatory authorities.

---

1 - *Conceptual Framework (2010)* Chapter 1, OB2. Under **U.S. GAAP**, the identical statement appears in Concept Statement 8, Chapter 1, OB2.

Standard-Setting Bodies

International Accounting Standards Board (IASB)

The IASB is the independent standard-setting body of the IFRS Foundation, which is an independent, not-for-profit private sector organization. The principal objectives of the **IFRS** Foundation are to develop and promote the use and adoption of a single set of high-quality financial standards; to ensure the standards result in transparent, comparable, and decision-useful information while taking into account the needs of a range of sizes and types of entities in diverse economic settings; and to promote the convergence of national accounting standards and **IFRS**.

- The IFRS Interpretations Committee is responsible for reviewing accounting issues that arise in the application of **IFRS** and are not specifically addressed by **IFRS**.
- The IFRS Advisory Council provides advice to the IASB on agenda decisions and priorities among other items.

Financial Accounting Standards Board (FASB)

The FASB issues new and revised standards with the aim of improving standards of financial reporting so that information provided to users is useful for decision-making. The FASB standards are contained in the FASB Accounting Standard Codification™ (Codification). The Codification is the source of all authoritative U.S. generally accepted accounting principles (**U.S. GAAP**) for nongovernmental entities. **U.S. GAAP** is officially recognized as authoritative by the Securities and Exchange Commission (SEC). However, the SEC retains the authority to establish standards.

Desirable Attributes of an Accounting Standards Board

- The responsibilities of all parties involved in the standard-setting process should be clearly defined.
- All parties involved in the standard-setting process should observe high professional and ethical standards, including standards of confidentiality.
- The organization should have adequate authority, resources, and competencies.
- There should be clear and consistent processes to guide the organization and formation of standards.
- There should be a well-articulated framework with a clearly stated objective to guide the board.
- The board should seek and consider input from all stakeholders. However, it should operate independently and make decisions that are in line with the stated objective of the framework.
- The board should not succumb to pressure from external forces.
- Final decisions should be in public interest, and should lead to a set of high-quality standards that will be recognized and adopted by regulatory authorities.

Regulatory Authorities

Regulatory authorities are governmental entities that have the legal authority to enforce the financial reporting requirements set forth by the standard-setting bodies, and to exert control over entities that participate in capital markets within their jurisdiction.

IOSCO (International Organization of Securities Commission) is not a regulatory authority, but its members regulate a large portion of the world's financial capital markets. IOSCO sets out three core objectives of securities regulation:[2]

1. Protection of investors.
2. Ensuring that markets are fair, efficient, and transparent.
3. Reducing systematic risk.

IOSCO's principles are grouped into nine categories, including principles for regulators, for enforcement, for issuers, and for auditors. With increasing globalization, the organization aims to assist its members in the development of internationally comparable financial reporting standards. Further, it assists in attaining uniform regulation and cross-border cooperation in combating violations of securities and derivatives laws. Finally, it provides guidance regarding the use of Self-Regulatory Organizations (SROs) in overseeing their respective areas of expertise.

The U.S. Securities and Exchange Commission

Any company issuing securities in the United States, or otherwise involved in U.S. capital markets is subject to the rules of the SEC. The SEC requires companies to submit numerous forms periodically. These filings, which are available on the SEC website (www.sec.gov), are a key source of information for analysis of listed firms. The forms most relevant for financial analysts include:

- All companies that issue new securities are required to file a Securities Offerings Registration Statement. Required information includes disclosures about the securities, the relationship of these new securities to the issuer's other capital securities, the information typically provided in annual filings, recent audited financial statements, and risk factors involved in the business.

- Forms 10-K, 20-F, and 40-F must be filed annually. In these forms, companies provide a comprehensive business overview and disclose important financial data (historical overview of performance, management discussion & analysis (MD&A) report, and audited financial statements). This information is also available in a company's annual report. However, annual reports are prepared for shareholders and are not required by the SEC.

- Forms 10-Q and 6-K: U.S. companies file form 10-Q quarterly while non-U.S. firms file form 6-K semiannually. These submissions require unaudited financial statements, MD&A reports, and disclosure of any nonrecurring events.

---

2 - Objectives and Principles of Securities Regulation, IOSCO, June 2010.

- Proxy Statement/ Form DEF-14A: The SEC requires that shareholders of a company be sent a proxy statement before any shareholder meeting. A proxy is an authorization from a shareholder granting another party the right to vote on her behalf. The following information is contained in a proxy statement:
  - Details of proposals that require shareholder vote.
  - Ownership stakes of senior management and principal owners.
  - Director biographies.
  - Executive compensation disclosures.

  The proxy statement that is filed with the SEC is known as Form DEF-14A.

- Form 8-K: This form must be filed for significant events that include the acquisition or disposal of corporate assets, changes in management or corporate governance, changes in securities and trading markets, and matters related to accountants and financial statements.

- Form 144: This form is filed to announce a possible sale of restricted securities or the sale of securities held by affiliates of the issuer.

- Forms 3, 4, 5, and 11-K: These forms are used to examine purchases and sales of securities by management, directors, employees, and other affiliates of the company.

Capital Market Regulation in Europe: Each country in the European Union (EU) regulates its own capital market. However, certain regulations have been adopted at the EU level to achieve some consistency in securities regulation among the different member states. In 2002 the EU agreed that from January 1, 2005, listed companies would prepare their consolidated accounts in accordance with the **IFRS**.

LOS 24c: Describe the status of global convergence of accounting standards and ongoing barriers to developing one universally accepted set of financial reporting standards. **Vol 3, pp 112–115**

The IASB and FASB, along with other standard setters, are working to achieve convergence of financial reporting standards.

- In 2002, the IASB and FASB both acknowledged their commitment to develop high quality, compatible accounting standards that can be used for both domestic as well as cross-border financial reporting.
- In 2004, both the boards agreed to align their conceptual frameworks and to work together in developing any significant accounting standards in the future. In the short term they aimed to remove selected differences, while in the medium term they agreed to issue joint standards in areas where significant improvements were required.
- In 2009, both the boards affirmed their commitment to achieve convergence in selected major projects by June 2011. This date was later revised to late 2011.

Convergence between **U.S. GAAP** and **IFRS** is underway. Time and again, the SEC has reiterated its commitment to global accounting standards and is looking into incorporating **IFRS** into the financial reporting system for U.S. issuers. Convergence between **IFRS** and other local GAAP (e.g., Japanese GAAP) is also underway.

However, the move toward developing one set of universally accepted financial reporting standards is impeded by two factors:

- Standard-setting bodies and regulators have different opinions regarding appropriate accounting treatments due to differences in institutional, regulatory, business, and cultural environments.
- Powerful lobbyists and business groups, whose reported financial performance would be affected adversely by changes in reporting standards, exert pressure against the adoption of unfavorable standards.

LOS 24d: Describe the International Accounting Standards Board's conceptual framework, including the objective and qualitative characteristics of financial statements, required reporting elements, and constraints and assumptions in preparing financial statements. **Vol 3, pp 116–128**

The IASB uses the Conceptual Framework for Financial Reporting 2010 (Conceptual Framework 2010) to develop reporting standards. The framework assists standard setters in developing and reviewing standards, assists preparers of financial statements in applying standards, helps auditors in forming an opinion on financial statements, and aids users in interpreting financial statement information. Table 1-1 summarizes the current status of **IFRS** adoption in selected countries, while Figure 1-1 summarizes the Conceptual Framework 2010.

Table 1-1: International Adoption Status of IFRS in Selected Locations as of June 2010[3]

Europe	• The EU requires companies listed in EU countries to adopt **IFRS** beginning with their 2005 financial statements.
	• Switzerland requires that Swiss multinational companies listed on the main board of the Swiss Exchange must choose either **U.S. GAAP** or **IFRS**.
	• Some countries (for example, Georgia, Macedonia, Moldova, Serbia) use **IFRS** as adopted locally. Georgia, for example, uses the **IFRS** 2007 edition.
	• Some countries (for example, Czech Republic, Finland, Germany, Ireland, Lithuania, Netherlands, Norway, and Poland) permit some foreign companies listing on local exchanges to use other specified and/or well-recognised standards.
North America	• The U.S. SEC accepts **IFRS** for non-U.S. registrants and no longer requires a reconciliation to **U.S. GAAP** for filers using **IFRS**.
	• The U.S. FASB is engaged in numerous projects with the IASB to achieve convergence of **U.S. GAAP** and **IFRS**.
	• The U.S. SEC announced its intention to decide by 2011 whether to incorporate **IFRS** into financial reporting by U.S. issuers.

(Table continued on next page. . .)

3 - Sources: Based on data from www.iasb.org, www.sec.gov, www.iasplus.com, and www.pwc.com

Table 1-1: (*continued*)

	• In Canada, listed companies are required to use **IFRS** beginning January 1, 2011. The year ending December 31, 2010 is the last year of reporting under current Canadian GAAP. • In November 2008, Mexico announced plans to move to **IFRS** in 2012. • Most of the island nations off the southeast coast of North America require or permit the use of **IFRS** by listed companies.
Central and South America	• Central America, Costa Rica, Honduras, and Panama require the use of **IFRS**. EI Salvador, Guatemala, and Nicaragua permit the use of **IFRS**. • Brazil requires that listed companies and financial institutions use **IFRS**, starting with periods ending in 2010. Brazilian GAAP continues to converge to **IFRS**. Ecuador requires listed companies, other than financial institutions, to use **IFRS** beginning in 2010. • Chile requires major listed companies to use **IFRS** for 2009 financial statements. Other companies are permitted to use **IFRS**. • Venezuela permits listed companies to use **IFRS**. The expectation is that listed companies will be required to use **IFRS** by 2011. • Peru and Uruguay require the use of **IFRS** as adopted locally. • In Argentina, convergence of ARG GAAP to **IFRS** is in progress. Listed foreign companies are permitted to use their primary GAAP, including **IFRS**, but should also include a reconciliation to ARG GAAP. • Bolivia is moving toward convergence with **IFRS**. • In Colombia and Paraguay, the adoption of **IFRS** is in early stages of consideration.
Asia and Middle East	• Listed companies in a number of countries—including India, Indonesia, and Thailand—report under local GAAP, and plans exist to either converge with or transition to **IFRS**. • Companies in China report under Chinese accounting standards (CAS). CAS are largely converged with **IFRS** and China's November 2009 proposed Roadmap targeted 2011 as the year for completion of convergence of **IFRS** and CAS. Financial institutions are required to prepare financial statements in accordance with **IFRS** in addition to their statements prepared using CAS. • In Japan, some companies that meet certain criteria may use **IFRS**, otherwise companies report using Japanese GAAP. Japan has launched a joint project with the IASB to reduce differences between Japanese GAAP and **IFRS**. • In Malaysia, domestic listed companies report using local GAAP and foreign companies listed on Malaysian exchanges are permitted to use **IFRS**. Malaysia plans to have full convergence with **IFRS** by January 2012. • In Hong Kong, companies incorporated in Hong Kong normally report under Hong Kong FRS. These are largely converged with **IFRS**. • Korea requires the use of **IFRS** beginning 2011. Early adoption was permitted from 2009.

(Table continued on next page. . .)

Table 1-1: (*continued*)

- Listed companies are required to report under **IFRS** in a number of other countries, including Kyrgyz Republic, Lebanon, and Turkey.
- A number of countries, including Pakistan, Philippines, and Singapore, require use of **IFRS** as adopted locally. In Singapore, **IFRS** is permitted for use by companies that list on other exchanges that require **IFRS** or if permission is given by the Accounting and Corporate Regulatory Authority.
- In a number of countries, **IFRS** is required for some types of entities and permitted for others. For example, Armenia requires **IFRS** for financial organizations and permits its use for others, Azerbaijan requires **IFRS** for banks and state-owned public interest entities, Israel requires **IFRS** for domestic listed companies except for banking institutions, Kazakhstan requires **IFRS** for domestic listed companies, large business entities and public-interest entities, Saudi Arabia requires **IFRS** for all banks regulated by the Saudi Arabian Monetary Agency (central bank), and Uzbekistan requires **IFRS** for all commercial banks and permits **IFRS** for others. Vietnam requires **IFRS** for state-owned banks and permits **IFRS** for commercial banks; all other listed companies report under Vietnamese accounting standards. Some countries, including Afghanistan and Qatar, permit the use of **IFRS**.

Oceana	- Australia requires Australian reporting entities to use **IFRS** as adopted locally. Foreign companies listing on local exchanges are permitted to use **IFRS** or their primary GAAP. The Australian regulator may require additional information. - New Zealand requires use of **IFRS** as adopted locally (NZ-IFRS).
Africa	- Many African countries, including Botswana, Ghana, Kenya, Malawi, Mauritius, Namibia, South Africa, Swaziland, Tanzania, Uganda, Zambia, and Zimbabwe, require **IFRS** for listed companies. - Morocco requires the use of **IFRS** for consolidated financial statements of bank and financial institutions and permits its use for others. - Mozambique requires the use of **IFRS** for financial and lending institutions and for certain large entities. Use of **IFRS** is permitted by other entities beginning in 2010. - Egypt requires the use of local GAAP, which is partially converged with **IFRS**. - The Nigerian Federal executive Council approved January 1, 2012 as the effective date for convergence of accounting standards in Nigeria with **IFRS**. - In some countries, financial statements are required to be prepared in accordance with the Organization for the Harmonization of Business Law in Africa accounting framework. These countries include Cameroon, Cote D'Ivoire, and Equatorial Guinea.

Figure 1-1: IFRS Framework for the Preparation and Presentation of Financial Reports[4]

Reporting Elements

Qualitative Characteristics

Objective

To Provide Financial Information Useful in Making Decisions about Providing Resources to the Entity

- Relevance*
- Faithful Representation

- Comparability, Verifiability, Timeliness, Understandability

- Performance
  ○ Income
  ○ Expenses
  ○ Capital Maintenance Adjustments
  ○ Past Cash Flows

- Financial Position
  ○ Assets
  ○ Liabilities
  ○ Equity

Constraint
- Cost (cost/benefit considerations)

Underlying Assumption
- Accrual Basis
- Going Concern

*Material is an aspect of relevance.

4 - Exhibit 2, pg 119, Vol 3, CFA Program Curriculum 2014

Objective of Financial Statements

Under the Conceptual Framework, the objective of general purpose financial reporting is to provide financial information that is useful in making decisions about providing resources to the entity to existing and potential providers of resources (e.g., investors, lenders, and creditors) to the entity.

Qualitative Characteristics

The Conceptual Framework identifies two fundamental qualitative characteristics that make financial information useful; relevance and faithful representation:

Relevance: The information presented in the financial statements should be useful in making forecasts (have predictive value) and/or be useful to evaluate past decisions or forecasts (have confirmatory value). Further, the criterion of materiality states that information should be timely and sufficiently detailed with no material omissions or misstatements of information that could make a difference to users' decisions.

Faithful Representation: This requires that the information presented is:
- Complete (i.e., all the information necessary to understand the phenomenon is included);
- Neutral (i.e., information presented is free from any bias); and
- Free from error (i.e., there are no errors of commission or omission in the description of the economic phenomenon). Further, an appropriate process is adhered to, without error, in order to arrive at the reported information.

The Conceptual Framework also identifies four supplementary qualitative characteristics that increase the usefulness of relevant and faithfully represented financial information. These are:

- Comparability: The presentation of financial statements should be consistent over time and across firms to facilitate comparisons.
- Verifiability: Different knowledgeable and independent observers should be able to verify that the information presented faithfully represents the economic phenomena that it is supposed to represent.
- Timeliness: Information should be available to users in a timely manner.
- Understandability: Users with basic business and accounting knowledge, who are willing to make reasonable efforts to study the information presented, should be able to easily understand the information presented.

Constraints on Financial Statements

While it would be ideal for financial statements to exhibit all the desirable characteristics listed earlier, there are several constraints to achieving this goal:

- There may be a tradeoff between certain desirable characteristics. For example, companies must estimate bad debts (amount of credit sales that the company will not be able to collect) when presenting financial information so that financial statements can be released in a timely manner. However, the fact estimated expenses must be included reduces the verifiability of the statements.

- There is a cost of providing useful financial information. The benefits from information should exceed the costs of providing it.
- Intangible aspects (e.g., company reputation, brand name, customer loyalty, and corporate culture) cannot be quantified and reflected in financial statements. Unfortunately, nonquantifiable information is omitted from financial statements.

Reporting Elements

The elements of financial statements that are related to the measurement of financial position are:

- Assets: Resources owned and controlled by a company from which it expects to realize future benefits.
- Liabilities: Obligations of a company that are expected to result in future outflow of resources.
- Equity: The residual claim of owners on assets of the company after subtracting all liabilities.

Elements related to the measurement of financial performance are:

- Income: Increases in economic benefits in the form of inflows or enhancement of assets or reductions in liabilities that result in increases in equity (other than increases resulting from contributions by owners). Income includes revenues and gains. Revenue refers to income generated through ordinary activities of the business (e.g., sale of products). Gains may result from ordinary activities or other activities (e.g., sale of surplus machinery).
- Expenses: Decreases in economic benefits in the form of outflows or depletion of assets or increases in liabilities that result in reductions in equity (other than reductions due to distributions to owners). Expenses include normal expenditures that occur in day-to-day business activities (e.g., wages) and losses.

Underlying Assumptions in Financial Statements

Two important assumptions that determine how financial statement elements are recognized and measured are:

- Accrual basis accounting requires that transactions should be recorded on the financial statements (other than on the cash flow statement) when they actually occur, irrespective of when the related exchange of cash occurs.
- Going concern refers to the assumption that the company will continue operating for the foreseeable future. If this is not the case, fair representation would require all assets to be written down to their liquidation values. The value of a company's year-end stock of inventory would be higher if it were allowed to sell it over a normal period of time, compared to its value if the company were forced to liquidate it immediately.

Recognition and Measurement of Financial Statement Elements

An element should be recognized on the financial statements if the future benefit from the item (flowing into or out of the firm) is probable, and if its value/cost can be estimated with reliability. The monetary value of the item recognized on the financial statements depends on the measurement base used. The following bases of measurement are typically used:

- Historical cost: For an asset, historical cost refers to the amount that it was originally purchased for. For liabilities, it refers to the amount of proceeds that were received initially in exchange for the obligation.
- Amortized cost: Historical cost adjusted for amortization, depreciation, or depletion and/or impairment.
- Current cost: For an asset, current cost refers to the amount that the asset can be purchased for today. For liabilities, it refers to the total undiscounted amount of cash that would be required to settle the obligation today.
- Realizable (settlement) value: In reference to assets, realizable value refers to the amount that the asset can be sold for in an ordinary disposal today. For liabilities, it refers to the undiscounted amount of cash expected to be paid to settle the liability in the normal course of business.
- Present value: For assets, present value refers to the discounted value of future net cash flows expected from the asset. For liabilities, it refers to the present discounted value of future net cash outflows that are expected to be required to settle the liability.
- Fair value: This is mentioned in the Conceptual Framework, but not specifically defined. It refers to the amount that the asset can be exchanged for, or a liability can be settled for, in an arm's length transaction. Fair value may be based on market value or present value.

LOS 24e: Describe general requirements for financial statements under IFRS. Vol 3, pp 123–127

International Accounting Standard (IAS) No. 1, Presentation of Financial Statements, specifies which financial statements are mandatory and how they must be presented. (See Table 1-2.)

Required Financial Statements

- Statement of financial position (balance sheet).
- Statement of comprehensive income (in a single statement or in two separate statements, i.e., the income statement + statement of comprehensive income).
- Statement of changes in equity.
- Statement of cash flows.
- Significant accounting policies and explanatory notes to facilitate the understanding of financial statements.
- In certain cases, a statement of financial position from earliest comparative period.

General Features of Financial Statements

- **Fair presentation:** This requires faithful representation of transactions, in compliance with the definitions and recognition criteria for reporting elements (assets, liabilities, equity, income, and expenses) set out in the Conceptual Framework.
- **Going concern:** Financial statements should be prepared on a going concern basis unless management has plans to liquidate the company.
- **Accrual basis:** All financial statements, except the cash flow statement, should be prepared on an accrual basis.
- **Materiality and aggregation:** Financial statements should be free from omissions and misrepresentations that could influence decisions taken by users. Similar items should be grouped and presented as a material class. Dissimilar items, unless immaterial, should be presented separately.
- **No offsetting:** Assets and liabilities and income and expenses should not be used to offset each other, unless a standard requires or allows it.
- **Frequency of reporting:** Financial statements must be prepared at least annually.
- **Comparative information:** Comparative amounts should be presented for prior periods unless a specific standard permits otherwise.
- **Consistency:** Items should be presented and classified in the same manner in every period.

Structure and Content Requirements

- **Classified statement of financial position:** Current and noncurrent assets and current and noncurrent liabilities should be shown separately on the balance sheet.
- **Minimum information on the face of financial statements:** Certain items must be explicitly disclosed on the face of the financial statements. For example, property, plant & equipment (PP&E) must be disclosed as a separate line item on the face of the balance sheet.
- **Minimum information in the notes (or on the face of financial statements):** Disclosures relating to certain items must be in the notes to the financial statements (e.g., measurement bases used). (See Table 1-3.)
- **Comparative information:** Comparative amounts should be presented for prior periods unless a specific standard permits otherwise.

Table 1-2: IAS No. 1: Minimum Required Line Items in Financial Statements[5]

On the face of the Statement of Financial Position	• Plant, property, and equipment • Investment property • Intangible assets • Financial assets (not listed in other line items) • Investments accounted for using the equity method • Biological assets • Inventories • Trade and other receivables • Cash and cash equivalents • Total of assets classified as held for sale • Trade and other payables • Provisions • Financial liabilities (not listed in other line items) • Liabilities and assets for current tax • Deferred tax assets and deferred tax liabilities • Liabilities included in disposal groups classified as held for sale • Noncontrolling interests, presented within equity • Issued capital and reserves attributable to owners of the parent
On the face of the Statement of Comprehensive Income, presented either in a single statement or in two statements (Income statement + Statement of comprehensive income)	• Revenue • Specified gains and losses for financial assets • Finance costs • Share of the profit or loss of associates and joint ventures accounted for using the equity method • Pretax gain or loss recognized on the disposal of assets or settlement of liabilities attributable to discontinued operations • Tax expense • Profit or loss • Each component of other comprehensive income • Amount of profit or loss and amount of comprehensive income attributable to noncontrolling interest (minority interest) • Amount of profit or loss and amount of comprehensive income attributable to the parent
On the face of the Statement of Changes in Equity	• Total comprehensive income for the period attributable to noncontrolling interests, and to owners of the parent • For each component of equity, the effects of changes in accounting policies and corrections of errors • For each component of equity, a reconciliation between the beginning and ending carrying amounts, separately disclosing changes resulting from profit or loss, each item of other comprehensive income, and transactions with owners in their capacity as owners

---

5 - Exhibit 4, pg 127–128, Vol 3, CFA Program Curriculum 2014

Table 1-3: Summary of IFRS Required Disclosures in the Notes to the Financial Statements[6]

Disclosure of accounting policies	• Measurement bases used in preparing financial statements • The other accounting policies used that are relevant to an understanding of the financial statements • Judgments made in applying accounting policies that have the most significant effect on the amounts recognized in the financial statements
Estimation uncertainty	• Key assumptions about the future and other key sources of estimation uncertainty that have a significant risk of causing material adjustment to the carrying amount of assets and liabilities within the next year
Other disclosures	• Information about capital and about certain financial instruments classified as equity • Dividends not recognized as a distribution during the period, including dividends declared before the financial statements were issued and any cumulative preference dividends • Description of the entity, including its domicile, legal form, country of incorporation, and registered office or business address • Nature of operations and its principal activities • Name of parent and ultimate parent

LOS 24f: Compare key concepts of financial reporting standards under IFRS and U.S. GAAP reporting systems. Vol 3, p 128

Most of the differences between **IFRS** and **U.S. GAAP** are discussed in the readings that follow. A brief summary of the differences regarding financial statement elements (definition, recognition, and measurement) are:

- FASB, in addition to the financial performance elements recognized under the IASB Framework (revenues and expenses), also identifies gains, losses, and comprehensive income.

- Reporting elements relating to financial position are defined differently. Under FASB, assets are the "future economic benefits" rather than "resources" from which future economic benefits are expected to flow under IASB.

- Under FASB, the word "probable" is not discussed in its revenue recognition criteria, while under IASB it is required that it is probable that a future economic benefit flow to/from the entity. FASB also has a separate recognition criterion of relevance.

- Regarding measurement of financial elements, both frameworks are broadly consistent. However, FASB does not allow upward revaluation of assets except for certain categories of financial instruments that must be reported at fair value.

---

6 - Exhibit 5, pg 128, Vol 3, CFA Program Curriculum 2014

Companies around the world follow different frameworks in preparing their financial statements. Until recently, companies were required to report reconciliation statements and disclosures to allow construction of financial statements as they would have been under alternative reporting standards. For example, the SEC used to (but no longer does) require reconciliation for foreign private issuers that do not prepare financial statements in accordance with **U.S. GAAP**. Now that reconciliation disclosures are not required, analysts must be aware of areas where accounting standards have not yet converged.

LOS 24g: Identify characteristics of a coherent financial reporting framework and the barriers to creating such a framework. **Vol 3, pp 129–130**

Characteristics of an Effective Financial Reporting Framework

- Transparency: A transparent reporting framework should reflect the underlying economics of the business. Full disclosure and fair representation create transparency.
- Comprehensiveness: A comprehensive reporting framework is one that is based on universal principles that provide guidance for recording all kinds of financial transactions—those already in existence and others that emerge with time.
- Consistency: Financial transactions of a similar nature should be measured and reported in a similar manner, irrespective of industry type, geography, and time period. However, there is also a need for flexibility to allow companies discretion to be able to report results in accordance with their underlying economic activity.

Barriers to Creating a Single Coherent Framework

- Valuation: When choosing a measurement base, it is important to remember the tradeoff between reliability and relevance. Historical cost is a more reliable measure of value, but fair value is more relevant over time.

- Standard-setting approach: Reporting standards can be based on one of the following approaches:
    - A principles-based approach provides a broad financial reporting framework with limited guidance on how to report specific transactions. It requires the use of subjective judgment in financial reporting.
    - A rules-based approach provides strict rules for classifying elements and transactions.
    - An objectives-oriented approach is a combination of a principles-based and rules-based approach. This approach includes a framework of principles and appropriate levels of implementation guidance.
  IFRS has a principles-based approach. FASB has historically followed a rules-based approach, but recently explicitly stated that it is moving toward an objectives-oriented approach.

- Measurement: Reporting of financial statement elements can be based on the asset/liability approach (where the elements are properly valued at a point in time) or the revenue/expense approach (where changes in the elements are properly valued over a period of time). The former gives preference to proper valuation of the balance sheet, while the latter focuses on the income statement. The use of one of these approaches will result in more reliable information on one statement and less on the other. In recent years, standard-setters have preferred the asset/liability approach.

LOS 24h: Describe implications for financial analysis of differing financial reporting systems and the importance of monitoring developments in financial reporting standards. Vol 3, pp 131–134

LOS 24i: Analyze company disclosures of significant accounting policies. Vol 3, pp 134–137

It is important for analysts to be aware of developments in financial reporting standards and to assess their implications for security analysis and valuation. They need to understand how changes and developments affect financial reports from a user's perspective.

1. New products and transactions in capital markets: Certain economic events have led to the development of new products and new transactions. For example, online stores have led to the advent of e-commerce and related transactions that did not exist earlier.

   Analysts should evaluate companies' financial reports to understand new transactions or products being used and implemented. Business journals, magazines, and capital markets can provide information on new transactions and financial instruments being used by various companies in an industry. Further information can always be obtained from company management regarding any products that they may have used or transactions that they might have undertaken during the year. As products or transactions become more common in the industry, it becomes imperative to understand their implications, usefulness, and impact on cash flows.

2. Actions of standard-setting bodies, such as IASB and FASB, must be monitored because changes in regulations and financial reporting standards affect reported financial performance. Investment decision-making can be improved by keeping track of enacted and proposed changes.

3. Company disclosures are a good source of information regarding the effects of financial reporting standards on a company's performance. Under **IFRS** and **U.S. GAAP**, companies are required to disclose accounting policies and estimates in the footnotes to the financial statements. Public companies also discuss accounting policies and estimates that require significant material judgment in the MD&A section.

   Companies must also disclose information relating to changes in accounting policies. **IFRS** requires discussion about pending implementation of new standards and any known or estimable information relevant to assessing the impact of those standards. Clear indications regarding the expected impact of changes in standards provide the most useful information and are very helpful to analysts. Vague statements like "management is still evaluating the impact of the standard" might be red flags that analysts should be wary of. Quantified disclosures (when companies are able to quantify the expected impact of standards that have changed but are not yet effective as of the reporting date) are extremely useful to analysts.

READING 25: UNDERSTANDING INCOME STATEMENTS

LESSON 1: INCOME STATEMENT: COMPONENTS AND FORMAT

LOS 25a: Describe the components of the income statement and alternative presentation formats of that statement. Vol 3, pp 151–155

Under **IFRS**, the income statement may be presented as:
- A section of a single statement of comprehensive income; or
- A separate statement (showing all revenues and expenses) followed by a statement of comprehensive income (described later) that begins with net income.

Under **U.S. GAAP**, the income statement may be presented as:
- A section of a single statement of comprehensive income.
- A separate statement followed by a statement of comprehensive income that begins with net income.
- A separate statement with the components of other comprehensive income presented in the statement of changes in shareholders' equity.

Exhibits 1-1 and 1-2 show the income statements of Van Dort Inc. (a European company) and Johnson Inc. (an American company).

Exhibit 1-1:

VAN DORT INCORPORATED
Income Statement
For the Year Ended December 31, 2008

		2007 €	2008 €
1	**Net revenue**	**55,000**	**59,250**
	Cost of goods sold	−39,000	−41,250
	Selling expenses	−6,500	−7,150
	General and administrative expenses	−2,250	−3,350
	Research and development expenses	−1,050	−1,100
	Other revenue (expense)	−675	−650
	Trading operating income	**5,525**	**5,750**
	Other operating income (expense)	−105	250
3	**Operating income**	**5,420**	**6,000**
	Interest revenue	60	85
	Interest expense	−350	−275
	Cost of net debt	−290	−190
	Other financial revenue expense	−450	−750
	Income before tax	**4,680**	**5,060**
	Income tax	−2,125	−1,950
	Income from fully consolidated companies	**2,555**	**3,110**
	Share of profits from associates	20	−50
	Net income from continuing operations	2,575	3,060
	Net income from discontinued operations	235	0
5	**Net income**	**2,810**	**3,060**
4	Attributable to the group	2,529	2,754
	Attributable to minority interests	281	306

Following net income, the income statement may also present earnings per share, the amount of earnings per common share of a company. Earnings per share will be discussed in detail later in this reading, and the per-share display has been omitted from these exhibits to focus on the core income statement.

Exhibit 1-2:   **JOHNSON INCORPORATED**
                                          Income Statement
                                 For the Year Ended December 31, 2008

	2008	2007
	$	$
1 — Net revenue	**15,000**	**13,500**
Cost of sales	11,050	10,075
2 — Gross profit	**3,950**	**3,425**
Marketing, administrative and research expenses	975	695
Loss (gain) on sale of equipment	250	0
Impairment expense	175	105
Loss (gain) on sale of old vehicles	225	275
Amortization of intangibles	25	55
3 — Operating income	**2,300**	**2,295**
Net interest expense	450	430
Earnings from continuing operations before income taxes	**1,850**	**1,865**
Provision for income taxes	240	135
Earnings from continuing operations	**1,610**	**1,730**
Earnings and gain from discontinued operations, net of income taxes	0	55
5 — Net earnings	**1,610**	**1,785**
4 — Noncontrolling interest	16	18
Net earnings attributable to Johnson Incorporated	**1,594**	**1,767**

1 — Revenue: Usually reported on the first line of the income statement, revenues are amounts charged (and expected to be received) for goods and services in the ordinary activities of a business. Net revenue is total revenue adjusted for product returns and amounts that are unlikely to be collected. Other commonly used terms for revenue include sales and turnover.

Expenses reflect outflows, depletions of assets, and incurrences of liabilities in the course of the activities of a business.

2 — Gross profit or gross margin is the difference between revenues and cost of goods that were sold. When an income statement explicitly calculates gross profit, it uses a multi-step format as opposed to a single-step format. Van Dort uses a single step format, while Johnson uses a multi-step format.

3 — Operating income is calculated after subtracting all direct and indirect (period) costs from revenues. It represents the profit earned by a company from its ordinary business activities before accounting for taxes and, in the case of nonfinancial companies, before deducting interest expense. Operating profits are useful in evaluating the profitability of individual businesses as they are not affected by financing decisions of the firm. Exhibits 1-1 and 1-2 contain income statements of nonfinancial companies. For financial firms, interest income and expense are part of ordinary business activities, so they are included in operating profits.

> Operating income is sometimes referred to as EBIT. However, they are not always equal.

Net income is the "bottom-line" of the income statement. It includes profits earned from ordinary business activities as well as gains and losses (increases and decreases in economic benefits) from nonoperating activities.

5

> Net income = Revenue – Expenses in the ordinary activities of the business
> + Other income – Other expenses + Gains – Losses

If a company owns the majority of the shares of a subsidiary, it must present consolidated financial statements. Consolidation requires the parent to combine all the revenues and expenses of the subsidiary with its own and present the combined results on its income statement. If the subsidiary is not wholly owned, the share of noncontrolling interests in net income is deducted from total income, as it represents the proportionate share in the subsidiary's net income that belongs to minority shareholders.

4

Some subtotals are required by **IFRS** (especially nonrecurring items), while others are not explicitly required. Examples of items that are required to be separately stated on the face of the income statement are revenues, finance costs, and taxes.

Under **IFRS,** revenue from rendering of services is recognized when:
1. The amount of revenue can be measured reliably;
2. It is probable that the economic benefits associated with the transaction will flow to the entity;
3. The stage of completion of the transaction at the balance sheet date can be measured reliably; and
4. The costs incurred for the transaction and the costs to complete the transaction can be measured reliably.

IFRS permits the grouping of expenses by nature or by function. An example of grouping by nature would be combining depreciation of factory equipment with depreciation of transport vehicles and stating a single aggregate amount for depreciation on the income statement. An example of grouping by function would be combining direct product costs (raw material costs and freight charges) under costs of goods sold.

Income statement presentation formats: Van Dort's and Johnson's income statements also highlight the following differences that we might run into when analyzing financial statements of various companies:
- Van Dort presents the latest year in the extreme right column, while Johnson presents the most recent year on the extreme left.
- Van Dort presents expense items (e.g., costs of goods sold and interest expense) in parenthesis to show that they are being deducted. In contrast, Johnson does not present its expenses in parenthesis or with negative signs. It assumes that users know that expense items are subtracted from revenues.
- Van Dort deducts cost of goods sold from sales, while Johnson deducts cost of sales. Such differences in terminology are common across sets of financial statements.

> When solving questions related to financial statement reporting and analysis, make sure you make a note of whether the most recent year is given in the right-most column or in the left-most. The convention used in exam questions can be different from what some of you are used to. Making an arrow indicating the movement from the oldest to the most recent accounting period will help you avoid careless mistakes in answering questions related to changes in accounting elements over the period.

LOS 25b: Describe general principles of revenue recognition and accrual accounting, specific revenue recognition applications (including accounting for long-term contracts, installment sales, barter transactions, gross and net reporting of revenue), and implications of revenue recognition principles for financial analysis. Vol 3, pp 155–168

LOS 25c: Calculate revenue given information that might influence the choice of revenue recognition method. Vol 3, pp 155–168

The IASB framework defines income as "increases in economic benefits during the accounting period in the form of inflows or enhancements of assets, or decreases in liabilities that result in increases in equity, other than those relating to contributions from equity participants."[1] Income includes revenues and gains. Revenues arise from ordinary, core business activities, whereas gains arise from noncore or peripheral activities. For example, for a software development company the sale of software to customers is considered revenue, but the profit on the sale of some old office furniture is classified as a gain.

The most important principle of revenue recognition is accrual accounting, which requires that revenues and costs are recognized independently of the timing of related cash flows. For example, under accrual accounting, rent expense is recognized in the month that a company uses the premises for its operations, not when the actual cash payment for rent is made. Accrual accounting allows firms to manipulate net income by recognizing revenue earlier or later, or by accelerating or deferring recognition of expenses.

Under **IFRS**, revenue is recognized for a sale of goods when:[2]
1. Significant risks and rewards of ownership are transferred to the buyer.
2. The entity retains no managerial involvement or effective control over the goods sold.
3. The amount of revenue can be measured reliably.
4. It is probable that the economic benefits from the transaction will flow to the entity.
5. Costs incurred or to be incurred for the transaction can be measured reliably.

IFRS specify similar criteria for recognizing revenue for the rendering of service. Revenue can be estimated reliably when all the following:[3]
1. The amount of revenue can be measured reliably.
2. It is probable that the economic benefits associated with the transaction will flow to the entity.
3. The stage of completion of the transaction at the balance sheet date can be measured reliably.
4. The costs incurred for the transaction and the costs to complete the transaction can be measured reliably.

IFRS also specifies the criteria for recognizing interest, royalties, and dividends. These may be recognized when it is probable that the economic benefits associated with the transaction will flow to the entity and that the amount of the revenue can be measured reliably.

---

1 - IASB, *International Framework for the Preparation and Presentation of Financial Statements,* paragraph 70.
2 - IASB, IAS No. 18, *Revenue,* paragraph 14.
3 - IAS No. 18, *Revenue,* paragraph 20.

Under **U.S. GAAP**, revenue is recognized on the income statement when it is "realized or realizable and earned."[4] The SEC provides specific guidelines to determine when these two conditions are met:[5]

1. There is evidence of an arrangement between the buyer and seller.
2. The product has been delivered or the service has been rendered.
3. The price is determined or determinable.
4. The seller is reasonably sure of collecting money.

Revenue Recognition in Special Cases

The principles of revenue recognition listed above cater to most cases. However, there are some special circumstances in which revenue may be recognized *prior* to the sale of a good/service or even *after* the sale.

Long-Term Contracts

Long-term contracts are contracts that extend over more than one accounting period, such as construction projects. In long-term contracts, questions arise as to how revenues and expenses should be allocated to each accounting period. The treatment of these items depends on how reliably the outcome of the project can be measured.

Under both **IFRS** and **U.S. GAAP**, if the outcome of the contract can be measured *reliably*, the percentage of completion revenue recognition method is used. Under this method, revenues, costs, and profits are allocated to each accounting period in proportion to the percentage of the contract completed during the given period. The percentage that is recognized during a period is calculated by dividing the total cost incurred during the period by the estimated total cost of the project.

If the outcome *cannot be measured reliably*, the completed-contract method is used under **U.S. GAAP**. Under this method, no revenues or costs are recognized on the income statement until the project is substantially finished. In the meantime, billings and costs are accumulated on the balance sheet (under a Construction-in-progress asset), rather than expensed on the income statement.

Under **IFRS**, when the outcome *cannot be measured reliably*, revenue is recognized on the income statement to the extent of costs incurred during the period. No profits are recognized until all costs have been recovered.

Example 2-1 illustrates the differences between the percentage of completion and the completed contract method.

> Under **U.S. GAAP**, the completed contract method is also appropriate when the contract is not a long-term contract. Note however, that when a contract is started and completed is the same period, there is no difference between the percentage-of-completion and completed contract methods.

---

4 - See Statement of Financial Accounting Concepts No. 5, paragraph 83(b).
5 - See SEC Staff Accounting Bulletin 101.

Example 2-1: Revenue Recognition for Long-Term Contracts

Paxel Construction Company has a $30 million contract to construct a building. It estimates that it will take 3 years to complete the project. The estimated cost of the project is $21 million. Paxel incurs costs amounting to $10.5 million in Year 1, $7.35 million in Year 2, and $3.15 million in Year 3. Determine the amount of revenue and profit that the company will recognize each year under **IFRS** and **U.S. GAAP** if:

1. The outcome of the contract can be reliably measured.
2. The outcome of the contract cannot be reliably measured.

Solution

Under both **IFRS** and **U.S. GAAP**, if the outcome of the contract can be measured *reliably*, the percentage of completion revenue recognition method is used.

Percentage of Completion Method

First we calculate the percentage of total costs incurred in each year.

	Year 1	Year 2	Year 3
Cost incurred	$10.50	$7.35	$3.15
Total cost	$21.00	$21.00	$21.00
Percentage of total cost incurred	**50%**	**35%**	**15%**

Then we multiply the percentage of total costs incurred each year by the total revenue earned over the term of the project to determine the amount of revenue recognized each year.

	Year 1	Year 2	Year 3
Percentage of total cost incurred	50%	35%	15%
Total revenue	$30	$30	$30
Revenue recognized	**$15**	**$10.5**	**$4.5**

Net income equals revenues recognized minus costs recognized:

	Year 1	Year 2	Year 3	Total
Revenue	$ 15	$ 10.5	$ 4.5	$ 30
Costs	$10.5	$7.35	$3.15	$ 21
Net income	$4.5	$3.15	$1.35	$9

Under **IFRS**, if the outcome of the contract cannot be measured reliably and it is probable that costs will be recovered, revenue may only be recognized to the extent of contract costs incurred.

Year 1: The company will recognize construction costs amounting to $10.5 million as well as revenue of $10.5 million and hence, $0 income.

Year 2: The company will recognize construction costs amounting to $7.35 million as well as revenue of $7.35 million and hence, $0 income.

Year 3: The company will recognize construction costs amounting to $3.15 million. Further, since the contract is complete, the company will also recognize the remaining revenue of $12.15 million, and therefore, report $9 million in net income.

	Year 1	Year 2	Year 3
Revenue	$10.5	$7.35	$12.15
Costs	$10.5	$7.35	$3.15
Net income	$0.00	$0.00	$9.00

Completed Contract Method

Under this method, no revenues or costs are recognized until the contract is completed. Therefore, for the first two years, Paxel will not recognize any revenues and costs. The entire amount of revenues, costs, and net income will be recognized in Year 3 on the income statement. On the balance sheet, for Years 1 and 2, Paxel would report all incurred costs under a "Construction-in-progress" head, which would be eliminated in Year 3.

	Year 1	Year 2	Year 3
Revenue	$0	$0	$30
Costs	$0	$0	$21
Net income	$0	$0	$9

The percentage of completion method is a more aggressive (less conservative) approach to revenue recognition. It is also more subjective as it depends on management estimates and judgment relating to the reliability of estimates. However, the percentage of completion method matches revenues with costs over time and provides smoother, less volatile earnings. Remember, cash flows are exactly the same under both methods.

Important: Under **IFRS** and **U.S. GAAP**, if a loss is expected on the contract, the loss must be recognized immediately, regardless of the revenue recognition method used.

Installment Sales

An installment sale occurs when a company finances a customer's purchase of its products and customers make payments (installments) to the company over an extended period.

Under **IFRS**, installment sales are separated into the selling price (discounted present value of installment payments) and an interest component. Revenue attributable to the sale price is recognized at the date of sale, while the interest component is recognized over time.[6] However, the standards provide that revenue should be recognized in light of local laws regarding the sale of goods. For transactions that require deferral of revenue and profit recognition (like sales of real estate on an installment basis) revenue recognition depends on specific aspects of the transaction.

Under **U.S. GAAP**, a sale of real estate is reported at the time of sale using the normal revenue recognition conditions if the seller:[7]
- Has completed the significant activities in the earnings process; and
- Is either assured of collecting the selling price or able to estimate amounts that will not be collected.

When these two conditions are not fully met, some of the profit must be deferred and one of the following two methods may be used.

6 - IAS No. 18 IE, Illustrative Examples, paragraph 8.
7 - FASB ASC Section 360–20–55 [Property, Plant, and Equipment - Real Estate Sales - Implementation Guidance and Illustrations].

Installment method: This method is used when collectability of revenues *cannot be reasonably estimated.* Under this method, profits are recognized as cash is received. The percentage of profit recognized in each period equals the proportion of total cash received in the period.

$$\text{Profit for the period} = (\text{Cash collected in the period}/\text{Selling price}) \times \text{Total profit}$$

Cost-recovery method: This method is used when collectability of revenues is *highly uncertain.* Under this method, profits are only recognized once total cash collections (including principal and interest on any financing provided to the buyer) exceed total costs. The revenue recognition method under international standards is similar to the cost recovery method, but the term "cost recovery method" is not used.

Example 2-2: The Installment Sales and Cost Recovery Methods of Revenue Recognition

Bingo Inc. sold property worth $500,000 and allowed the buyer to make the payment in installments. The cost of the property sold is $300,000. The first installment of $250,000 has been received in Year 1, while the rest of the payment is expected to be received in Year 2. Calculate the amount of profit that will be recognized each year using the:
1) Installment sales method.
2) Cost-recovery method.

Solution

<u>Installment Sales Method</u>

$$\text{Profit for the period} = (\text{Cash collected in the period}/\text{Selling price}) \times \text{Total profit}$$

Profit (Year 1) = (250,000 /500,000) × 200,000 = $100,000.

Profit (Year 2) = (250,000 /500,000) × 200,000 = $100,000.

<u>Cost-Recovery Method</u>

Under the cost-recovery method, the company will not recognize any profits in Year 1 because total cash received from the buyer ($250,000) does not exceed the cost of the property ($300,000). If the second installment of $250,000 is received in Year 2, Bingo will recognize a profit of $200,000 in Year 2.

Installment sales and cost recovery treatment of revenue recognition are rare for financial reporting purposes, especially for assets other than real estate.

Barter Transactions

In barter transactions, goods are exchanged between two parties and there is no exchange of cash. One form of barter transaction is a *round-trip* transaction, in which a good is sold by one party in exchange for the purchase of an identical good. The issue with these transactions is whether revenue should be recognized.

- Under **IFRS**, revenue from barter transactions can be reported on the income statement based on the fair value of revenues from similar *nonbarter* transactions with *unrelated parties.*
- Under **U.S. GAAP**, revenue from barter transactions can be reported on the income statement at fair value only if the company has a history of making or receiving cash payments for such goods and services and hence, can use its historical experience to determine fair value. Otherwise, revenue should be reported at the carrying amount of the asset surrendered.

Gross Versus Net Reporting

Under gross revenue reporting, sales and cost of sales are reported separately, while under net reporting, only the difference between sales and cost of sales is reported on the income statement. Under **U.S. GAAP**, only if the following conditions are met can a company recognize revenue based on gross reporting:

- The company is the primary obligor under the contract.
- The company bears inventory and credit risk.
- The company can choose its suppliers.
- The company has reasonable latitude to establish price.

Example 2-3: Gross Versus Net Reporting of Revenues

A travel agent purchases discounted tickets and sells them to customers. The agent only pays for the tickets that she manages to sell to customers. She purchases a ticket for $1,000 and sells it for $1,100. Assume that there are no other revenues and expenses involved. Demonstrate the reporting of revenues under gross and net reporting.

Solution

	Gross Reporting	Net Reporting
Revenues	$1,100	$100
Cost of sales	−$1,000	$0
Gross margin	**$100**	**$100**

The travel agent should report revenue on a *net basis* because:
- She only pays for tickets that she is able to sell to customers. Therefore, she does not bear any inventory risk.
- The airline, not the travel agent, is the primary obligator under the contract.

Companies are required to disclose their revenue recognition policies in the footnotes to their financial statements. The impact of a chosen policy on financial analysis depends on how conservative and objective the revenue recognition policy is. A conservative policy would recognize revenue later rather than sooner, and an objective policy would not leave too many estimates to management discretion. While it is difficult to attach a monetary value to differences in revenue recognition policies, analysts should be able to assess qualitative differences between sets of financial statements and evaluate how these differences affect important financial ratios.

LOS 25d: Describe general principles of expense recognition, specific expense recognition applications, and implications of expense recognition choices for financial analysis. Vol 3, pp 168–178

The IASB framework defines expenses as "decreases in economic benefits during the accounting period in the form of outflows or depletions of assets or incurrences of liabilities that result in decreases in equity, other than those relating to distributions to equity participants."[8]

> **IFRS** does not specifically refer to a "matching principle," but rather to a "matching concept," or to a process resulting in "matching of costs with revenues."

Expenses also include losses, which may or may not result from the ordinary activities of the business. The most important principle of expense recognition is the matching principle, which requires that expenses be matched with associated revenues when recognizing them on the income statement. If goods bought in the current year remain unsold at the end of the year, their cost is not included in the cost of goods sold for the current year to calculate current period profits.

Instead, the cost of these goods will be subtracted from next period's revenues once they are sold. Certain expenses (e.g., administrative costs) cannot be directly linked to the generation of revenues. These expenses are called period costs and are allocated systematically with the passage of time.

8 - IASB *Framework for the Preparation and Presentation of Financial Statements*, paragraph 70.

Example 2-4: Matching of Inventory Costs with Revenues

In its first year of business (2008), Brainiac Inc. made following purchases:

	Units Purchased	Cost per Unit	Total Cost
First Quarter	2,500	$20	$50,000
Second Quarter	3,550	$22	$78,100
Third Quarter	4,200	$25	$105,000
Fourth Quarter	3,500	$26	$91,000
TOTAL	13,750		$324,100

A detailed discussion of the various inventory accounting methods is presented in Reading 29.

9,100 units were sold during 2008 at a price of $30 per unit. Ending inventory consists of 4,650 units from the most recent purchases. Calculate total revenue and the cost of goods sold during the year.

Solution

Total revenue = 9,100 × $30 per unit = **$273,000**

The cost of the 9,100 units sold during 2008 will be expensed (included in COGS and matched against 2008 revenues). The cost of the remaining 4,650 units will remain in inventory.

Calculation of cost of goods sold:

	Units Purchased	Cost per Unit	Total Cost
First Quarter	2,500	$20	$50,000
Second Quarter	3,550	$22	$78,100
Third Quarter	3,050	$25	$76,250
TOTAL	9,100		$204,350

Calculation of ending inventory:

	Units	Cost per Unit	Total Cost
Third Quarter	1,150	$25	$28,750
Fourth Quarter	3,500	$26	$91,000
TOTAL	4,650		$119,750

To confirm that all costs ($324,100) are accounted for, we add the cost of inventory apportioned to COGS and the cost allocated to ending inventory.

$204,350 + $119,750 = $324,100

In 2008, cost of goods sold will be matched against revenues as follows:

Total revenue	$273,000
Cost of goods sold	$(204,350)
Gross profit	$68,650

Ending inventory ($119,750) will be matched against revenues in 2009 when these units are sold.

Inventory Methods

If a company can specifically identify which units of inventory have been sold over the year and which ones remain in stock, it can use the specific identification method for valuing its inventory. Automobiles, for example, can be valued using this method. However, if sales are composed of identical units that are sold in high volumes (e.g., pencils), the separate identification method becomes difficult to administer. In such situations, the following methods of inventory valuation can be used:

> The various inventory cost flow assumptions are demonstrated in Reading 29.

First-in, first-out (FIFO): This method assumes that items purchased first are sold first. Therefore, ending inventory is composed of the most recent purchases. FIFO is an appropriate method for valuing inventory that has a limited shelf life. For example, older food products will be sold first to ensure that available stock is fresh.

> All three methods are allowed under **U.S. GAAP. IFRS** allows FIFO and weighted-average cost methods, but does not permit use of LIFO.

Last-in, first-out (LIFO): This method assumes that items purchased most recently are sold first. Therefore, ending inventory is composed of the earliest purchases. The LIFO method is suitable when the physical flow of the item is such that the latest item must be sold first, for example, stacks of lumber in a lumberyard. This method is popular in the United States because of its income tax benefits.

Weighted-average cost: Under this method, total inventory costs are allocated evenly across all units. Inventory valuation and analysis is covered in detail in Reading 29.

Inventory Costing Methods

Method	Description	Cost of Goods Sold	Ending Inventory
FIFO	Costs of the earliest items purchased are included in cost of goods sold first.	Earliest purchases	Most recent purchases
LIFO	Costs of the most recent purchases are included in cost of goods sold first.	Most recent purchases	Earliest purchases
Weighted-average cost	Distributes total costs over total units available for sale.	Average cost	Average cost

Issues in Expense Recognition

Doubtful Accounts

When sales are made on credit, there is a possibility that some customers will not be able to meet their payment obligations. Companies can choose to wait for actual customer defaults to recognize these losses (direct write-off method). However, the matching principle requires companies to estimate bad debts at the time of revenue recognition. These estimated uncollectable amounts are expensed on the income statement for the period during which the related sales were made (they are not directly adjusted to revenues).

Warranties

When companies provide warranties for their products, there is a possibility that they might have to pay for repairing or replacing defective products in the future. Rather than recognizing these expenses only when they are actually incurred (when warranty claims are made), the matching principle requires companies to estimate future warranty-related expenses and recognize these amounts on the income statement in the period of sale, and to update this amount to bring in line with actual expenses incurred over the life of the warranty.

Depreciation

Companies incur significant costs to acquire long-lived assets that provide economic benefits over an extended period of time. Under **IFRS**, long-lived assets may either be valued using the cost model or the revaluation model. On the other hand, **U.S. GAAP** only permits the use of the cost model.

> Depreciation and amortization are covered in detail in Reading 30.

Under the cost model, the asset is reported at a cost less than any accumulated depreciation. Depreciation is the process of allocating the cost of long-lived assets across the accounting periods that they provide economic benefits for. The allocation of costs to several periods matches these costs with associated revenues. With regard to depreciation, **IFRS** requires the following:

- Each component of an asset should be depreciated separately.
- Estimates of residual value and useful life should be reviewed annually.

> Note that these are not required under **U.S. GAAP**.

The choice of depreciation method depends on how a company expects to utilize the benefits from a long-lived asset over time.

Under the straight-line method, the cost of the asset less its estimated residual value is spread evenly over the estimated useful life of the asset. This method requires estimates of residual value and useful life. Residual value is the amount that the company expects to receive upon sale of the asset at the end of its useful life.

Under accelerated methods of recording depreciation, a greater proportion of the asset's cost is allocated to the initial years of its use and a lower proportion of the cost is allocated to later years. Accelerated methods are used when the asset is expected to be utilized more heavily in the years immediately following its purchase.

Accelerated methods of depreciation result in higher depreciation expense and lower net income in the early years of an asset's life. In later years, accelerated methods recognize less depreciation expense in every accounting period, resulting in higher net income.

Amortization

Amortization refers to the allocation of the cost of an intangible asset over its useful life.

- Intangible assets with identifiable useful lives are amortized evenly over their lives in the same way as long-term assets are depreciated using the straight-line method. However, there are no estimates for residual value involved in the calculation.

- Intangible assets with indefinite lives (e.g., goodwill) are not amortized; instead they are tested annually for impairment. An asset is impaired when its current value is lower than its book value. If an asset is deemed impaired, an impairment charge (expense) is made on the income statement to bring its value down to its true current value.

Demonstration of Depreciation Methods

A variety of methods can be used to calculate depreciation expense. While annual depreciation expense might vary from method to method, total depreciation expense over the life of the asset will be the same under all methods.

Straight-line depreciation: An equal amount of depreciation expense is charged every year during the asset's useful life. Annual depreciation expense is calculated as:

$$\boxed{(\text{Cost} - \text{Residual value}) / \text{Useful life}}$$

Declining balance depreciation: This is an accelerated method of depreciation, which applies a constant rate of depreciation to a declining book value. To compute depreciation expense, we must determine the *straight-line rate*, which equals 100% divided by the number of years that the asset is expected to remain in use. For example, if the asset's useful life is 5 years, the straight-line rate would be 20% (100/5). Next, we must determine the acceleration factor, which is multiplied by the straight-line rate. The product of the two is then applied to the net book value of the asset to determine depreciation expense.

The double-declining balance method uses an acceleration factor of 200 (it depreciates the asset at a rate that is two times the straight-line rate). Depreciation expense under the double-declining balance (DDB) method is calculated as:

$$\boxed{(2 / \text{Useful life}) \times (\text{Cost} - \text{Accumulated depreciation})}$$

Unlike straight-line depreciation, the declining balance method does not explicitly take into account the residual value of the asset in determining depreciation expense each year. Under the declining balance method, the asset is only depreciated until its net book value equals its residual value.

Example 2-5 demonstrates the depreciation of long-term assets under the straight-line and double-declining balance methods.

Example 2-5: Depreciation Methods

A company purchases a new generator for its factory. The following data is available:

Cost of the generator $38,000
Estimated useful life   5 years
Residual value $3,000

Calculate the annual depreciation expense under the straight-line method and the double-declining balance method.

Solution

1. Straight-line depreciation = [38,000 − 3,000]/5 = $7,000

2. Double-declining balance depreciation

$$\text{DDB Depreciation} = (2/\text{useful life}) \times (\text{Cost} - \text{Accumulated depreciation})$$

Every year, a 40% (2/5) depreciation rate is applied to the declining book value to determine depreciation expense.

Net book value =
Historical cost − Accumulated depreciation

Net book value at the end of Year 1
= $38,000 − $15,200 = $22,800

In year 5 only $1,925 of depreciation is charged against the generator even though 4,925 × 40% equals 1,970. This is because under DDB depreciation, the asset is only depreciated until its book value equals its residual value.

DDB Depreciation Schedule

Year	Calculation $	Depreciation Expense $	Accumulated Depreciation $	Net Book Value $
				38,000
1	38,000 × 40%	15,200	15,200	22,800
2	22,800 × 40%	9,120	24,320	13,680
3	13,680 × 40%	5,472	29,792	8,208
4	8,208 × 40%	3,283	33,075	4,925
5	4,925 −3,000	1,925	35,000	3,000
Total		**$35,000**		

Depreciation expense for Year 2
= [2/5]×[$38,000 − $15,200] = $9,120

Accumulated depreciation equals total depreciation expense charged against the asset to date.

Accumulated depreciation at the end of Year 2 = $15,200 + $9,120 = $24,320

Annual depreciation expense is sensitive to two estimates—residual value and useful life. An increase in the value of these two estimates would decrease yearly depreciation expense and increase reported net income. Let's tweak the information provided in Example 2-5 to illustrate this. If the residual value of the generator is increased to $6,000 (from $3,000) and the useful life is increased to 8 years (from 5 years), annual depreciation expense under the straight-line method would equal $4,000 [(38,000 – 6,000)/8]. The increase in residual value and useful life estimates leads to a reduction in depreciation expense (from $7,000 to $4,000).

Implications for Financial Analysis

A company's estimates for doubtful accounts and warranties and estimates of useful lives and salvage values of long-lived assets directly affect net income. The subjective nature of these estimates allows management to manipulate reported financial statements. Therefore, when analyzing financial statements, analysts must carefully scrutinize the validity of used estimates. For example, if a company reports lower warranty expense in the current year compared to the previous year, an analyst should consider whether this is due to better and more reliable products, or because management had recognized an artificially high warranty expense in the previous period to inflate net income in the current period.

Accounting estimates should also be compared to those of other companies that operate in the same industry to check their validity and evaluate management integrity. If a company has a lower provision for doubtful accounts compared to a peer company, an analyst should assess whether this is because of stricter credit policies or because the company has a more aggressive accounting approach. As with revenue recognition, relative conservatism in expense recognition has a direct impact on reported financial ratios.

Accounting policies and estimates are disclosed in the footnotes to the financial statements and the management discussion and analysis (MD&A) section of the annual report.

LESSON 3: NON-RECURRING ITEMS, NON-OPERATING ITEMS

LOS 25e: Describe the financial reporting treatment and analysis of non-recurring items (including discontinued operations, extraordinary items, unusual or infrequent items) and changes in accounting standards. Vol 3, pp 178–184

In order to forecast a company's future earnings, analysts must project the company's revenues and expenses into the future. The most popular way of doing this is to use prior years' income and expense items as base figures, and to separate revenues and expenses that are likely to continue in the future from those that are not as likely to occur in the future (nonrecurring items). Two examples of nonrecurring items are discontinued operations and extraordinary items.

Discontinued Operations

Under both **IFRS** and **U.S. GAAP**, the income statement must separately report an operation as a "discontinued operation" when the company disposes of, or decides to dispose of, one of its component operations, and the component is operationally and physically separable from the rest of the firm.
- Discontinued operations are reported *net of tax* as a *separate* line item *after* income from continuing operations (this treatment is permitted under **IFRS** and **U.S. GAAP**).

- *As the disposed operation will not earn revenue for the company going forward, it will not be taken into account when formulating expectations regarding the future performance of the company.*

Extraordinary Items

IFRS does not allow any items to be classified as extraordinary. **U.S. GAAP** defines extraordinary items as being **both** unusual in nature **and** infrequent in occurrence. A significant degree of judgment is involved in classifying an item as extraordinary. For example, losses caused by Hurricane Katrina in the Unites States were not classified as extraordinary items because natural disasters could reasonably be expected to reoccur.

- Extraordinary items are reported *net of tax* and as a *separate* line item *after* income from continuing operations (below discontinued operations).
- *Analysts can eliminate extraordinary items from expectations about a company's future financial performance unless there is an indication that these extraordinary items may reoccur.*

The likelihood of certain other items continuing in the future is not as clear and requires analysts to make judgments regarding their impact on future profits. Two examples of such items are unusual or infrequent items and changes in accounting standards.

Unusual or Infrequent Items

These items are **either** unusual in nature **or** infrequent in occurrence. Examples of such items include restructuring charges and gains and losses arising from selling an asset for more or less than its carrying value.

> **IFRS** requires that income and expense items that are material and/or relevant to the understanding of a company's financial performance should be disclosed separately. Unusual or infrequent items meet these criteria.

- These items are listed as separate line items on the income statement but are *included* in income from continuing operations and hence, reported *before-tax*.
- *Analysts should not ignore all unusual items. When forecasting future profits, analysts should assess whether each of them is likely to reoccur.*

Changes in Accounting Policies

- A change in accounting policy could be required by standard setters or be decided on by management to provide a better reflection of the company's performance. An example of change in accounting policy is moving away from LIFO to the FIFO method of inventory valuation. Changes in accounting policies are applied *retrospectively*, unless it is impractical to do so. This means that financial data for all periods shown in the financial report must be presented as if the new principal were in use through the entire period. This retrospective change facilitates comparisons across reporting periods. Further, a description of and justification for the change are provided in the footnotes to the financial statements.
- A change in an accounting estimate (e.g., a change in the residual value of an asset), is applied *prospectively* and only affects financial statements for the current and future periods. No adjustments are made to prior statements and the adjustment is not shown on the face of the income statement. Significant changes in accounting estimates should be disclosed in the footnotes.
- A correction of prior-period errors is made by restating all prior-period financial statements presented in the financial report. In addition, disclosure about the error is required in the footnotes. Analysts should carefully assess these disclosures, as they may point to weaknesses in the company's accounting system or financial controls.

LOS 25f: Distinguish between the operating and non-operating components of the income statement. **Vol 3, pp 183–184**

IFRS does not define operating activities. Therefore, companies that choose to report operating income or the results of operating activities need to ensure that such activities would normally be regarded as operating.

On the other hand, **U.S. GAAP** defines operating activities as those that generally involve producing and delivering goods and providing services, and include all transactions and other events that are not defined as investing or financing activities.[9]

For example, a cloth manufacturer might receive dividend and interest income from investments in securities issued by other entities. These sources of income do not relate to the core business operations of the manufacturer and will be listed under nonoperating components of net income. Interest payments on loans taken by the manufacturer are also nonoperating items because interest expense is incurred due to a financing decision. Analysts typically use a firm's earnings before interest and taxes (EBIT) as a measure of its operating income. For financial services companies however, interest expense and income are related to their core businesses and constitute operating components of their business.

LESSON 4: EARNINGS PER SHARE, ANALYSIS OF THE INCOME STATEMENT AND COMPREHENSIVE INCOME

LOS 25g: Describe how earnings per share is calculated and calculate and interpret a company's earnings per share (both basic and diluted earnings per share) for both simple and complex capital structures. **Vol 3, pp 184–193**

LOS 25h: Distinguish between dilutive and antidilutive securities, and describe the implications of each for the earnings per share calculation. **Vol 3, pp 184–193**

Earnings per share is one of the most important profitability measures for publicly listed firms. Earnings refer to the share of net income of a company that is owned by common shareholders only.

A firm can have a simple capital structure or a complex capital structure. A company has a simple capital structure when it does not have any financial instruments outstanding that can be converted into common stock. Firms with simple capital structures are required to report basic earnings per share (EPS) only.

$$\text{Basic EPS} = \frac{\text{Income available to common shareholders}}{\text{Weighted average number of shares outstanding}}$$

$$\text{Basic EPS} = \frac{\text{Net income} - \text{Preferred dividends}}{\text{Weighted average number of shares outstanding}}$$

Preferred dividends are subtracted from net income to calculate earnings available to common shareholders. This is because preferred dividends are not included in expenses on the income statement in the calculation of net income.

---

9 - FASB ASC Master Glossary.

The weighted average number of shares outstanding refers to the number of shares that were outstanding over the year (adjusted for stock splits and stock dividends), weighted according to the proportion of the year that they were outstanding.

Example 4-1: Basic EPS

The information provided below pertains to Liu Plc. for the year ended December 31, 2008. Calculate basic EPS for the company.

Net income for 2008	$2,625,000
Preferred dividends for the year	$420,000
Weighted average number of common shares outstanding	600,000

Solution

$$\text{Basic EPS} = (\$2,625,000 - \$420,000)/600,000$$
$$= \$3.68$$

Stock repurchases result in a *decrease* in the number of shares outstanding. Therefore, reacquired shares are excluded from the computation of weighted average number of shares from the date of repurchase. For example, if a company had 1,000 shares outstanding at the start of the year and repurchased 100 shares in July, the weighted average number of shares outstanding would be calculated as:

Weighted average number of shares = $(1,000 \times 12/12) - (100 \times 6/12) = 950$

In contrast, stock splits and stock dividends (stock bonus) result in an *increase* in the number of shares outstanding.

- In a stock split, existing shares in a company are "split" into more shares. A 2-for-1 stock split will increase the number of shares held by a holder of 1,000 shares by 1,000 shares to 2,000 shares. After a 3-for-2 stock split, the owner of 1,000 shares will see her shareholding increase by 500 shares to 1,500 shares.
- A stock dividend is a dividend paid as additional shares of stock rather than cash. These additional shares are granted to each shareholder in proportion to her current holding. After a 25% stock dividend, the holder of 1,000 shares will get 250 (25%) more shares to take her total shareholding to 1,250 shares.

> We multiply the 100 repurchased shares by (6/12) because they were repurchased in July and were not a part of the company's outstanding capital for 6 months.

Important: If a company declares a stock split or a stock dividend, the weighted average number of shares outstanding should be calculated based on the assumption that the additional (newly granted) shares have been outstanding since the date that the original shares were outstanding. Example 4-2 will clarify this important point.

Example 4-2: Basic EPS Calculation

LEM Company has reported net income of $1,850,000 for the year ended December 31, 2008. The company declared preferred dividends of $150,000. The following information regarding shares outstanding is available:

Shares outstanding at January 1, 2008	1,000,000
2–1 Stock split on April 1, 2008	
Shares issued on June 30, 2008	500,000
10% Stock dividend on September 1, 2008	
Shares repurchased on October 1, 2008	150,000
Shares outstanding on December 31, 2008	2,600,000

Shares issued during the year enter the computation from the date of issuance.

The stock split and stock dividend are applied to all shares outstanding prior to the split or dividend announcement. They are not applied to any shares issued or repurchased after the announcement. The stock split applies only to the 1 million shares outstanding at Jan 1. The stock dividend applies to the 1 million shares outstanding since Jan 1, the additional shares issued on those 1 million shares in the stock split, and to the 500,000 shares that were issued on June 30.

Calculate 2008 basic EPS for LEM.

Solution

Shares outstanding on January 1	**1,000,000**
2–for-1 stock split	1,000,000
	2,000,000
10% stock dividend.	200,000
Shares outstanding since January 1 (for 12 months)	2,200,000
Shares issued on June 30	**500,000**
10% stock dividend	50,000
Shares outstanding since June 30 (for 6 months)	550,000
Shares repurchased on October 1	
Not outstanding for 3 months	150,000

VERY IMPORTANT

When weighting the shares, assume that the new shares issued from the stock split or stock dividend were outstanding NOT since date of split or stock dividend declaration, but from the date that the original shares were outstanding from.

Weighted average number of shares outstanding

$$= (2,200,000 \times 12/12) + (550,000 \times 6/12) - (150,000 \times 3/12) = \mathbf{2{,}437{,}500}$$

$$\text{Basic EPS} = \frac{(\text{Net income} - \text{Preferred dividends})}{\text{Weighted average number of shares outstanding}}$$

Basic EPS = ($1,850,000 − $150,000)/2,437,500 = **$0.70**

The if converted method is used to calculate diluted EPS when the company has convertible securities outstanding.

A complex capital structure is one that contains certain financial instruments that can be converted into common stock (e.g., convertible bonds, convertible preferred stock, warrants, and options). These financial instruments are potentially dilutive, so companies with complex capital structures are required to report basic and diluted EPS. A dilutive security is one whose conversion into shares of common stock would result in a reduction in EPS. EPS calculated after taking into account all dilutive financial instruments in the capital structure is known as diluted EPS. Financial instruments that can be converted into common stock, but whose conversion does not reduce EPS below basic EPS, are anti-dilutive. Anti-dilutive financial instruments are not considered in the calculation of diluted EPS. Accounting standards require companies to disclose diluted EPS because this information is important for existing common shareholders.

Diluted EPS when a Company has Convertible Preferred Stock Outstanding

If convertible preferred shares were converted into common shares:

- We would add back dividends paid to convertible preferred shareholders to our numerator (earnings available to common shareholders). This is because the company would not be required to pay any preferred dividends on convertible preferred shares if these shares were converted into ordinary shares.
- We would increase the number of shares outstanding by the number of common shares that would be issued to convertible preferred shareholders upon conversion.

$$\text{Diluted EPS} = \frac{\text{Net income} - \text{Preferred dividends} + \text{Convertible preferred dividends}}{\text{Weighted average number of shares outstanding} + \text{New common shares issued upon conversion}}$$

Example 4-3: Diluted EPS

Xingia Inc. earns profits of $2,500,000 for the year ended December 31, 2008. Xingia has 1,000,000 weighted average shares outstanding during the year and pays taxes at the rate of 40%. Xingia also has 1,000 convertible preferred shares outstanding, which pay a dividend of $50 per share every year. Each convertible preferred share can be converted into 100 common shares. Calculate Xingia's basic and diluted EPS for 2008.

Solution

Basic EPS = ($2,500,000 − $50,000) / 1,000,000 = **$2.45**

Each preferred share can be converted into 100 shares of common stock. Therefore:

Number of common shares issued upon conversion = 100 × 1,000 = **100,000**

Diluted EPS = ($2,500,000 − $50,000 + $50,000) / (1,000,000 + 100,000) = **$2.27**

Since basic EPS equals $2.45 and EPS assuming that convertible preferred shares are converted is lower ($2.27), the convertible preferred shares are dilutive. If EPS after conversion were greater than basic EPS, these shares would be anti-dilutive and would not be included in the calculation of diluted EPS.

A quick way to determine whether convertible preferred shares are dilutive is by calculating:

$$\frac{\text{Convertible preferred dividends}}{\text{New shares issued upon conversion}}$$

If this per share figure is lower than basic EPS, the convertible preferred shares are dilutive, and should be included in the calculation of diluted EPS. If this figure is greater than basic EPS, the convertible preferred shares are anti-dilutive and should be ignored in the calculation of diluted EPS.

Diluted EPS when a Company has Convertible Debt Outstanding

If convertible bonds were converted into ordinary shares:

- We would add interest payments that were made to bondholders back to the numerator. This is because the company would not be required to make any interest payments to holders of convertible bonds if these bonds were converted to ordinary shares. However, the increase in earnings available to common shareholders is not the entire amount of interest savings from inversion. Recall that interest expense is deducted from operating profits before the calculation of net income before tax, so interest expense results in a tax shield for the company. Interest savings adjusted for the tax shield benefits that have already been realized will be added to the numerator.
- The number of shares outstanding will increase by the number of common shares that would be issued to convertible debt holders upon conversion.

$$\text{Diluted EPS} = \frac{\text{Net income} - \text{Preferred dividends} + \text{Convertible debt interest} \times (1 - t)}{\text{Weighted average number of shares outstanding} + \text{New common shares issued upon conversion}}$$

Example 4-4: Diluted EPS

Xingia Inc. earns profits of $2,500,000 for the year ended December 31, 2008. Xingia has a weighted average of 1,000,000 shares outstanding during the year and pays taxes at the rate of 40%. Xingia has 1,000 preferred shares outstanding, which offer a dividend of $50 per share every year. Xingia also has $75,000 par of 10% convertible bonds outstanding, which are convertible into 7,000 shares of common stock. Calculate Xingia's basic and diluted EPS for 2008.

Solution

Basic EPS = ($2,500,000 − $50,000) / 1,000,000 Shares = **$2.45**

To determine diluted EPS, we must first calculate the after-tax interest on convertible debt.

After tax interest on convertible debt = $7,500 (1 − 0.40) = **$4,500**

The convertible bonds can be converted into **7,000** shares of common stock.

Diluted EPS = ($2,500,000 − $50,000 + $4,500) / (1,000,000 + 7,000) = **$2.43**

Since basic EPS is $2.45 and EPS assuming that convertible bonds are converted is lower ($2.43), the company's outstanding convertible bonds are dilutive, and diluted EPS for 2008 equals $2.43.

> The preference shares in this example cannot be converted into ordinary shares so they are not considered in the calculation of diluted EPS.

A quick way to determine whether convertible bonds are dilutive is by calculating:

$$\frac{\text{Convertible bond interest } (1-t)}{\text{New shares issued upon conversion}}$$

If this per share figure is lower than basic EPS, the convertible bonds are dilutive and should be included in the calculation of diluted EPS. If this figure is greater than basic EPS, the convertible bonds are anti-dilutive and should be ignored in the calculation of diluted EPS.

Diluted EPS when a Company has Stock Options, Warrants, or their Equivalents Outstanding

In the calculation of diluted EPS, stock options and warrants are accounted for using the treasury stock method (required under **U.S. GAAP**). The treasury stock method assumes that all the funds received by the company from the exercise of options and warrants are used by the company to repurchase shares at the average market price for the period. The resulting net increase in number of shares outstanding equals the increase in shares from the exercise of options and warrants minus the number of shares repurchased.

Stock options and warrants are assumed to be exercised if the strike or exercise price is lower than the average market price during the year. The proceeds to the company from the exercise of the options equal the exercise price multiplied by the number of options. These proceeds are used to repurchase shares at the average market price. In calculating diluted EPS:

> Year-end stock prices do NOT matter in determining whether options and warrants are exercised.

- No adjustment must be made to the numerator because the exercise of options or warrants has no impact on income available to common shareholders.
- The number of shares outstanding increases by the number of shares issued upon exercise of options minus the number of shares repurchased with the proceeds of option exercise. A shortcut for calculating the net increase in the number of shares is:

$$\frac{\text{Market price} - \text{Exercise price}}{\text{Market price}} \times \begin{array}{l}\text{Number of shares created}\\\text{from the exercise of options}\end{array}$$

$$\text{Diluted EPS} = \frac{\text{Net income}}{\begin{array}{c}\text{Weighted average number of shares outstanding} + \text{New shares issued at}\\\text{option exercise} - \text{Shares repurchased from proceeds of option exercise}\end{array}}$$

> **IFRS** requires the use of a similar method, but does not refer to it as the treasury stock method. The proceeds of option exercise are assumed to be used to repurchase shares at the average market price and these shares are known as inferred shares. The excess of new issued shares over inferred shares is added to the weighted average number of shares outstanding.

Example 4-5: Diluted EPS

Xingia Inc. earns profits of $2,500,000 for the year ended December 31, 2008. Xingia has 1,000,000 shares outstanding during the year and pays taxes at the rate of 40%. Xingia paid preference dividends amounting to $50,000 in 2008. The average market price of Xingia's stock over the year was $50. Xingia has 10,000 stock options outstanding, which have an exercise price of $30. Calculate Xingia's diluted EPS for 2008.

Solution

Since the average market price exceeds the exercise price of the options, they should be assumed to have been exercised.

Number of common shares issued to option holders = **10,000**

Cash proceeds from exercise of options = **$300,000** (10,000 shares × $30)

Number of shares that can be purchased at average market price with these funds = $300,000/$50 = **6,000**

Net increase in common shares outstanding from the exercise of options = 10,000 − 6,000 = **4,000**

Diluted EPS = $2,500,000 − $50,000 / (1,000,000 + 10,000 − 6,000) = **$ 2.44**

Diluted EPS ($2.44) is lower than basic EPS ($2.45). Therefore, the options are dilutive and should be considered in the calculation of diluted EPS.

When options/warrants are exercised (average market price is greater than exercise price) they result in an increase in the number of shares outstanding. Because their exercise only has an impact on the denominator of the EPS formula, options and warrants are always dilutive if exercised.

Now let's calculate diluted EPS for Xingia assuming that all three types of potentially dilutive financial instruments are present in its capital structure.

Important: In determining which potentially dilutive financial instruments should be included in the diluted EPS calculation, each of the financial instruments must be evaluated individually and independently to determine whether they are dilutive. If there are any anti-dilutive financial instruments, they must be ignored from the diluted EPS calculation.

Example 4-6: Diluted EPS

Xingia Inc. earns profits of $2,500,000 for the year ended December 31, 2008. Xingia has 1,000,000 weighted average shares outstanding during the year and pays taxes at the rate of 40%. The average market price of Xingia's stock over the year was $50. Xingia has 1,000 convertible preferred shares outstanding with each share convertible into 100 shares of common stock. It pays a dividend of $50 per share on these shares. Xingia also has $75,000 par of 10% convertible bonds outstanding which are convertible into 7,000 shares of common stock. Further, it has 10,000 stock options outstanding, which have an exercise price of $30. Calculate Xingia's basic and diluted EPS for 2008.

Solution

Basic EPS = ($2,500,000 − $50,000) / 1,000,000 shares = **$2.45**

Diluted EPS

In Examples 4-3, 4-4, and 4-5, we have already determined that all three potentially dilutive financial instruments are, in fact, dilutive. Xingia's diluted 2008 EPS is calculated as:

$$\text{Diluted EPS} = \frac{\left[\text{Net income} - \begin{array}{c}\text{Preferred}\\\text{dividends}\end{array}\right] + \begin{array}{c}\text{Convertible}\\\text{preferred}\\\text{dividends}\end{array} + \left[\begin{array}{c}\text{Convertible}\\\text{debt}\\\text{interest}\end{array} \times (1-t)\right]}{\begin{array}{c}\text{Weighted}\\\text{average}\\\text{shares}\end{array} + \begin{array}{c}\text{Shares from}\\\text{conversion of}\\\text{convertible}\\\text{preferred shares}\end{array} + \begin{array}{c}\text{Shares from}\\\text{conversion of}\\\text{convertible}\\\text{debt}\end{array} + \begin{array}{c}\text{Shares}\\\text{issuable from}\\\text{stock options}\end{array}}$$

$$\text{Diluted EPS} = \frac{2,500,000 - 50,000 + 50,000 + 7,500(1-0.4)}{1,000,000 + 100,000 + 7,000 + 4,000} = \textbf{\$2.25}$$

Example 4-7: Anti-Dilutive Financial Instruments

Acme Inc. reported a net income of $2,500,000 over the year. During the year its weighted average number of common shares outstanding was 1,000,000. Acme also had 25,000 convertible preferred shares outstanding on which it paid a dividend of $7 per share. Each of these shares are convertible into 2 shares of common stock. Calculate basic EPS and diluted EPS for Acme for the year.

Solution

Basic EPS = [(2,500,000 − 175,000)/1,000,000] = **$2.33**

Diluted EPS

If the convertible preferred shares were converted into common shares, EPS would equal:

$$(\$2,500,000 - \$175,000 + \$175,000) / (1,000,000 + 50,000) = \textbf{\$2.38}$$

EPS assuming the convertible preferred shares are converted into common stock ($2.38) is greater than basic EPS ($2.33). The convertible preferred shares are anti-dilutive, and should not be included in the calculation of diluted EPS. The firm's diluted EPS is therefore, the same as its basic EPS of $2.33.

One final note: If dilutive financial instruments were issued during the year, the denominator of the diluted EPS formula would increase by the number of shares issued upon conversion/ exercise multiplied by the proportion of the year that they were outstanding for. For example, if dilutive convertible preferred shares that can be converted into 10,000 shares of common stock were issued after 9 months of the accounting year had passed, the denominator of the diluted EPS formula would be increased by $10,000 \times (3/12) = 2,500$.

*Note: Both **U.S. GAAP** and **IFRS** require the presentation of EPS (basic EPS and diluted EPS) on the face of the income statement.*

LESSON 5: ANALYSIS OF THE INCOME STATEMENT AND COMPREHENSIVE INCOME

LOS 25i: Convert income statements to common-size income statements.
Vol 3, pp 193–198

LOS 25j: Evaluate a company's financial performance using common-size income statements and financial ratios based on the income statement.
Vol 3, pp 193–198

Analysis of the Income Statement

Common-size income statements present each line item on the income statement as a percentage of *sales*. The standardization of each item removes the effect of company size and facilitates financial statement analysis, as the data can be used to conduct time-series (across time periods) and cross-sectional (across companies) analysis.

While common-size income statements present most items as a percentage of sales, it is more appropriate to present income taxes as a percentage of pre-tax income. This ratio is known as the company's effective tax rate. In cross-sectional analysis, effective tax rates are compared across companies and sources of any differences are analyzed in detail.

Exhibit 5-1 presents common-size income statement of Liuson Company. Notice that the provision for income taxes has been expressed as a percentage of income before tax.

Exhibit 5-1: Common-Size Income Statement

Liuson Company
Common Size Income Statement
For the year ended 2006 and 2007

	2006 $	2006 %	2007 $	2007 %
Total revenue	400,000	100.00	500,000	100.00
Cost of goods sold	(320,000)	80.00	(380,000)	76.00
Gross profit	80,000	20.00	120,000	24.00
Operating expenses				
General expenses	(28,000)	7.00	(29,000)	5.80
Depreciation	(8,000)	2.00	(12,000)	2.40
Operating income	44,000	11.00	79,000	15.8
Interest income	3,000	0.75	2,000	0.40
Interest expense	(400)	0.10	(1,800)	0.36
Other losses	(1,800)	0.45	(4,200)	0.84
Income before income taxes	44,800	11.20	75,000	15.00
Provision for income taxes	(16,000)	35.71	(21,000)	28.00
Net income	28,800	7.20	54,000	10.80

The things that stand out in Liuson's common-size statements are that:
- Cost of goods sold has decreased from 80% to 76% of sales, so the gross margin has increased.
- General expenses decreased from 7% to 6% of sales.
- The net profit margin has increased significantly from 7% to 11%.

This implies that management is effectively controlling costs in order to boost profitability. Common-size income statements are discussed in detail in Reading 28.

Income Statement Ratios

Items listed on the income statement are used to calculate ratios to evaluate a company's profitability. Gross profit margin and net profit margin are the two most commonly used indicators of profitability.

- Net profit margin = Net income / Revenue
- Gross profit margin = Gross profit / Revenue

Any sub-total on the income statement can also be expressed as a margin ratio by dividing it by total revenue. For example, operating margin is calculated as operating income (EBIT) divided by sales, and pre-tax margin is calculated as earnings before tax (EBT) divided by total revenue.

Income statement ratios are discussed in more detail in Reading 28.

LOS 25k: Describe, calculate, and interpret comprehensive income.
Vol 3, pp 198–201

LOS 25l: Describe other comprehensive income, and identify the major types of items included in it. Vol 3, pp 198–201

Most revenues, gains, expenses, and losses are reported on the income statement to determine a company's net income. However, there are certain income and expense items that are excluded from the income statement; instead these items are reported directly in shareholders' equity (**U.S. GAAP** only), or in a separate statement of comprehensive income (**IFRS** and **U.S. GAAP**) as a part of other comprehensive income.

IFRS defines total comprehensive income as "the change in equity during a period resulting from transaction and other events, other than those changes resulting from transactions with owners in their capacity as owners."[10]

Under **U.S. GAAP**, comprehensive income is defined as "the change in equity (net assets) of a business enterprise during a period from transactions and other events and circumstances from nonowner sources. It includes all changes in equity during a period except those resulting from investments by owners and distributions to owners."[11]

Comprehensive income includes both net income and *other* revenues and expenses that are excluded from the net income calculation (other comprehensive income). Both net income and other comprehensive income have an impact on retained earnings.

> Comprehensive income = Net income plus other comprehensive income

$$\text{Ending shareholders' equity} = \frac{\text{Beginning shareholders' equity} + \text{Net income} +}{\text{Other comprehensive income} - \text{Dividends declared}}$$

Suppose a company's beginning shareholders' equity was $100 million. Its net income for the period was $10 million, and it declared $1 million as dividends. There was no repurchase or issuance of common stock during the year and the company's year-end shareholders' equity stood at $130 million. The company's other comprehensive income will be calculated as:

Other comprehensive income = $130m − 100m − 10m + 1m = $21 million

Items Classified as Other Comprehensive Income

Four types of items are classified as other comprehensive income under both **IFRS** and **U.S. GAAP:**
- Foreign currency translation adjustments.
- Certain costs relating to the company's defined benefit post-retirement plans.
- Unrealized gains or losses on derivatives contracts, accounted for as hedges.
- Unrealized holding gains and losses on available-for-sale securities.

Under **IFRS**, certain changes in the value of long-lived assets that are measured using the revaluation model (as opposed to the cost model) at fair value are also included in other comprehensive income.

---

10 - IAS 1, Presentation of Financial Statements, paragraph 7.
11 - FASB ASC Section 220–10–05 [Comprehensive Income-Overall-Overview and Background]

Example 5-1: Calculating Comprehensive Income

Company XYZ – Selected Financial Statement Data

Net income	$1,000
Dividends received from available-for-sale securities	60
Unrealized gain from foreign currency translation adjustment	20
Dividends paid	(100)
Reacquisition of common stock	(300)
Unrealized loss on derivatives (those considered as hedges)	(20)
Unrealized gain on available-for-sale securities	15
Realized loss on sale of machinery	(50)

Comprehensive income equals net income plus other comprehensive income

Net income	$1,000	
Unrealized gain from foreign currency adjustment	20	Other
Unrealized loss on derivatives considered as hedges	(20)	Comprehensive
Unrealized gain on available-for-sale securities	15	Income = $15
Comprehensive Income	**$1,015**	

Important points:

- We do not include dividends from available-for-sale securities and the realized loss on machinery in other comprehensive income because they are already included in net income.

- We do not include reacquisition of common stock and dividends paid in the calculation because they are transactions that relate to owners. Other comprehensive income does not include the effect of investments by owners and distributions to owners. These transactions are accounted for in the statement of changes in shareholders' equity.

When comparing the financial performance of companies, it is very important for analysts to examine significant differences in overall comprehensive income (as opposed to simply focusing on net income).

READING 26: UNDERSTANDING BALANCE SHEETS

LESSON 1: BALANCE SHEET: COMPONENTS AND FORMAT

The balance sheet (also called the statement of financial position or statement of financial condition) provides users with information regarding a company's assets, liabilities, and equity at a specific point in time. It also provides insights into the future earnings capacity of the company as well as indications regarding expected cash flows.

LOS 26a: Describe the elements of the balance sheet: assets, liabilities, and equity. Vol 3, pp 212–213

Assets

Assets are resources under a company's control as a result of past transactions that are expected to generate future economic benefits for the company.

Liabilities

Liabilities are a company's obligations from previous transactions that are expected to result in outflows of economic benefits in the future.

Assets and liabilities may arise from business transactions (e.g., the purchase of a piece of equipment) or as a result of accrual accounting. As we saw in Reading 23, differences between the timing of revenue and expense recognition (based on accrual accounting) and the timing of related cash flows give rise to current assets and liabilities.

Assets and liabilities should only be recognized on the financial statements if it is probable that the future economic benefits associated with them will flow to or from the firm, and that the item's cost or value can be measured with reliability.

Equity

Equity represents the residual claim of shareholders on a company's assets after deducting all liabilities. Other terms commonly used for shareholders' equity include stockholders' equity, net assets, and owners' equity. Equity can be created as a result of operating activities (business transactions that yield operating profits) and financing activities (issuance of common stock).

LOS 26b: Describe the uses and limitations of the balance sheet in financial analysis. Vol 3, p 213

The balance sheet provides useful information regarding a company's financial position to both investors and lenders. However, balance sheet information should be interpreted carefully. Analysts should be careful not to view equity reported on the balance sheet as either the market or intrinsic value of a company's net assets because of the following reasons:

- Under current accounting standards, measurement bases of different assets and liabilities may vary considerably. For example, some assets and liabilities may be measured at historical cost, while others may be measured at current value. These differences can have a significant impact on reported figures.

- The value of items reported on the balance sheet reflects their value at the end of the reporting period, which may not necessarily remain "current" at a later date.
- The balance sheet does not include qualitative factors (e.g., reputation, management skills, etc.) that have an important impact on the company's future cash-generating ability and therefore, its overall value.

Latter sections of this reading and other subsequent readings will comprehensively illustrate the use of balance sheets in evaluating the financial strength of a company.

LOS 26c: Describe alternative formats of balance sheet presentation. Vol 3, pp 213–214

Balance sheets may be presented in any of the following formats:

- Report format: Assets, liabilities, and equity are presented in a single column. This format is the most commonly used balance sheet presentation format.
- Account format: Assets are presented on the left-hand side of the balance sheet, with liabilities and equity on the right-hand side.
- Classified balance sheet: Different types of assets and liabilities are grouped into subcategories to give a more effective overview of the company's financial position. Classifications typically group assets and liabilities into their current and non-current portions.
- Liquidity-based presentation: **IFRS** allows the preparation of a balance sheet using a liquidity-based presentation format (rather than a current/non-current format), if such a format provides more reliable and relevant information. In a liquidity-based presentation, all assets and liabilities are broadly presented in order of liquidity. This format is typically used by banks.

> For a company, liquidity refers to the company's ability to meet short-term cash requirements. For an individual asset, liquidity refers to how quickly the asset can be converted to cash at a price close to its fair market value.

We will use the balance sheet of Nexen Company (Exhibit 1-1) to describe current and non-current assets and liabilities that are typically found on balance sheets.

Exhibit 1-1: Sample Balance Sheet

Nexen Company
Balance Sheet

	2008 $	2007 $
ASSETS		
1 **Current Assets**	**22,000**	**18,500**
Cash and cash equivalents 1a	6,000	4,500
Marketable securities 1b	5,000	6,000
Trade receivables 1c	4,000	2,000
Inventories 1d	6,000	5,500
Other current assets 1e	1,000	500
2 **Noncurrent Assets**	**81,000**	**57,500**
Property, plant, and equipment 2a	50,000	40,000
Goodwill 2b	10,000	8,000
Other intangible assets	6,000	2,000
Non-current investments (subsidiaries)	15,000	7,500
TOTAL ASSETS	**103,000**	**76,000**
LIABILITIES AND EQUITY		
3 **Current Liabilities**	**24,500**	**14,000**
Trade and other payables 3a	7,000	3,000
Current borrowings 3b	6,000	2,000
Current portion of non-current borrowings 3c	3,000	2,000
Current taxes payable 3d	4,000	4,000
Accrued liabilities 3e	2,500	1,500
Unearned revenue 3f	2,000	1,500
4 **Non-current Liabilities**	**37,000**	**25,000**
Non-current borrowings	25,000	15,000
Deferred taxes	10,000	8,000
Noncurrent provisions	2,000	2,000
TOTAL LIABILITIES	**61,500**	**39,000**
5 **EQUITY**	**41,500**	**37,000**
Common stock	25,000	25,000
Preferred shares 5a	5,000	5,000
Reserves	2,000	0
Retained earnings 5b	12,500	9,000
Shares repurchased (Treasury stock) 5c	(3,000)	(2,000)
TOTAL LIABILITIES AND **SHAREHOLDERS' EQUITY**	**103,000**	**76,000**

Nexen uses the title Balance Sheet. Other companies use "Statement of Financial Position."

LOS 26d: Distinguish between current and non-current assets and current and non-current liabilities. Vol 3, pp 215–217

IFRS and U.S. GAAP Balance Sheet Presentation

Both **IFRS** and **U.S. GAAP** require that assets and liabilities be grouped separately into their current and non-current portions, which makes it easier for analysts to examine the company's liquidity position as of the balance sheet date. However, it is not required that current assets be presented before non-current assets, or that current liabilities be presented before non-current liabilities (even though this is the case in Nexen's balance sheet). Further, under **IFRS**, the current/non-current classifications are not required if a liquidity-based presentation provides more relevant and reliable information.

1 ← Current assets: These are liquid assets that are likely to be converted into cash or realized within one year or one operating cycle, whichever is longer. The operating cycle is the average time taken by a company to convert the funds used to purchase inventory or raw materials into cash proceeds from sales to customers. Current assets may be listed in order of liquidity, with cash being the first item listed.

2 ← Non-current assets (also known as long-term or long-life assets): These are less liquid assets and are not expected to be converted into cash within one year or within one operating cycle. They represent the infrastructure that the firm uses in its operations and other investments made from a strategic or long-term perspective.

3 ← Current liabilities: These are obligations that are likely to be settled within one year or one operating cycle, whichever is longer. Specifically, a liability may be classified as a current liability if:
- It is expected to be settled in the entity's normal operating cycle;
- It is primarily held for the purpose of trading;
- It is due to be settled within one year after the balance sheet date; or
- The entity does not have an unconditional right to defer settlement of the liability for at least one year after the balance sheet date.[1]

IFRS allow some liabilities such as trade payables and accruals for employees to be classified as current liabilities even though they might not be settled within one year.

4 ← Non-current liabilities: These liabilities are not expected to be settled within a year or within one operating cycle. Non-current liabilities are a source of long-term finance for a company.

> We shall study working capital management in greater detail in Reading 39.

Working capital: The difference between current assets and current liabilities is known as working capital. Working capital is necessary for the smooth functioning of a firm's daily operations. Low working capital levels suggest that the company might be unable to meet its short-term obligations. Excessively high levels of working capital indicate that the company is not utilizing its resources efficiently.

---

1 - IAS 1, Presentation of Financial Statements, paragraph 69.

LOS 26e: Describe different types of assets and liabilities and the measurement bases of each. Vol 3, pp 217–241

Individual assets and liabilities are reported on the balance sheet using different measurement bases. The challenge for analysts lies in understanding how the reported values of assets and liabilities relate to *economic reality* and to each other. As stated previously, balance sheet values should not be assumed to be accurate measures of the value of a company. For example, land is usually presented at its historical cost. If prices have increased significantly since the date of acquisition, the total value of assets is understated on the balance sheet. The balance sheet provides important information about the value of certain assets and information about expected future cash flows, but does not always accurately represent the value of the company as a whole.

Current Assets

These are assets that can be liquidated or consumed by the company within one year, or one operating cycle, whichever is greater. Accounting standards require that certain specific line items must be shown on a balance sheet if they are material (e.g., cash and cash equivalents, trade and other receivables, inventories, and financial assets [with short maturities]).   → 1

Cash and cash equivalents   → 1a

Cash equivalents are highly liquid securities that usually mature in less than 90 days. Since they are so close to maturity, there is minimal risk of any change in their value due to changes in interest rates. Since cash equivalents are financial assets, they may be measured at amortized cost or fair value.
- Amortized cost equals historical cost adjusted for amortization and impairment.
- Fair value under **IFRS** equals the amount at which the asset can be exchanged in an arm's length transaction between willing and informed parties. Under **U.S. GAAP**, fair value is based on exit price—the price received to sell an asset.

The amortized cost and fair values of cash equivalents are usually very similar.

Marketable securities   → 1b

These are also financial assets and include investments in debt and equity securities that are traded on public markets. Their balance sheet values are based on market price.

Trade receivables   → 1c

Also considered financial assets, trade receivables represent amounts owed to the company by customers to whom sales have been made. These amounts are usually reported at net realizable value (an estimate of fair value based on the company's expectations regarding collectability).

> The provision for doubtful accounts is called a contra-asset account as it is netted against accounts receivable (an asset account).

- The relation between accounts receivable and sales is important. A significant increase in accounts receivable relative to sales may imply that the company is having problems collecting cash from customers.
- An increase in the allowance for doubtful accounts (the company's estimate of uncollectable amounts) results in a lower value reported under trade receivables (assets), and bad debts (expense) being reported on the income statement.
- The more diversified the customer base, the lower the credit risk of accounts receivable.

1d ←— Inventories

Inventory valuation
methods, write-
downs, and analysis
are covered in depth
in Reading 29.

These are physical stocks held by the company in the form of finished goods, work-in-progress, or raw materials. Measurement of inventory differs under **IFRS** and **U.S. GAAP**.

- Under **IFRS**, inventory is reported at the lower of cost and net realizable value (NRV).
- Under **U.S. GAAP**, inventory is reported at the lower of cost and market.

NRV is calculated as selling price minus selling costs, while cost is determined by the cost flow assumption (LIFO, FIFO, or average cost) that is used. Market value (under **U.S. GAAP**) equals the current replacement cost of inventory, which must lie between NRV minus the normal profit margin and NRV.

Inventory costs should include direct materials, direct labor, and overheads. However, the following amounts should not be included when calculating inventory cost:

- Abnormal amounts of wasted materials, labor, and overheads.
- Storage costs incurred after the production process is complete.
- Administrative overheads.
- Selling costs.

In limited cases, standard cost or the retail method can be used for valuing inventory. Standard cost should take into account normal levels of materials, labor, and actual capacity. The retail method reduces selling price by gross profit margin to determine the cost of inventory.

Once inventory is sold, its cost is reported as an expense in the income statement under "cost of goods sold."

1e ←— Other current assets

Items that are not material enough to be reported as a separate line item on the balance sheet are aggregated into a single amount and reported as "other current assets." These may include the following:

Prepaid expenses are normal operating expenses that have been paid in advance, so they are recognized as assets on the balance sheet. Over time, they are expensed on the income statement and the value of the asset is reduced. For example, suppose that at the beginning of the year a company makes a payment of $60,000 as advance payment for a year's rent. This results in reduction in cash of $60,000 and a corresponding increase in prepaid expenses (asset). At the end of the first quarter, three months rent of $15,000 will be expensed and the prepaid rent asset will be decreased by $15,000. By the end of the year, the entire $60,000 would have been charged as an expense on the income statement and the balance of the prepaid rent asset account will be zero.

Deferred tax assets (DTA) usually arise when a company's taxes payable exceed its income tax expense. They represent a kind of prepayment of taxes and therefore, count as assets. DTA will be discussed in more detail in Reading 31.

Current Liabilities → 3

These are a company's obligations that are expected to be settled within one year or one operating cycle, whichever is greater. Current liabilities that are typically found on the balance sheet include the following:

Trade payables (accounts payable) → 3a

These are amounts owed by the business to its suppliers for purchases on credit. Analysts are usually interested in examining the trend in the levels of trade payables relative to purchases to gain insight into the company's relationships with its suppliers.

Notes payables (current borrowings) → 3b

These financial liabilities are borrowings from creditors that are documented by a loan agreement. Depending on the agreed repayment date, notes payable may also be included in non-current liabilities.

Current portion of long-term liabilities → 3c

These represent portions of long-term debt obligations that are expected to be paid within a year of the balance sheet date or within one operating cycle, whichever is greater.

Income taxes payable → 3d

These are taxes (based on taxable income) have not actually been paid yet.

Accrued liabilities → 3e

These are expenses that have been recognized on the income statement but have still not been paid for as of the balance sheet date.

Unearned revenue (deferred revenue or deferred income) → 3f

This arises when a company receives cash in advance for goods and services that are still to be delivered. The company is obligated to either provide the goods or services or to return the cash received.

Non-Current Assets → 2

Non-current assets typically include the following:

Property, plant, and equipment (PP&E) → 2a

These are long-term assets that have physical substance. Examples of tangible assets treated as PP&E include land, plant, machinery, equipment, and any natural resources owned by the company.

> The cost and revaluation models for PP&E along with impairment and investment property are discussed in more detail in Reading 30.

Under **IFRS**, PP&E may be valued using either the cost model or the revaluation model. However, companies need to ensure that the chosen method is applied to all the assets within a particular class of assets. **U.S. GAAP** only allows the cost model for reporting PP&E.

Investment property

IFRS defines investment property as property that is owned (or leased under a finance lease) for rental income and/or capital appreciation. Under **IFRS**, investment property may be valued using the cost model or the fair value model. The chosen model must be applied to all investment properties held by the company. Further, a company may only use the fair value model if it is able to determine the fair value of the investment property on a continuing basis with reliability. **U.S. GAAP** does not include a specific definition for investment property.

We will study the accounting standards related to intangible assets in detail in Reading 30.

Intangible assets

These are identifiable, non-monetary assets that lack physical substance. Under **IFRS**, intangible assets may be reported using either the cost model or the revaluation model. However, the revaluation model can only be selected if there is an active market for the asset. **U.S. GAAP** only allows the cost model.

- Intangible assets with finite useful lives are amortized systematically over their lives and may also be impaired depending on circumstances. Impairment principles for these assets are the same as those that apply to PP&E.
- Intangible assets with indefinite useful lives are not amortized, but are tested for impairment at least annually.

Financial statement disclosures provide important information (e.g., useful lives, amortization rates and methods) regarding a company's intangible assets.

Identifiable intangible assets can be acquired singly and are usually related to rights and privileges that accrue to the their owners over a finite period. Under **IFRS**, identifiable intangible assets may only be recognized if it is probable that future economic benefits will flow to the company and the cost of the asset can be measured reliably. A company may develop intangible assets internally, but such assets can only be recognized under certain circumstances. Under both **IFRS** and **U.S. GAAP**, costs related to the following are usually expensed:

- Start-up and training costs.
- Administrative and overhead costs.
- Advertising and promotion costs.
- Relocation and reorganization costs.

Acquired intangible assets may be reported as separately identifiable intangibles (rather than goodwill) if:

- They arise from contractual rights (e.g., licensing agreements), or other legal rights (e.g., patents); or
- Can be separated and sold (e.g., customer lists).

2b ← Goodwill (an example of an asset that is not separately identifiable) is the excess of the amount paid to acquire a business over the fair value of its net assets. The purchase price may exceed the fair value of the target company's identifiable (tangible and intangible) net assets because of the following reasons:

- Certain items of value (e.g., reputation, brand) are not recognized in a company's financial statements.
- The target company may have incurred research and development expenditures that may have not been recognized on its financial statements but do hold value for the acquirer.
- The acquisition may improve the acquirer's position against a competitor or there may be possible synergies.

Note that goodwill is only created (recognized) in a purchase acquisition. Internally generated goodwill is expensed.

Analysts must understand the difference between accounting and economic goodwill. Accounting goodwill is based on accounting standards and is only reported for acquisitions when the purchase price exceeds the fair value of the acquired company's net assets. Economic goodwill, which is not reflected on the balance sheet, is based on a company's performance and its future prospects. Analysts are more concerned with economic goodwill as it contributes to the value of the firm and should be reflected in its stock price.

Under **U.S. GAAP** and **IFRS**, accounting goodwill resulting from acquisitions is capitalized. Further, under both sets of standards, goodwill is not amortized, but is tested for impairment annually. An impairment charge reduces net income and decreases the carrying value of goodwill to its actual value. Impairment of goodwill is a non-cash expense and therefore does not affect cash flows.

Goodwill can significantly affect the comparability of financial statements of companies. When performing ratio analysis, income statement values should be adjusted by removing impairment expense (so that operating trends can be identified), and balance sheet values should be adjusted by excluding goodwill when computing financial ratios. Analysts should evaluate future acquisitions of a company in light of the price paid relative to net assets and earnings prospects of the acquired company (economic goodwill).

Companies are required to disclose information that assists users in evaluating the nature and financial impact of business combinations. Information such as the purchase price paid relative to the fair value of a company's net assets and earnings prospects of the acquired company help analysts to develop expectations about the company's performance following an acquisition.

Financial assets

Under **IFRS**, a financial instrument is defined as a contract that gives rise to a financial asset for one entity, and a financial liability or equity instrument for another entity.[2] Financial assets include investments in securities (e.g., stocks and bonds) and receivables, while financial liabilities include bonds payable and notes payable. A derivative is a complex financial instrument that derives its value from some underlying factor (e.g., interest rate, exchange rate, underlying asset price) and requires little or no initial investment. As we shall learn later, derivatives may be used for hedging purposes or for speculation.

Mark-to-market is a process of adjusting the values of trading assets and liabilities to reflect their current market values. These adjustments are usually made on a daily basis. Assets that are classified as held for trading and available for sale are subject to mark-to-market adjustments. Exhibit 2-1 breaks down various marketable and non-marketable financial instruments according to the measurement base used to value them.

Exhibit 2-1: Measurement Bases of Various Financial Assets[3]

Measured at Fair Value	Measured at Cost or Amortized Cost
Financial Assets Financial assets held for trading (stocks and bonds). Available-for-sale financial assets (stocks and bonds). Derivatives. Non-derivative instruments with face value exposures hedged by derivatives.	**Financial Assets** Unlisted instruments. Held-to-maturity investments. Loans and receivables.

---

2 - IAS 32, Financial Instruments: Presentation, paragraph 11.

3 - Exhibit 10, Volume 3, CFA Program Curriculum 2014.

Marketable investment securities can be classified under the following categories:

Available-for-sale securities: These are debt or equity securities that are neither expected to be traded in the near term, nor held till maturity. They may be sold to address the liquidity needs of the company. These securities are reported at fair market value on the balance sheet. While dividend income, interest income, and realized gains and losses on AFS securities are reported on the income statement, unrealized gains and losses are reported in other comprehensive income as a part of shareholders' equity.

The "available-for-sale" classification no longer appears in **IFRS** as of 2010, even though "IFRS 9: Financial Instruments" will be effective from 2013. However, even though the available-for-sale category will not exist, **IFRS** will still permit certain equity investments to be measured at fair value with any unrealized gains and losses recognized in other comprehensive income. This classification will be known as financial assets measured at fair value through other comprehensive income.

Held-to-maturity securities: These are debt securities that are purchased with the intent of holding them till maturity. Held-to-maturity securities are carried at amortized cost (Amortized cost = Face value − Unamortized discount + Unamortized premium). For these securities, unrealized gains or losses from changes in market value are ignored and not recognized on the financial statements. Only interest income and realized gains and losses (gains and losses when these securities are sold) are recognized on the income statement. See Exhibit 2-2.

Trading securities: These are debt and equity securities (e.g., stocks and bonds) that are acquired with the intent of earning trading profits over the near term. These securities are measured at fair market value on the balance sheet. Dividend income, interest income, realized gains and losses, and unrealized gains and losses are all reported on the income statement.

Exhibit 2-2: Accounting for Gains and Losses on Marketable Securities

	Held-to-Maturity Securities	Available-for-Sale Securities	Trading Securities
Balance Sheet	Reported at cost or amortized cost.	Reported at fair value. Unrealized gains or losses due to changes in market value are reported in other comprehensive income.	Reported at fair value.
Items recognized on the income statement	Interest income. Realized gains and losses.	Dividend income. Interest income. Realized gains and losses.	Dividend income. Interest income. Realized gains and losses. Unrealized gains and losses due to changes in market value.

Example 2-1 will help us understand the accounting of gains and losses on marketable securities under each of the different classifications.

Example 2-1: Marketable Securities

Panorama Inc. invests $5,000,000 in a 10% semiannual coupon fixed-income security. After six months, Panorama receives the first coupon payment of $250,000. Additionally, interest rates have declined over the period, and the value of the securities has increased by $1,000,000. Illustrate how ownership of this bond will affect Panorama's financial statements under each of the three classifications of marketable securities.

Solution

	Trading $	Available for Sale $	Held to Maturity $
Balance Sheet			
Assets			
Cash	250,000	250,000	250,000
Cost of securities	5,000,000	5,000,000	5,000,000
Unrealized gains (losses)	1,000,000	1,000,000	
	6,250,000	**6,250,000**	**5,250,000**
Liabilities			
Equity			
Paid-in-capital	5,000,000	5,000,000	5,000,000
Retained earnings	→1,250,000	→250,000	→250,000
Other comprehensive income		1,000,000	
	6,250,000	**6,250,000**	**5,250,000**
Income Statement			
Interest income	250,000	→250,000	→250,000
Unrealized gains (losses)	1,000,000		
	→**1,250,000**	**250,000**	**250,000**

Non-Current Liabilities

Non-current liabilities include the long-term financial liabilities and deferred tax liabilities.

Long-term financial liabilities

These may either be measured at fair value or amortized cost. Exhibit 2-3 lists some financial liabilities along with their measurement basis.

Exhibit 2-3: Measurement Basis of Various Financial Liabilities[3]

Measured at Fair Value	Measured at Cost or Amortized Cost
Financial Liabilities Derivatives. Financial liabilities held for trading. Non-derivative instruments with face value exposures hedged by derivatives.	**Financial Liabilities** All other liabilities (bonds payable and notes payable).

We shall study the accounting of financing liabilities in greater detail in Reading 32.

Deferred tax liabilities

These usually arise when a company's income tax expense exceeds taxes payable. The company pays less taxes based on its tax return than it should pay according to its financial statements. These unpaid taxes will be paid in future periods and are therefore a liability for the company. Deferred tax liabilities have current and non-current portions. These items will be discussed in more detail in Reading 31.

LESSON 3: EQUITY

LOS 26f: Describe the components of shareholders' equity. Vol 3, pp 242–244

5 ◄— U.S. GAAP and IFRS define equity as the owners' residual claim on the assets of an entity after deducting all liabilities. Various components of the owners' equity are described below.

> The first five components represent equity attributable to owners of the parent company, while the sixth component represents equity attributable to non-controlling interests.

- **Capital contributed by owners (common stock or issued capital):** Owners contribute capital to an entity by investing in common shares. Common shares have par (stated) values that are required to be listed separately in owners' equity. Required disclosures also include the number of authorized, issued, and outstanding shares for each class of stock issued by the company. Authorized shares are the maximum number of shares that can be sold under the company's Articles of Incorporation. Issued shares are the total number of shares that have been sold to shareholders. Outstanding shares equal the number of shares that were issued less the number of shares repurchased (treasury stock).

5a ◄—
- **Preferred shares:** Preferred shareholders receive dividends (at a specified percentage of par value) and have priority over ordinary shareholders in the event of liquidation. Preferred shares may either be classified as equity or financial liabilities depending on their characteristics. For example, perpetual, non-redeemable preferred shares are classified as equity, while preferred shares with mandatory redemption are classified as financial liabilities.

5c ◄—
- **Treasury shares:** These are shares that have been bought back by the company. Share repurchases result in a reduction in owners' equity and in the number of shares outstanding. These shares do not receive dividends and do not have voting rights. While Treasury shares may be reissued at a later date, no gain or loss is recognized when they are reissued.

5b ◄—
- **Retained earnings:** These are the cumulative earnings (net income) of the firm over the years that have not been distributed to shareholders as dividends.

- **Accumulated other comprehensive income:** This represents cumulative other comprehensive income.

- **Non-controlling interest (minority interest):** This is the minority shareholders' pro rata share of the net assets of a subsidiary that is not wholly owned by the company.

Statement of Changes in Owners' Equity

This statement presents the effects of all transactions that increase or decrease a company's equity over the period. Under **IFRS**, the following information should be included in the statement of changes in equity:
- Total comprehensive income for the period;
- The effects of any accounting changes that have been retrospectively applied to previous periods.
- Capital transactions with owners and distributions to owners; and
- Reconciliation of the carrying amounts of each component of equity at the beginning and end of the year.[4]

Under **U.S. GAAP**, companies are required to provide an analysis of changes in each component of stockholders' equity that is shown in the balance sheet.[5]

Exhibit 3-1 provides an example of a typical statement of changes in stockholders' equity.

Exhibit 3-1: Statement of Changes in Shareholders' Equity

Abel Company
Statement of Changes in Stockholders' Equity

	Common Stock $	Retained Earnings $	Accumulated Other Comprehensive Income $	Total $
Beginning balance	30,000	22,000	−3,000	**49,000**
Components of comprehensive income				
Net income		4,000		4,000
Unrealized loss on AFS Securities			−100	−100
Unrealized loss on cash flow hedge			−150	−150
Minimum pension liability adjustment			−75	−75
Translation adjustment			90	90
Comprehensive income				**3,765**
Issuance of common stock	3,000			**3,000**
Repurchases of common stock	−8,000			**−8,000**
Dividends		−2,500		**−2,500**
Ending balance	**25,000**	**23,500**	**−3,235**	**45,265**

---

4 - IAS 1, Presentation of Financial Statements, paragraph 80.
5 - FASB ASC 505-10-S99 [Equity-Overall-SEC materials] indicates that a company can present the analysis of changes in stockholders' equity in the notes or in a separate statement.

Uses and Analysis of Balance Sheets

Analysts can gain information regarding a company's liquidity, solvency, and the economic resources controlled by the company by examining its balance sheet.

- Liquidity refers to a company's ability to meet its short-term financial obligations.
- Solvency refers to a company's ability to meet its long-term financial obligations.

Two of the techniques that may be used to analyze a company's balance sheet are common-size analysis and ratio analysis.

LESSON 4: ANALYSIS OF THE BALANCE SHEET

LOS 26g: Convert balance sheets to common-size balance sheets and interpret common-size balance sheets. Vol 3, pp 246–254

LOS 26h: Calculate and interpret liquidity and solvency ratios. Vol 3, p 254

Common-Size Balance Sheets

A vertical common-size balance sheet expresses each balance sheet item as a percentage of total assets. This allows an analyst to perform historical analysis (time-series analysis) and cross-sectional analysis across firms within the same industry.

Exhibit 4-1 illustrates the construction of a common-size balance sheet.

Exhibit 4-1: The Construction of a Common-Size Balance Sheet

	Company A ('000)	Company B ('000)
ASSETS		
Current assets		
Cash and cash equivalents	400	3,000
Short-term marketable securities	200	1,300
Accounts receivable	500	1,000
Inventory	100	300
Total current assets	1,200	5,600
Property, plant, and equipment, net	2,050	2,650
Intangible assets	500	–
Goodwill	–	1,000
Total assets	**3,750**	**9,250**
LIABILITIES AND SHAREHOLDERS' EQUITY		
Current liabilities		
Accounts payable	800	600
Total current liabilities	800	600
Long-term bonds payable	10	8,500
Total liabilities	810	9,100
Total shareholders' equity	2,940	150
Total liabilities and shareholders' equity	**3,750**	**9,250**

Exhibit 4-1: (*continued*)

	Company A (%)	Company B (%)
ASSETS		
Current assets		
Cash and cash equivalents	10.7%	32.4%
Short-term marketable securities	5.3%	14.1%
Accounts receivable	13.3%	10.8%
Inventory	2.7%	3.2%
Total current assets	32.0%	60.5%
Property, plant, and equipment, net	54.7%	28.6%
Intangible assets	13.3%	0.0%
Goodwill	0.0%	10.8%
Total Assets	**100.0%**	**100.0%**
LIABILITIES AND SHAREHOLDERS' EQUITY		
Current liabilities		
Accounts payable	21.3%	6.5%
Total current liabilities	21.3%	6.5%
Long-term bonds payable	0.3%	91.9%
Total liabilities	21.6%	98.4%
Total shareholders' equity	78.4%	1.6%
Total Liabilities and Shareholders' Equity	**100.0%**	**100.0%**

The following important points should be noted:

- Company A has 16% of its assets in cash and short-term marketable securities, while Company B has 46.5% of its assets in cash and short-term marketable securities. Therefore Company B is more liquid than Company A.

- Company A's current liabilities exceed its cash on hand by $400,000. This means that Company A might need to raise cash through some other means (e.g., by selling inventory or collecting accounts receivable) to meet its short-term liabilities. On the other hand, Company B has sufficient cash on hand ($3 million) to meet its short-term liabilities ($600,000).

- The presence of goodwill on Company B's balance sheet shows that the company has grown via acquisitions. In contrast, Company A seems to have pursued a strategy of internal growth as evidenced by the lack of goodwill on its balance sheet.

- Company B has financed 98.4% of its total assets with liabilities. In contrast, Company A finances only 21.6% of its assets with liabilities. Therefore, Company A is more solvent than Company B. If Company B sees significant volatility in cash flows, it may struggle to meet its debt-servicing obligations.

Balance Sheet Ratios

These are ratios that have balance sheet items in the numerator and the denominator. The two main categories of balance sheet ratios are liquidity ratios, which measure a company's ability to settle short-term obligations, and solvency ratios, which evaluate a company's ability to settle long-term obligations.

The *higher* a company's liquidity ratios, the *greater* the likelihood that the company will be able to meet its short-term obligations.

Table 4-1: Liquidity Ratios

	Numerator	Denominator
Current ratio	Current assets	Current liabilities
Quick ratio (acid test ratio)	Cash + marketable securities + receivables	Current liabilities
Cash ratio	Cash + marketable securities	Current liabilities

Higher solvency ratios, on the other hand, are *undesirable* and indicate that the company is highly leveraged and risky.

Table 4-2: Solvency Ratios

	Numerator	Denominator
Long-term debt-to-equity ratio	Total long-term debt	Total equity
Debt-to-equity ratio	Total debt	Total equity
Total debt ratio	Total debt	Total assets
Financial leverage ratio	Total assets	Total equity

Ratio analysis is covered in detail in Reading 28. We also discuss the uses and limitations of ratio analysis in that reading.

READING 27: UNDERSTANDING CASH FLOW STATEMENTS

LESSON 1: THE CASH FLOW STATEMENT: COMPONENTS AND FORMAT

LOS 27a: Compare cash flows from operating, investing, and financing activities and classify cash flow items as relating to one of those three categories given a description of the items. Vol 3, pp 267–268

Under both **IFRS** and **U.S. GAAP**, cash flows are classified into the following categories (see Table 1-1):

Cash flow from operating activities (CFO): These are inflows and outflows of cash related to a firm's day-to-day business activities.

Cash flow from investing activities (CFI): These are inflows and outflows of cash generated from the purchase and disposal of long-term investments. Long-term investments include plant, machinery, equipment, intangible assets, and nontrading debt and equity securities.

Note: Investments in securities that are considered highly liquid (cash equivalents) are not included in investing activities. Neither are securities held for trading. Cash flows associated with the purchase and sale of highly liquid cash equivalents and of securities for trading purposes are classified under cash flow from operating activities.

Cash flow from financing activities (CFF): These are cash inflows and outflows generated from issuance and repayment of capital (interest-bearing debt and equity).

Note: Indirect short-term borrowings from suppliers that are classified as accounts payable, and changes in receivables from customers are not considered financing activities; they are classified as operating activities.

Table 1-1: Cash Flow Classification Under U.S. GAAP

CFO

Inflows	Outflows
Cash collected from customers.	Cash paid to employees.
Interest and dividends received.	Cash paid to suppliers.
Proceeds from sale of securities held for trading.	Cash paid for other expenses.
	Cash used to purchase trading securities.
	Interest paid.
	Taxes paid.

CFI

Inflows	Outflows
Sale proceeds from fixed assets.	Purchase of fixed assets.
Sale proceeds from long-term investments.	Cash used to acquire LT investment securities.

CFF

Inflows	Outflows
Proceeds from debt issuance.	Repayment of LT debt.
Proceeds from issuance of equity instruments.	Payments made to repurchase stock.
	Dividends payments.

*Note: There is a difference in how some cash flows are classified under **IFRS** and **U.S. GAAP**. These differences are discussed in LOS 27c and are very important from the examination perspective.*

LOS 27b: Describe how non-cash investing and financing activities are reported. Vol 3, pp 267–268

Noncash investing and financing activities are not reported on the cash flow statement because these transactions do not involve any receipt or payment of cash. Examples of noncash investing and financing activities include:

- Barter transactions where one nonmonetary asset is exchanged for another.
- Issuance of common stock for dividends or when holders of convertible bonds or convertible preferred stock convert their holdings into ordinary shares of the company.
- Acquisition of real estate with financing provided by the seller.

Remember that companies are required to disclose any significant noncash investing and financing activities in a separate note or a supplementary schedule to the cash flow statement.

LOS 27c: Contrast cash flow statements prepared under International Financial Reporting Standards (IFRS) and U.S. generally accepted accounting principles (U.S. GAAP). Vol 3, pp 269–270

Cash flow statements prepared under **IFRS** and **U.S. GAAP** differ along the following lines:

- Classification of cash flows: Certain cash flows are classified differently under **IFRS** and **U.S. GAAP**. **IFRS** offers more flexibility regarding the classification of certain cash flows.

- Presentation format: There is a difference in the presentation requirements for cash flow from operating activities.

Table 2 highlights important differences between **IFRS** and **U.S. GAAP** with respect to cash flow statements.

Table 1-2: Cash Flow Statements: Differences Between IFRS and U.S. GAAP[1]

Topic	IFRS	U.S. GAAP
Classification of cash flows:		
Interest received	Operating or investing	Operating
Interest paid	Operating or financing	Operating
Dividends received	Operating or investing	Operating
Dividends paid	Operating or financing	Financing
Bank overdrafts	Considered part of cash equivalents	Not considered part of cash and cash equivalents and classified as financing
Taxes paid	Generally operating, but a portion can be allocated to investing or financing if it can be specifically identified with these categories	Operating
Format of statement	Direct or indirect; direct is encouraged	Direct or indirect; direct is encouraged. A reconciliation of net income to cash flow from operating activities must be provided regardless of method used

LOS 27d: Distinguish between the direct and indirect methods of presenting cash from operating activities and describe arguments in favor of each method. Vol 3, pp 270–280

Under both **IFRS** and **U.S. GAAP**, there are two acceptable formats for presenting the cash flow statement—the direct method and the indirect method. These methods differ only in the *presentation* of the *CFO* section of the cash flow statement; calculated values for CFO are the same under both. Further, the presentation of CFF and CFI are exactly the same under both formats.

Direct method: Under the direct method, income statement items that are reported on an accrual basis are all converted to cash basis. All cash receipts are reported as inflows, while cash payments are reported as outflows. Exhibit 1-1 illustrates the presentation of CFO under the direct method.

1 - Sources: IAS 7; FASB ASC Topic 230; and "**IFRS** and **U.S. GAAP**: Similarities and Differences," PricewaterhouseCoopers (September 2009), available at www.pwc.com.

Exhibit 1-1

Company XYZ
Cash Flow from Operating Activities

Cash collected from customers	$100,000
Cash paid to suppliers	(30,000)
Cash paid to employees	(12,000)
Cash paid for interest	(5,000)
Cash paid for taxes	(3,000)
Operating cash flow	$50,000

Presentation of CFO under the direct method has similarities with the presentation of the income statement. The income statement starts with total sales and deducts direct and indirect costs to arrive at net income. The direct method of calculating CFO starts with cash sales and deducts all cash payments for direct and indirect costs to arrive at cash flow from operations.

Indirect method: Under the indirect method, cash flow from operations is calculated by applying a series of adjustments to net income. These adjustments are made for noncash items (e.g., depreciation), nonoperating items (e.g., gains on sale of noncurrent assets), and changes in working capital accounts resulting from accrual accounting. Exhibit 1-2 illustrates the presentation of CFO under the indirect method.

Exhibit 1-2

Company ABC
Cash Flow from Operating Activities

Net income	$120,000
Adjustments:	
Depreciation	10,000
Gain on sale of machinery	(1,000)
Increase in inventory	(2,000)
Decrease in accounts receivable	3,000
Decrease in accounts payable	(1,000)
Operating cash flow	$129,000

The Direct Method Versus Indirect Method

- The direct method explicitly lists the actual sources of operating cash inflows and outflows, whereas the indirect method only provides net results for these inflows and outflows. The argument is similar to the one for having an income statement that lists all revenue and expense items, as opposed to one that only provides the end result (i.e., net income). The information provided in the direct format is very useful in evaluating past performance and making projections of future cash flows.

- The indirect method provides a list of items that are responsible for the difference between net income and operating cash flow. These differences can then be used when estimating future operating cash flows. The indirect method facilitates forecasting of future cash flows since forecasts of future net income simply have to be adjusted for changes in balance sheet accounts that are caused by differences between accrual and cash accounting.

LOS 27e: Describe how the cash flow statement is linked to the income statement and the balance sheet. **Vol 3, pp 280–294**

Links Between the Cash Flow Statement and the Income Statement and Balance Sheet

The sum of cash flow from operating, investing, and financing activities equals the change in cash over the year.

> CFO + CFI + CFF = Change in cash
> Year-end cash balance – Beginning-of-year cash balance = Change in cash

| Previous year's balance sheet |

| Current year's balance sheet |

Operating income and expense items are recognized on the income statement on an accrual basis, which means that revenues and expenses are recognized when incurred, irrespective of when the associated cash flows occur. When the timing of an expense or revenue item differs from the associated cash flow, it is reflected in changes in balance sheet accounts. For example, if revenue is recognized prior to the receipt of cash, accounts receivable will increase.

> Beginning accounts receivable + Revenues – Cash received from customers
> = Ending accounts receivable

| Previous year's balance sheet |

| Current year's income statement |

| Current year's cash flow statement |

If an expense is incurred but not paid for, it is charged on the income statement and accounts payable increase.

> Beginning accounts payable + Purchases – Cash paid to suppliers
> = Ending accounts payable

| Purchases = COGS + Ending inventory – Beginning inventory |

These changes in current assets and current liabilities are then used to reconcile net income to operating cash flows under the indirect method.

CFI is calculated from changes in asset balances under the noncurrent assets section of the balance sheet.

CFF is calculated from changes in the equity and noncurrent debt sections of the balance sheet.

A company's retained earnings (on the balance sheet) represent cumulative net income that has not been distributed to shareholders. Every year, if the company makes a profit, some of it may be distributed to shareholders as dividends, while the rest is added to retained earnings.

> Beginning retained earnings + Net income – Dividends declared
> = Ending retained earnings.

| Previous year's balance sheet |

| Current year's income statement |

| Notes to the financial statements |

Understanding these links between the balance sheet, income statement, and statement of cash flows facilitates the evaluation of a company's financials and the detection of accounting irregularities.

Sources Versus Uses of Cash

Let's consider an **asset** account, inventory.
- If inventory levels have *increased* from the previous year, *more* liquidity of the firm is tied up in inventories. This is a *use of cash* for the firm.
- If inventory levels have *decreased* over the year, *less* of the firm's cash is tied up in inventory. This is a *source of cash* for the firm.

Increases in current assets are *uses* of cash and *decreases* in current assets are *sources* of cash. Changes in asset balances and cash are *negatively* related.

Now let's move on to a **liability** account, accounts payable.
- If the total amount due to the firm's creditors has *increased* over the year, it implies that the firm has borrowed *more* money. This represents a *source of cash* to the firm.
- If the amount payable to creditors has *fallen* over the year, some creditors have been paid back, which is a *use of cash* for the firm.

Increases in current liabilities are *sources* of cash, while *decreases* in current liabilities are *uses* of cash. Changes in liability balances and cash are *positively* related.

The Direct Method

Step 1: Start with sales on the income statement. Go through each income statement account and adjust it for changes in related working capital accounts on the balance sheet. This serves to remove the effects of the timing difference between the recognition of revenues and expenses and the actual receipt or payment of cash.

Step 2: Determine whether changes in these working capital accounts indicate a source or use of cash. Make sure you put the right sign in front of the income statement item. Sales are an inflow item so they have a *positive* effect on cash flow, while COGS, wages, taxes, and interest expense are all outflow items that have *negative* effects on cash flow.

Step 3: Ignore all nonoperating items (e.g., gain/loss on sale of plant and equipment) and noncash charges (e.g., depreciation and amortization).

The Indirect Method

Step 1: Start with net income. Go up the income statement and remove the effects of all noncash expenses and gains from net income. For example, the *negative* effect of depreciation is removed from net income by *adding* depreciation back to net income. Cash-based net income will be higher than accrual-based net income by the amount of noncash expenses.

Step 2: Remove the effects of all nonoperating activities from net income. For example, the *positive* effect of a gain on sale of fixed assets on net income is removed by *subtracting* the gain from net income.

Step 3: Make adjustments for changes in all working capital accounts. Add all sources of cash (increases in current liabilities and declines in current assets) and subtract all uses of cash (decreases in current liabilities and increases in current assets).

The income statement and balance sheet for ABC Company are presented below. We will use these statements to construct the cash flow statement for the company using the direct and indirect methods.

INCOME STATEMENT
Year ended Dec 31 2008

Revenues		23,000
Cost of goods sold		11,500
Gross profit		**11,500**
Salary and wages expense	4,000	
Depreciation expense	1,000	
Other operating expenses	3,500	
Total operating expenses		8,500
Operating profit		**3,000**
Other revenues (expenses)		
Gain on sale of equipment		200
Interest expense		(300)
Income before tax		**2,900**
Income tax expense		(1,400)
Net income		**1,500**

LEGEND:
Amounts used in calculating CFO are filled with color.
Amounts used in calculating CFI are written in color.
Amounts used in calculating CFF are boxed in color.

BALANCE SHEET
As at Dec 31 2008

	2008	2007	Net Change
Cash	2,300	1,150	1,150
Accounts receivable	1,000	950	50
Inventory	3,900	3,250	650
Prepaid expenses	100	250	(150)
Total current assets	**7,300**	**5,600**	**1,700**
Land	500	500	
Buildings	3,600	3,600	
Equipment	7,700	8,500	(800)
Less accumulated depreciation	(3,400)	(2,900)	500
Total long-term assets	**8,400**	**9,700**	**(1,300)**
Total assets	**15,700**	**15,300**	**400**
Accounts payable	3,500	3,300	200
Salary and wages payable	80	70	10
Interest payable	60	85	(25)
Income tax payable	60	45	15
Other accrued liabilities	1,200	1,100	100
Total current liabilities	**4,900**	**4,600**	**300**
Long-term debt	3,000	3,600	(600)
Common stock	4,550	4,850	(300)
Retained earnings	3,250	2,250	1,000
Total liabilities and equity	**15,700**	**15,300**	**400**

Note: The book value of the equipment sold was $300.

The Direct Method to Compute CFO

Total sales adjusted for changes in related working capital accounts are known as cash collections from customers:

$$\text{Cash collections} = \text{Sales} - \text{Increase in accounts receivable} = +23{,}000 - 50 = \$22{,}950$$

Cost of goods sold adjusted for changes in related working capital items is known as cash payments to suppliers:

$$\text{Cash paid to suppliers} = -\text{COGS} - \text{Increase in inventory} + \text{Increase in A/C payable}$$
$$= -11{,}500 - 650 + 200 = -\$11{,}950$$

Salaries and wages adjusted for related working capital accounts:

$$\text{Cash salaries and wages} = -\text{Wages and salaries} + \text{Increase in wages and salaries payable}$$
$$= -4{,}000 + 10 = -\$3{,}990$$

Depreciation is a noncash expense so it is ignored altogether.

Other operating expenses adjusted for changes in related working capital accounts:

$$\text{Other operating expenses (cash)} = -\text{Other operating expenses (accrual basis)} +$$
$$\text{Decrease in prepaid expenses} + \text{Increase in other accrued liabilities}$$
$$= -3{,}500 + 150 + 100 = -\$3{,}250$$

Gain on sale of equipment relates to the sale of a long-lived asset. The proceeds from this transaction are classified under investing activities and ignored in the calculation of CFO.

Interest expense adjusted for related working capital accounts:

$$\text{Cash interest paid} = -\text{Interest expense} - \text{Decrease in interest payable}$$
$$= -300 - 25 = -\$325$$

Income tax expense adjusted for related working capital accounts:

$$\text{Cash taxes paid} = -\text{Income tax expense} + \text{Increase in taxes payable}$$
$$= -1{,}400 + 15 = -\$1{,}385$$

Cash flow from operating activities under the direct method:

Cash received from customers	22,950
Cash paid to suppliers	−11,950
Cash paid to employees	−3,990
Cash paid for other operating expenses	−3,250
Cash paid for interest	−325
Cash paid for income taxes	−1,385
Net cash flow from operating activities	**$2,050**

Calculating CFO Using the Indirect Method:

On the income statement, the only noncash expense is depreciation expense of $1,000, and the only nonoperating income/expense is the gain on sale of equipment of $200. We start by removing the effects of these two items from net income:

Net income	1,500
Add: Depreciation expense	1,000
Less: Gain on sale of equipment	−200
	2,300

Next, we adjust the figure calculated above for changes in all working capital accounts, adding sources of cash and subtracting uses of cash.

	2,300
Increase in accounts receivable (use)	−50
Increase in inventory (use)	−650
Decrease in prepaid expenses (source)	150
Increase in accounts payable (source)	200
Increase in salaries and wages payable (source)	10
Decrease in interest payable (use)	−25
Increase in income tax payable (source)	15
Increase in accrued liabilities (source)	100
Net cash flow from operating activities	2,050

Notice that we obtain the same answer for CFO under both methods.

Exhibit 2-1: Adjustments to Net Income Using the Indirect Method

Additions	
	• Noncash items
	○ Depreciation expense of tangible assets
	Amortization expense of intangible assets
	Depletion expense of natural resources
	Amortization of bond discount
	• Nonoperating losses
	○ Loss on sale or write-down of assets
	○ Loss on retirement of debt
	○ Loss on investments accounted for under the equity method
	• Increase in deferred income tax liability
	• Changes in working capital resulting from accruing higher amounts for expenses than the amounts of cash payments or lower amounts for revenues than the amounts of cash receipts
	○ Decrease in current operating assets (e.g., accounts receivable, inventory, and prepaid expenses)
	○ Increase in current operating liabilities (e.g., accounts payable and accrued expense liabilities)

(Exhibit continued on next page . . .)

Exhibit 2-1: *(continued)*

Subtractions	
	• Noncash items (e.g., amortization of bond premium)

- Nonoperating items
  - ○ Gain on sale of assets
  - ○ Gain on retirement of debt
  - ○ Income on investments accounted for under the equity method

- Decrease in deferred income tax liability

- Changes in working capital resulting from accruing lower amounts for expenses than for cash payments or higher amounts for revenues than for cash receipts
  - ○ Increase in current operating assets (e.g., accounts receivable, inventory, and prepaid expenses)
  - ○ Decrease in current operating liabilities (e.g., accounts payable and accrued expense liabilities)

Calculating CFI and CFF :

Calculating cash flow from investing activities requires us to consider the effects of transactions relating to long-lived assets and long-term investments on cash.

Before we get into calculating cash flow from investing activities, let's go through some fundamental accounting:

The value of **gross fixed assets** indicates the *historical cost* of the fixed assets owned by the company at the balance sheet date. If the figure for gross fixed assets changes from one year to the next, there has been an investing activity. If gross fixed assets increase, there has been a fixed asset purchase, and if gross fixed assets decrease, there has been a fixed asset disposal.

> Beginning gross fixed assets + Purchase price of new fixed assets – Historical cost of disposed fixed assets = Ending gross fixed assets.

Net fixed assets equal gross fixed assets minus accumulated depreciation.

Going back to our example, the gross amounts recorded for land and for buildings are the same across both years ($500 and $3,600, respectively). Therefore, we conclude that there have been no purchases or sales of land and buildings during the year.

However, the gross amount recorded for equipment has decreased by $800. This suggests that there has been a sale of equipment over the year. Our belief is confirmed by the fact that the company also recognized a gain of sale of equipment on its income statement.

Calculation of historical cost of sold equipment:

> Beginning gross fixed assets + Purchase price of new fixed assets – Historical cost of disposed fixed asset = Ending gross fixed assets.
>
> $8,500 + 0 – Historical cost of sold equipment = $7,700
>
> Historical cost of sold equipment = **$800**

The historical cost and accumulated depreciation of a long-lived asset is removed from the balance sheet once it is sold.

Calculation of accumulated depreciation on sold equipment:

Beginning accumulated depreciation + Current year's depreciation on all assets − Accumulated depreciation on sold asset = Ending accumulated depreciation.

$2,900 + $1,000 − Accumulated depreciation on sold equipment = **$3,400**

Accumulated depreciation on sold equipment = **$500**

Calculation of book value of sold equipment:

Book value of sold equipment = Historical cost − Accumulated depreciation

Book value of sold equipment = $800 − $500 = **$300**

Calculation of proceeds from sale of equipment:

Selling price − Book value = Gain/loss on sale of equipment

Selling price − $300 = $200

Cash proceeds from the sale of equipment equal $500. These proceeds are classified as inflows from investing activities.

Cash flow from investing activities:

Cash received from sale of equipment	500
Net cash flow from investing activities	500

Calculating CFF

Cash flow from financing activities is generated from the issuance and repayment of capital (long-term debt and equity) and distributions in the form of dividends to shareholders.

Long-term debt: An increase in long-term debt from one year to the next implies cash inflows from new borrowings. A decrease implies debt repayment and an outflow of cash.

Over the course of the year, ABC's long-term debt fell by $600. This implies that $600 was *used* by the company to retire debt.

Equity: An increase in common stock from one year to the next implies cash inflows from issuance of new shares. A decrease implies a share repurchase that results in a cash outflow.

ABC has repurchased $300 of common stock over the year, which *reduces* cash flow from financing activities.

Dividends: Cash dividends paid out can be computed from the following relationship:

Cash dividends paid out = Beginning dividends payable + Dividends declared − Ending dividends payable.

Dividends declared = Beginning retained earnings + Net income − Ending retained earnings.

Notice that ABC's retained earnings increased by only $1,000 even though income was $1,500. This implies that $500 of net income was appropriated to the company's shareholders as dividends. Even though our example never explicitly mentions dividends, we must ensure that net income reconciles with the change in retained earnings. ABC declared $500 of dividends and paid them out as well. If the company had not paid them, we would have seen an increase in dividends payable of $500 over the year.

Cash flow from financing activities

Cash paid to retire long-term debt	−600
Repurchase of common stock	−300
Cash paid as dividends	−500
Net cash flow from financing activities	**−1,400**

Combining the effects of CFO, CFI, and CFF gives us change in cash and cash equivalents over the year:

Net cash provided by operating activities	**2,050**
Net cash provided by investing activities	500
Net cash used for financing activities	**−1,400**
Net change in cash over the year	**1,150**

The net increase in cash on the cash flow statement must equal the difference between the cash balances for 2007 and 2008. The company's cash balance in 2007 was $1,150, and in 2008 was $2,300. Notice that the difference between the two amounts ($1,150) is also the net increase in cash calculated on the cash flow statement.

LOS 27g: Convert cash flows from the indirect to the direct method.
Vol 3, pp 293–294

There is a three-step process for converting an indirect cash flow statement into a direct statement.

Step 1: Aggregate all revenues and all expenses

- Aggregate all operating and nonoperating revenues and gains such as sales and gains from sale of assets.
- Aggregate all operating and nonoperating expenses such as wages, depreciation, interest, and taxes.

Step 2: Remove the effect of noncash items from aggregated revenues and expenses and separate the adjusted revenues and expenses into their respective cash flow items.

- Deduct noncash revenue items such as gain on sales of assets from total revenue.
- Deduct noncash expense items such as depreciation from total expenses.
- Break down the adjusted expenses into cash outflow items, such as cost of goods sold, wages, interest expense, and tax expense.

Step 3: Convert the accrual-based items into cash-based amounts by adjusting for changes in corresponding working accounts.

An increase (decrease) in an asset account is a cash outflow (inflow). An increase (decrease) in a liability account is a cash inflow (outflow).

- Convert revenue into cash receipts from customers by adjusting for accounts receivable and unearned revenue.
- Convert COGS into cash payments to suppliers by adjusting for inventory and accounts payable.
- Convert wages, interest, and tax expenses into cash amounts by adjusting for wages payable, interest payable, taxes payable, and deferred taxes.

Conversion from Indirect to the Direct Method:

Step 1

Aggregate all revenue and all expenses:

Total revenues (23,000 + 200)	$23,200
Total expenses (11,500 + 8,500 + 300 + 1,400)	$21,700
Net income	$1,500

Step 2

Remove all noncash items from aggregated revenues and expenses and break out remaining items into relevant cash flow items:

Total revenue less noncash item revenues: (23,200 – 200)	$23,000
Total expenses less noncash item expenses: (21,700 – 1,000)	$20,700
Cost of goods sold	$11,500
Salary and wage expenses	$4,000
Other operating expenses	$3,500
Interest expense	$300
Income tax expense	$1,400
Total	**$20,700**

Step 3

Convert accrual amounts to cash flow amounts by adjusting for working capital changes:

Cash received from customers	$22,950
Cash paid to suppliers	($11,950)
Cash paid to employees	($3,990)
Cash paid for other operating expenses	($3,250)
Cash paid for interest	($325)
Cash paid for income tax	($1,385)
CFO	**$2,050**

LOS 27h: Analyze and interpret both reported and common-size cash flow statements. Vol 3, pp 296–302

Cash flow analysis helps us evaluate how well a business is being run and to estimate its future cash flows. The analysis begins with understanding the sources and uses of cash and determining which components of the cash flow statement these sources and uses can be attributed to. The analysis also includes an evaluation of the determinants of each of the components.

Major Sources and Uses of Cash

Sources and uses of cash depend upon the company's stage of growth.

- Companies in the early stages of growth may have negative operating cash flows as cash is used by the company to finance inventory rollout and receivables. These negative operating cash flows are supported by financing inflows from issuance of debt or equity.
- Inflows of cash from financing activities are not sustainable. Over the long term, a company must generate positive cash flows from operating activities that exceed capital expenditures and payments to providers of debt and equity capital.
- Companies in the mature stage of growth usually have positive cash flows from operating activities. These inflows can be used for debt repayment and stock repurchases. They can also be used by the company to expand its scale of operations (investing activities).

Operating Cash Flow

- Changes in relevant asset and liability accounts should be used to determine whether business operations are a source or use of cash.
- Operating cash flow should be compared to net income. If high net income is not being translated into high operating cash flow, the company might be employing aggressive revenue recognition policies.
- Companies should ideally have operating cash flows that exceed net income.
- The variability of operating cash flow and net income is an important determinant of the overall risk inherent in the company.

Investing Cash Flow

- Changes in long-term asset and investment accounts are used to determine sources and uses of investing cash flows.
- Increasing outflows may imply capital expenditures. Analysts should then evaluate how the company plans to finance these investments (i.e., with excess operating cash flow or by undertaking financing activities).

Financing Cash Flow

- Changes in interest-bearing debt and equity are used to determine sources and uses of financing cash flow.
- If debt issuance contributes significantly to financing cash flow, the repayment schedule must be considered.
- Increasing use of cash to repay debt, repurchase stock, or make dividend payments might indicate a lack of lucrative investment opportunities for the company.

Common-size analysis: There are two ways to construct common-size cash flow statements:

1. Express each item as a percentage of net revenues. This is the most commonly used format.
2. Express each cash inflow item as a percentage of total cash inflows, and each cash outflow item as a percentage of total cash outflows.

Common-size cash flow statements make it easier to identify trends in cash flows, and help in forecasting future cash flows as individual items are expressed as a percentage of revenues.

Exhibit 3-1 contains Rhodson Company's common-size cash flow statement:

Exhibit 3-1: Common-Size Cash Flow Statement

Rhodson Company
Cash Flow Statement
Percent of Revenues

	2008	2008	2007	2007
	$	%	$	%
Net income	55,000	18.33	45,000	18.00
Depreciation	10,000	3.33	10,000	4.00
Increase in accounts receivable	–5,000	–1.67	–4,000	–1.60
Increase in inventory	–3,000	–1.00	–2,000	–0.80
Decrease in prepaid expenses	1,500	0.50	3,000	1.20
Increase in accrued expenses	2,000	0.67	2,500	1.00
Operating cash flow	**60,500**	**20.17**	**54,500**	**21.80**
Cash from sale of fixed assets	12,000	4.00	5,000	2.00
Purchase of plant and equipment	–10,000	–3.33	0	0.00
Investing cash flow	**2,000**	**0.67**	**5,000**	**2.00**
Sale of bonds	7,500	2.50	5,000	2.00
Cash dividends	–2,000	–0.67	–2,000	–0.80
Financing cash flow	**5,500**	**1.83**	**3,000**	**1.20**
Total cash flows	**68,000**	**22.67**	**62,500**	**25.00**

Net revenue in 2008 = $300,000
Net revenue in 2007 = $250,000

Brief Analysis

- CFO has *fallen* as a percentage of revenues in 2008.
- CFI is *lower* in 2008 due to the purchase of plant and equipment.
- CFF has contributed more significantly to total cash flow in 2008. The company has issued more debt.
- Total cash flow has decreased as a percentage of sales.

LOS 27i: Calculate and interpret free cash flow to the firm, free cash flow to equity, and performance and coverage cash flow ratios. **Vol 3, pp 302–305**

Free cash flow is the excess of a company's operating cash flows over capital expenditure undertaken during the year. Free cash flow to the firm and free cash flow to equity are more precise measures of free cash flow as they identify specifically whom the cash is available to.

Free cash flow to the firm (FCFF) is cash that is available to equity and debt holders after the company has met all its operating expenses and satisfied its capital expenditure and working capital requirements.

$$FCFF = NI + NCC + [Int \times (1 - tax\ rate)] - FCInv - WCInv$$

where:
NI = net income
NCC = noncash charges
FCInv = fixed capital investment (net capital expenditure)
WCInv = working capital investment
Int = Interest expense

Notice that net income that has been adjusted for noncash charges and changes in working capital accounts equals the company's operating cash flows. Therefore:

$$FCFF = CFO + [Int \times (1 - tax\ rate)] - FCInv$$

Example 3-1: Calculating FCFF

Continuing from our previous example of ABC Company and assuming a tax rate of 40%, calculate FCFF.

Solution

Recall the following information regarding ABC Company:
- CFO = $2,050
- Interest expense = $300
- Fixed capital investment = –$500 (the company sold noncurrent assets for $500)

Therefore:

$$FCFF = CFO + Interest\ expense\ (1 - Tax\ rate) - FCInv$$

$$FCFF = 2,050 + 300\ (1 - 0.4) - (-500) = \$2,730$$

---

*Note: Under **IFRS**, if the company has classified interest and dividends received as investing activities, they should be added to CFO to determine FCFF. If dividends paid were deducted from CFO, they should be added back to CFO to calculate FCFF. Dividends must not be adjusted for taxes as dividends paid are not tax-deductible.*

Free cash flow to equity (FCFE) refers to cash that is available only to common shareholders.

$$FCFE = CFO - FCInv + Net\ borrowing$$

Example 3-2: Calculating FCFE

Continuing from our previous example of ABC Company and assuming a tax rate of 40%, calculate FCFE.

Solution

Recall the following information regarding ABC Company:
- CFO = $2,050
- Fixed capital investment = –$500 (the company sold noncurrent assets for $500)
- Net borrowing = –$600 (the company repaid $600 worth of debt)

Therefore:

$$FCFE = CFO - FCInv + Net\ borrowing$$

$$FCFE = 2,050 - (-500) + (-600) = \$1,950$$

A positive FCFE suggests that the company has operating cash flows available after payments have been made for capital expenditure and debt repayment. This excess belongs to common shareholders.

Note: Under **IFRS**, if the company has deducted dividends paid in calculating CFO, dividends must be added back to calculated FCFE.

Cash Flow Ratios

The information available on cash flow statements can be used to compute cash flow ratios. These ratios, like income statement and balance sheet ratios, can be used for comparing the company's performance over time (time-series analysis) or against other companies within the same industry (cross-sectional analysis). Cash flow ratios can be categorized as performance (profitability) ratios and coverage (solvency) ratios. See Table 3-1.

Table 3-1: Cash Flow Ratios[2]

Performance Ratio	Formula	What it Measures
Cash flow to revenue	CFO / Net revenue	Cash generated per unit of revenue.
Cash return on assets	CFO / Average total assets	Cash generated from all resources, equity, and debt.
Cash return on equity	CFO / Average shareholders' equity	Cash generated from owner resources.
Cash to income	CFO / Operating income	The ability of business operations to generate cash.
Cash flow per share	(CFO – Preferred dividends) / Number of common shares outstanding	Operating cash flow available for each shareholder.

Coverage Ratios	Formula	What it Measures
Debt coverage	CFO / Total debt	Leverage and financial risk.
Interest coverage	(CFO + Interest paid + Taxes paid) / Interest paid	Ability to satisfy interest obligations.
Reinvestment	CFO / Cash paid for long-term assets	Ability to buy long-term assets with operating cash flows.
Debt payment	CFO / Cash paid for long-term debt repayment	Ability to meet debt obligations with operating cash flows.
Dividend payment	CFO / Dividends paid	Ability to make dividend payments with operating cash flows.
Investing and financing	CFO / Cash outflows for investing and financing activities	Ability to buy long-term assets, settle debt obligations and make dividend payments from operating cash flows.

2 - Exhibit 15, Volume 3, CFA Program Curriculum 2014

READING 28: FINANCIAL ANALYSIS TECHNIQUES

LESSON 1: ANALYTICAL TOOLS AND TECHNIQUES

Financial statement analysis applies analytical tools to financial statements and related data to make investment decisions. It involves transforming accounting data into information useful for analysis, forecasting, and decision-making.

Financial statement analysis reduces reliance on hunches and guesses in decision-making. It does not lower the need for expert judgment, but provides an effective and systematic basis for making investment decisions.

It is important for an analyst to understand the financial analysis process. A general framework for financial statement analysis is presented in Exhibit 1-1.

Exhibit 1-1: Framework for Financial Statement Analysis

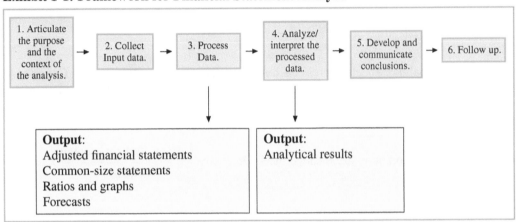

The primary focus of this reading is on Steps 3 and 4, processing and analyzing data.

LOS 28a: Describe the tools and techniques used in financial analysis, including their uses and limitations. Vol 3, pp 322–338

A ratio expresses a mathematical relationship between two quantities in terms of a percentage or a proportion. Ratios may be computed using data directly from companies' financial statements or from other available databases. Computation of a ratio is a simple arithmetic operation but its interpretation may not be that simple. To be meaningful, a ratio must refer to an economically important relation.

The value of ratio analysis lies in its ability to assist an equity or credit analyst in the evaluation of a company's past performance, assessment of its current financial position, and forecasting its future cash flows and profitability trends.

Uses of Ratio Analysis

Financial ratios provide insights into:
- Microeconomic relationships within the company that are used by analysts to project the company's earnings and cash flows.
- A company's financial flexibility.
- Management's ability.
- Changes in the company and industry over time.
- How the company compares to peer companies and the industry overall.

Common-Size Analysis

Common-size statements allow analysts to compare a company's performance with that of other firms and to evaluate its performance over time.

Common-Size Income Statements

A common-size income statement expresses all income statement items as a percentage of revenues. Common-size income statements are extremely useful in identifying trends in costs and profit margins. Further, certain financial ratios are explicitly stated on these statements (e.g., the gross profit margin and the net profit margin).

$$\text{Vertical common-size income statement percentage} = \frac{\text{Income statement account}}{\text{Revenue}} \times 100$$

Common-Size Balance Sheets

Common-size balance sheets express each item as a percentage of total assets. Common-size balance sheets are prepared to highlight changes in the mix of assets, liabilities, and equity.

$$\text{Vertical common-size balance sheet percentage} = \frac{\text{Balance sheet account}}{\text{Total assets}} \times 100$$

Exhibit 1-2 contains the income statement and balance sheet of XYZ Company in terms of dollar amounts and common-size percentages.

Exhibit 1-2: Vertical Common-Size Income Statement and Balance Sheet for XYZ

Income Statement

	2006 $	2006 %	2007 $	2007 %	
Sales	400,000	100.0	475,000	100.0	
Cost of goods sold (COGS)	320,000	80.0	377,625	79.5	
Gross profit	80,000	20.0	97,375	20.5	
Selling, general, & administrative expenses (SG&A)	28,000	7.0	30,875	6.5	[2]
Depreciation	20,000	5.0	7,125	1.5	[3]
Interest expense	20,000	5.0	33,250	7.0	[4]
	68,000		71,250		
Profit before taxes	12,000	3.0	26,125	5.5	
Income taxes (30% of pretax profits)	3,600	0.9	7,838	1.7	
Net income	8,400	2.1	18,288	3.9	[1]

Balance Sheet

	2006 $	2006 %	2007 $	2007 %	
Assets					
Current Assets					
Cash	21,000	8	10,000	3	6
Short-term investments	15,000	5	12,000	4	
Accounts receivable	27,000	10	34,000	11	
Inventories	44,000	16	33,000	11	
Prepaid expenses	2,500	1	3,500	1	
Other current assets	19,000	7	24,000	8	
Total Current Assets	128,500	46	116,500	39	8
Fixed Assets					
Net property and equipment	110,000	40	110,000	37	
Long-term investments	10,000	4	4,000	1	
Intangible assets	16,000	6	56,000	19	7
Other long-term assets	12,000	4	12,000	4	
Total Fixed Assets	148,000	54	182,000	61	
Total Assets	276,500	100	298,500	100	
Liabilities					
Current Liabilities					
Accounts payable	27,000	10	20,000	7	
Accrued expenses	12,700	5	17,000	6	
Total Current Liabilities	39,700	14	37,000	12	
Long Term Debt	21,800	8	21,800	7	5
Shareholders Equity					
Common stock	120,000	43	135,000	45	
Accumulated other comprehensive income	500	0	−300	0	
Retained earnings*	95,000	34	100,000	34	
Other equity	−500	0	5,000	2	
Total Shareholders' Equity	215,000	78	239,700	80	
Total Liabilities and Shareholders' Equity	276,500	100	298,500	100	

* The company paid out $13,288 in dividends for the year 2007.

Analysis of the common-size income statement for ABC Company indicates that:

1. The profitability of the company has improved.
2. Decrease in COGS and SG&A as a percentage of sales only explain a small proportion of the improvement in profit margins.
3. Reduction in depreciation has contributed significantly to the improvement in profitability.
4. The drastic reduction in depreciation has masked the effect of a significant increase in interest expense over the period.
5. Interest expense has risen despite the fact that the long-term liabilities of the firm have remained constant. This tells us that the company has probably issued floating-rate bonds and is now paying a higher effective interest rate on its loans.
6. Although the income statement shows improved profitability, the firm might run into some cash flow issues going forward. Higher interest expense has drained cash from the firm. On the income statement, the effect of higher interest expense is offset by significantly lower depreciation. While it helps reported profits, lower depreciation does not bring in any cash.
7. The company's intangible assets now form a more significant proportion of its total assets. These must be scrutinized in detail.
8. More of the company's assets are now concentrated in long-term assets. Current assets' share of total assets has declined significantly.

While common-size analysis does not tell us the entire story behind the company's financials, it does lead us in the right direction and prompt us to ask relevant questions in assessing the company's operating performance over the period, and evaluating its prospects going forward.

Cross-Sectional Analysis

Cross-sectional analysis, also known as relative analysis, compares a specific metric for one company with the same metric for another company or group of companies over a period of time. This allows comparisons even though the companies might be of significantly different sizes and/or operate in different countries. Consider two companies from the same industry. If one of them has accounts receivable representing 20% of its total assets, while the other has 40% of its assets in the form of accounts receivable, we might conclude that the latter has a greater proportion of credit sales or that it uses aggressive accounting policies for revenue recognition.

Trend Analysis

Trend analysis provides important information about a company's historical performance. It can also offer assistance in forecasting the financial performance of a company. When looking for trends over time, horizontal common-size financial statements are often prepared. Dollar values of accounts are divided by their base-year values to determine their common-size values. Horizontal common-size statements can also help identify structural changes in the business.

Example 1-1: Relationships Among Financial Statements

Consider the following information:

	2011 ($)	2010 ($)	2009 ($)
Revenue	7,604,186	6,336,822	5,510,280
Net income	1,260,477	1,008,381	826,542
Operating cash flow	942,258	1,046,953	1,102,056
Total assets	10,637,596	7,879,700	6,061,308

Based on the given information, comment on the financial performance of the company.

Solution

We can use horizontal common-size analysis to evaluate the financial performance of the company. The year-on-year percentage changes for various financial variables are calculated below:

	2011	2010
Revenue	20.00%	15.00%
Net income	25.00%	22.00%
Operating cash flow	−10.00%	−5.00%
Total assets	35.00%	30.00%

The percentage growth figures allow us to draw the following conclusions:
- *Net income is growing faster than revenue.* This indicates increasing profitability. However, the analyst should dig deeper and identify the source of this higher net income (i.e., whether it results from continuing operations, or from nonoperating, nonrecurring items).
- *The company's operating cash flow is decreasing.* This is a cause for concern and requires further investigation. The fact that operating cash flow is declining in spite of the positive growth in revenues may indicate a problem with the company's earnings quality (e.g., aggressive recognition of revenue).
- *Total assets are growing faster than revenue.* This suggests that the company's efficiency levels are declining. The analyst should look to identify the reason for the high growth rate in assets and also examine the composition of the increase in assets.

Uses of Charts in Financial Analysis

Graphs facilitate comparisons of firm performance and financial structure over time, highlighting changes in significant aspects of business operations. They may also be used to communicate important conclusions of financial analysis.

Pie charts are most useful in illustrating the composition of a total value. For example, a pie chart should be used when presenting the components of total expenses for the year (COGS, SG&A, depreciation).

Line graphs help identify trends and detect changes in direction or magnitude. For example, a line graph that illustrates a marked increase in accounts receivable while cash balances are falling indicates that the firm might have problems managing its working capital going forward.

A stacked common graph illustrates the changes in various items over the period in graphical form. Figure 1-1 illustrates the asset mix of Bilan Company. It is quite clear from this graph that while total assets are generally increasing over the 5-year period, an increasing proportion of the company's assets are composed of receivables.

Figure 1-1: Stacked Column Graph

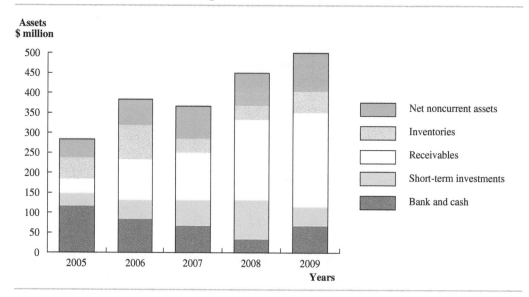

Regression analysis can help identify relationships between variables (e.g., between sales and inventory) over time and assist analysts in making forecasts (e.g., the relationship between GDP and sales can be used to make revenue forecasts).

Limitations of Ratio Analysis

- Companies may have divisions that operate in different industries. This can make it difficult to find relevant industry ratios to use for comparisons.

- One set of ratios may suggest that there is a problem, but another set may indicate that the potential problem is only short term.

- There are no set ranges within which particular ratios for a company must lie. An analyst must use her own judgment to evaluate the implications of a given value for a ratio. This usually involves examining the operations of a company, the external, industry and economic scenario before interpreting results and drawing conclusions.

- Firms enjoy significant latitude in the choice of accounting methods that are acceptable given the jurisdiction in which they operate. For example, under **U.S. GAAP**, companies can:
  - Use the FIFO, AVCO, or LIFO inventory cost flow assumption.
  - Choose from a variety of depreciation methods.

- Comparing ratios of firms across international borders is even more difficult in that most countries use **IFRS**. Despite the growing convergence between **IFRS** and **U.S. GAAP**, significant differences remain, which make it very difficult for analysts to compare ratios of firms that use different accounting standards.

It is also important to understand that the exact definitions of certain ratios vary across the analyst community. For example, in measuring leverage, some analysts use total liabilities, while others using only interest-bearing debt.

LESSON 2: COMMON RATIOS USED IN FINANCIAL ANALYSIS

LOS 28b: Classify, calculate, and interpret activity, liquidity, solvency, profitability, and valuation ratios. **Vol 3, pp 338–359**

Ratios are typically classified into the following categories:

Activity ratios measure how productive a company is in using its assets and how efficiently it performs its everyday operations.

Liquidity ratios measure the company's ability to meet its short-term cash requirements.

Solvency ratios measure a company's ability to meet long-term debt obligations.

Profitability ratios measure a company's ability to generate an adequate return on invested capital.

Valuation ratios measure the quantity of an asset or flow (e.g., earnings) associated with ownership of a specific claim (e.g., common stock).

These categories are not mutually exclusive. Some ratios are useful in evaluating multiple aspects of the business. Certain profitability ratios, for example, also reflect the operating efficiency of the business.

> Research has shown that in addition to being useful in evaluating the past performance of a company, ratios can be useful in predicting future earnings and equity returns.

Interpretation and Context

The financial ratios of a company are compared to those of its major competitors in cross-sectional analysis. A company's ratios for a given year can also be compared to its own prior period ratios to identify trends. The goal of ratio analysis is to understand the causes of material differences in ratios of a company compared to its peers. An analyst should evaluate financial ratios based on the following:

- Actual ratios should be compared to the company's stated objectives. This helps in determining whether the company's operations are moving in line with its strategy.

- A company's ratios should be compared with those of others in the industry. When comparing ratios between firms from the same industry, analysts must be careful because:
  - Not all ratios are important to every industry.
  - Companies may have several lines of business, which can cause aggregate financial ratios to be distorted. In such a situation, analysts should evaluate ratios for each segment of the business in relation to relevant industry averages.
  - Companies might be using different accounting standards.
  - Companies could be at different stages of growth or may have different strategies. This can result in different values for various ratios for firms in the same industry.

- Ratios should be studied in light of the current phase of the business cycle.

Exhibit 2-1 contains the financial statements of ABC Company, which we will use to calculate and interpret various financial ratios.

Exhibit 2-1: Financial Statements for ABC Company

Income Statement

	2006 $	2007 $
Total revenue	400,000	500,000
Cost of goods sold (COGS)	(320,000)	(380,000)
Gross profit	80,000	120,000
General expenses	(28,000)	(29,000)
Depreciation	(8,000)	(12,000)
Operating income	44,000	79,000
Interest income	3,000	2,000
Interest expense	(400)	(1,800)
Other losses	(1800)	(4,200)
Income before income taxes	44,800	75,000
Provision for income taxes	(16,000)	(21,000)
Net income	**28,800**	**54,000**

Balance Sheet

	2006 $	2007 $
Assets		
Current Assets		
Cash	21,000	32,000
Short-term investments	15,000	22,000
Accounts receivable	27,000	34,000
Inventories	16,000	34,000
Prepaid expenses	21,500	27,500
Total Current Assets	**100,500**	**149,500**
Fixed Assets		
Property and equipment	110,000	180,000
Long-term investments	13,000	4,000
Intangible assets	16,000	56,000
Other long-term assets	12,000	14,000
Total Fixed Assets	**151,000**	**254,000**
Total Assets	**251,500**	**403,500**
Liabilities		
Current Liabilities		
Accounts payable	27,000	20,000
Accrued expenses	12,700	17,000
Total Current Liabilities	**39,700**	**37,000**
Long-Term Debt	**21,800**	**83,000**
Shareholders' Equity		
Common stock	120,000	180,000
Accumulated other comprehensive income	0	−1,500
Retained earnings	70,000	100,000
General reserves	0	5,000
Total Shareholders' Equity	**190,000**	**283,500**
Total Liabilities and Shareholders' Equity	**251,500**	**403,500**

Activity Ratios

Activity ratios are also known as **asset utilization ratios** or **operating efficiency** ratios. They measure how well a company manages its operations and particularly how efficiently it manages its assets—working capital and long-lived assets. See Table 2-1.

$$\text{Inventory turnover} = \frac{\text{Cost of goods sold}}{\text{Average inventory}}$$

This ratio is used to evaluate the effectiveness of a company's inventory management. Generally, this ratio is benchmarked against the industry average.

- A high inventory turnover ratio relative to industry norms might indicate highly effective management. Alternatively, it could also indicate that the company does not hold adequate inventory levels, which can hurt sales incase shortages arise. A simple comparison of the company's sales growth to the industry's growth in sales can indicate whether sales are suffering because too little stock is available for sale at any given point in time.
- A low inventory turnover relative to the rest of the industry can be an indicator of slow moving or obsolete inventory. It suggests that the company has too many resources tied up in inventory.

$$\textbf{Inventory turnover} \text{ of ABC Company} = \frac{380,000}{(16,000 + 34,000)/2} = \textbf{15.2}$$

$$\textbf{Days of inventory on hand (DOH)} = \frac{365}{\text{Inventory turnover}}$$

This ratio is *inversely* related to inventory turnover.

- The *higher* the inventory turnover ratio, the *shorter* the length of the period that inventory is held on average.

$$\textbf{Days of Inventory on hand} \text{ of ABC Company} = \frac{365}{15.2} = \textbf{24.0 days}$$

$$\textbf{Receivables turnover} = \frac{\text{Revenue}}{\text{Average receivables}}$$

- A high receivables turnover ratio might indicate that the company's credit collection procedures are highly efficient. However, a high ratio can also result from overly stringent credit or collection policies, which can hurt sales if competitors offer more lenient credit terms to customers.
- A low ratio relative to industry averages will raise questions regarding the efficiency of a company's credit or collection procedures.
- As with the inventory turnover ratio, a simple comparison of the company's sales growth with industry sales growth can help determine whether the reason behind a high receivables turnover ratio is strict credit terms or efficient receivables management.
- Analysts can also compare current estimates of the company's bad debts and credit losses with its own past estimates and peer companies' estimates to assess whether low receivables turnover is the result of credit management issues.

$$\textbf{Receivables turnover} \text{ of ABC Company} = \frac{500,000}{(27,000 + 34,000)/2} = \textbf{16.4}$$

$$\text{Days of sales outstanding (DSO)} = \frac{365}{\text{Receivables turnover}}$$

- The receivables turnover ratio and days of sales outstanding are *inversely* related.
- The *higher* the receivables turnover ratio, the *lower* the DSO.

$$\textbf{DSO} \text{ of ABC Company} = \frac{365}{16.4} = \textbf{22.3 days}$$

$$\text{Payables turnover} = \frac{\text{Purchases}}{\text{Average trade payables}}$$

The amount for purchases over the year is usually not explicitly stated on the income statement; it is typically only disclosed in the footnotes to the financial statements. You might be expected to calculate purchases using the following formula:

$$\text{Purchases} = \text{Ending inventory} + \text{COGS} - \text{Opening inventory}$$

Payables turnover measures how many times a year the company theoretically pays off all its creditors.

- A high ratio can indicate that the company is not making full use of available credit facilities and repaying creditors too soon. However, a high ratio could also result from a company making payments early to avail early payment discounts.
- A low ratio could indicate that a company might be having trouble making payments on time. However, a low ratio can also result from a company successfully exploiting lenient supplier terms. If the company has sufficient cash and short-term investments, the low payables turnover ratio is probably not an indication of a liquidity crisis. It is probably a result of lenient supplier credit and collection policies.

$$\textbf{Payables turnover} \text{ of ABC Company} = \frac{34,000 + 380,000 - 16,000}{(27,000 + 20,000)/2} = \textbf{16.9}$$

$$\text{Number of days of payables} = \frac{365}{\text{Payables turnover}}$$

- The number of days of payables is *inversely* related to the payables turnover ratio.
- The *higher* the payables turnover, the *lower* the number of days of payables.

$$\textbf{Number of days of payables} \text{ of ABC Company} = \frac{365}{16.9} = \textbf{21.6 days}$$

$$\text{Working capital turnover} = \frac{\text{Revenue}}{\text{Average working capital}}$$

Working capital turnover indicates how efficiently the company generates revenue from its working capital. Working capital equals current assets minus current liabilities

- A higher working capital turnover ratio indicates higher operating efficiency.

For 2007, ABC's opening working capital equals $60,800 ($100,500 − $39,700), and ending working capital equals $112,500 ($149,500 − $37,000). Therefore, average working capital for 2007 equals $86,650.

$$\text{\textbf{Working capital turnover} of ABC Company} = \frac{\$500,000}{\$86,650} = \textbf{5.77}$$

$$\text{\textbf{Fixed asset turnover}} = \frac{\text{Revenue}}{\text{Average fixed assets}}$$

This ratio measures how efficiently a company generates revenues from its investments in long-lived assets.

- A higher ratio indicates more efficient use of fixed assets in generating revenue.
- A low ratio could be an indicator of operating inefficiency. However, a low fixed asset turnover can also be the result of a capital intensive business environment. Companies that have recently entered a new business that is not fully operational also report low fixed asset turnover ratios.
- The fixed asset turnover ratio will be lower for a firm whose assets are newer than for a firm whose assets are relatively older. The older-asset firm will have depreciated its assets for a longer period so the book value of its fixed assets will be lower.

$$\text{\textbf{Fixed asset turnover} of ABC Company} = \frac{500,000}{(151,000+254,000)/2} = \textbf{2.47}$$

$$\text{\textbf{Total asset turnover}} = \frac{\text{Revenue}}{\text{Average total assets}}$$

Total asset turnover measures the company's overall ability to generate revenues with a given level of assets.

- A high ratio indicates efficiency, while a low ratio can be an indicator of inefficiency or the level of capital intensity of the business.
- This ratio also identifies strategic decisions by management. For example, a business that uses highly capital-intensive techniques of production will have a lower total asset turnover compared to a business that uses labor-intensive production methods.

$$\text{\textbf{Total asset turnover} of ABC Company} = \frac{500,000}{(251,500+403,500)/2} = \textbf{1.53}$$

Table 2-1: Definitions of Commonly Used Activity Ratios[1]

Activity Ratios	Numerator	Denominator
Inventory turnover	Cost of goods sold	Average inventory
Days of inventory on hand (DOH)	Number of days in period	Inventory turnover
Receivables turnover	Revenue	Average receivables
Days of sales outstanding (DSO)	Number of days in period	Receivables turnover
Payables turnover	Purchases	Average trade payables
Number of days of payables	Number of days in period	Payables turnover
Working capital turnover	Revenue	Average working capital
Fixed asset turnover	Revenue	Average net fixed assets
Total asset turnover	Revenue	Average total assets

Liquidity Ratios

Analysis of a company's liquidity ratios aims to evaluate a company's ability to meet its short-term obligations. Liquidity measures how quickly a company can convert its assets into cash at prices that are close to their fair values. See Table 2-2.

$$\text{Current ratio} = \frac{\text{Current assets}}{\text{Current liabilities}}$$

- A higher ratio is desirable because it indicates a higher level of liquidity.
- A current ratio of 1.0 indicates that the book value of the company's current assets equals the book value of its current liabilities.
- A low ratio indicates less liquidity and implies a greater reliance on operating cash flow and outside financing to meet short-term obligations.
- The current ratio assumes that inventory and accounts receivable can readily be converted into cash at close to their fair values.

$$\text{Current ratio of ABC Company} = \frac{149,500}{37,000} = 4.04$$

$$\text{Quick ratio} = \frac{\text{Cash} + \text{Short-term marketable investments} + \text{Receivables}}{\text{Current liabilities}}$$

---

1 - Exhibit 10, Volume 3, CFA Program Curriculum 2014

The quick ratio recognizes that certain current assets (such as prepaid expenses) represent costs that have been paid in advance in the current year and cannot usually be converted into cash. This ratio also considers the fact that inventory cannot be immediately liquidated at its fair value. Therefore, these current assets are excluded from the numerator in the calculation of the quick ratio. When inventory is illiquid, this ratio is a better indicator of liquidity than current ratio.

- A high quick ratio indicates greater liquidity.

$$\textbf{Quick ratio} \text{ of ABC Company} = \frac{32,000 + 22,000 + 34,000}{37,000} = \textbf{2.38}$$

$$\boxed{\textbf{Cash ratio} = \frac{\text{Cash} + \text{Short-term marketable investments}}{\text{Current liabilities}}}$$

The cash ratio is a very reliable measure of an entity's liquidity position in the event of an unforeseen crisis. This is because it only includes cash and highly liquid short-term investments in the numerator.

$$\textbf{Cash ratio} \text{ of ABC Company} = \frac{54,000}{37,000} = \textbf{1.46}$$

$$\boxed{\textbf{Defensive interval ratio} = \frac{\text{Cash} + \text{Short-term marketable investments} + \text{Receivables}}{\text{Daily cash expenditures}}}$$

This ratio measures how long the company can continue to meet its daily expense requirements from its existing liquid assets without obtaining any additional financing. A defensive interval of 40 indicates that the company can pay its operating expenses for 40 days by liquidating its quick assets.

- A high defensive interval ratio is desirable as it indicates greater liquidity.
- If a company's defensive interval ratio is very low compared to the industry average, the analyst might want to determine whether significant cash inflows are expected in the near future to meet expense requirements.

$$\boxed{\textbf{Cash conversion cycle} = \text{DSO} + \text{DOH} - \text{Number of days of payables}}$$

The cash conversion cycle (also known as net operating cycle) measures the length of the period between the point that a company invests in working capital and the point that the company collects cash proceeds from sales. Specifically, it is the time between the outlay of cash (to pay off accounts payable for credit purchases) and the collection of cash (from accounts receivable for goods sold on credit).

- A shorter cycle is desirable, as it indicates greater liquidity.
- A longer cash conversion cycle indicates lower liquidity. It implies that the company has to finance its inventory and accounts receivable for a longer period of time.

Cash conversion cycle of ABC Company = $24 + 22.3 - 21.6 = \textbf{24.7 days}$

Table 2-2: Definitions of Commonly Used Liquidity Ratios[2]

Liquidity Ratios	Numerator	Denominator
Current ratio	Current assets	Current liabilities
Quick ratio	Cash + Short-term marketable investments + Receivables	Current liabilities
Cash ratio	Cash + Short-term marketable investments	Current liabilities
Defensive interval ratio	Cash + Short-term marketable investments + Receivables	Daily cash expenditures
Additional Liquidity Measure		
Cash conversion cycle (net operating cycle)	DOH + DSO – Number of days of payables	

Solvency Ratios

Solvency refers to a company's ability to meet its long-term debt obligations. Solvency ratios measure the relative amount of debt in a company's capital structure and the ability of earnings and cash flows to meet debt-servicing requirements. The amount of debt in the capital structure is important to assess a company's degree of financial leverage (its financial risk). If the company can earn a return on borrowed funds that is greater than interest costs, the inclusion of debt in the capital structure will increase shareholder wealth. See Table 2-3.

$$\text{Debt-to-assets ratio} = \frac{\text{Total debt}}{\text{Total assets}}$$

Important: In this reading, we take total debt in this context to be the sum of interest-bearing short-term and long-term debt. The debt-to-asset ratio measures the proportion of the firm's total assets that have been financed by debt.

- A higher D/A ratio is undesirable because it implies higher financial risk and a weaker solvency position.

$$\textbf{Debt to assets ratio} \text{ of ABC Company} = \frac{83,000}{403,500} = \textbf{0.21}$$

ABC has no short-term debt.

---

2 - Exhibit 12, Volume 3, CFA Program Curriculum 2014

$$\text{Debt-to-capital ratio} = \frac{\text{Total debt}}{\text{Total debt} + \text{Shareholders' equity}}$$

This ratio measures the proportion of a company's total capital (debt plus equity) that is composed of debt.

- A higher ratio indicates higher financial risk and is undesirable.

$$\text{Debt to capital ratio of ABC Company} = \frac{83,000}{83,000 + 283,500} = \textbf{0.23}$$

$$\text{Debt-to-equity ratio} = \frac{\text{Total debt}}{\text{Shareholders' equity}}$$

This ratio measures the amount of debt capital relative to a firm's equity capital.

- A higher ratio is undesirable and indicates higher financial risk.
- A ratio of 1.0 indicates equal amounts of debt and equity in the company's capital structure.

$$\text{Debt to equity ratio of ABC Company} = \frac{83,000}{283,500} = \textbf{0.29}$$

$$\text{Financial leverage ratio} = \frac{\text{Average total assets}}{\text{Average total equity}}$$

This ratio measures the amount of total assets supported by each money unit of equity. For example, a leverage ratio of 2 means that each dollar of equity supports $2 worth of assets. This ratio uses *average* values for total assets and total equity and plays an important role in Dupont decomposition, which we study later in this reading.

- The higher the leverage ratio, the more leveraged (dependent on debt for finance) the company.

$$\text{Financial leverage ratio of ABC Company} = \frac{(403,500 + 251,500)/2}{(283,500 + 190,000)/2} = \textbf{1.38}$$

$$\text{Interest coverage ratio} = \frac{\text{EBIT}}{\text{Interest payments}}$$

This ratio measures the number of times a company's operating earnings (earnings before interest and tax, or EBIT) cover its annual interest payment obligations. This very important ratio is widely used to gauge how comfortably a company can meet its debt-servicing requirements from operating profits.

- A higher ratio provides assurance that the company can service its debt from operating earnings.

$$\text{Interest coverage ratio of ABC Company} = \frac{79,000}{1,800} = \textbf{44 times}.$$

$$\text{Fixed charge coverage ratio} = \frac{\text{EBIT} + \text{Lease payments}}{\text{Interest payments} + \text{Lease payments}}$$

This ratio relates the fixed charges or obligations of the company to its earnings. It measures the number of times a company's operating earnings can cover its interest and lease payments.

- A higher ratio suggests that the company is comfortably placed to service its debt and make lease payments from the earnings it generates from operations.

$$\text{Fixed charge coverage ratio for ABC Company} = \frac{79{,}000}{1{,}800} = \textbf{44 times.}$$

*ABC has no lease payments.

Table 2-3: Definitions of Commonly Used Solvency Ratios[3]

Solvency Ratios	Numerator	Denominator
Debt Ratios		
Debt-to-assets ratio	Total debt	Total assets
Debt-to-capital ratio	Total debt	Total debt + Total shareholders' equity
Debt-to-equity ratio	Total debt	Total shareholders' equity
Financial leverage ratio	Average total assets	Average total equity
Coverage Ratios		
Interest coverage	EBIT	Interest payments
Fixed charge coverage	EBIT + Lease payments	Interest payments + Lease payments

"Total debt ratio" is another name sometimes used for the debt-to-assets ratio.
In this reading, we take total debt in this context to be the sum of interest-bearing short-term and long-term debt.

> When evaluating a company's solvency ratios, it is important to consider the volatility of the company's cash flows. Companies with stable cash flow streams are typically able to take on more debt.

Profitability Ratios

The ability of a company to generate profits is a key driver of the company's overall value and the value of the securities it issues. Therefore, many analysts consider profitability to be the focus of their analysis.

Before moving on to any profitability ratios, you should be familiar with a few terms, such as gross profit, operating profit, net profit, and so on. These are linked in the income statement as follows:

	Net sales
−	Cost of goods sold
=	Gross profit
−	Operating expenses
=	Operating profit (EBIT)
−	Interest
=	Earnings before tax (EBT)
−	Taxes
=	Earnings after tax (EAT)
+/−	Below the line items adjusted for tax
=	Net income
−	Preferred dividends
=	Income available to common shareholders

$$\textbf{Gross profit margin} = \frac{\text{Gross profit}}{\text{Revenue}}$$

The gross profit margin tells us the percentage of a company's revenues that are available to meet operating and nonoperating expenses. A high gross profit margin can be a combination of high product prices (reflected in high revenues) and low product costs (reflected in low COGS).

$$\textbf{Gross profit margin} \text{ of ABC Company} = \frac{120,000}{500,000} = \textbf{24\%}$$

$$\textbf{Operating profit margin} = \frac{\text{Operating profit}}{\text{Revenue}}$$

Operating profits are calculated as gross profit minus operating costs.

- An operating profit margin that is increasing at a higher rate than the gross profit margin indicates that the company has successfully controlled operating costs.
- A decreasing operating profit margin when gross profit margins are rising indicates that the company is not efficiently controlling operating expenses.

$$\textbf{Operating profit margin} \text{ of ABC Company} = \frac{79,000}{500,000} = \textbf{15.8\%}$$

$$\textbf{Pretax margin} = \frac{\text{EBT (earnings before tax, but after interest)}}{\text{Revenue}}$$

Pretax income is also called earnings before tax (EBT). It is calculated as operating income minus nonoperating expenses plus nonoperating income.

- If a company's pretax margin is rising primarily due to higher nonoperating income, the analyst should evaluate whether this source of income will continue to bring in significant earnings going forward.

Pretax margin of ABC Company $= \dfrac{75,000}{500,000} = \textbf{15\%}$

$$\textbf{Net profit margin} = \frac{\text{Net profit}}{\text{Revenue}}$$

Net profit margin shows how much profit a company makes for every dollar it generates in revenue.

- A low net profit margin indicates a low margin of safety. It alerts analysts to the risk that a decline in the company's sales revenue will lower profits or even result in a net loss (reduction in shareholder wealth).

Net profit margin of ABC Company $= \dfrac{54,000}{500,000} = \textbf{10.8\%}$

$$\textbf{ROA} = \frac{\text{Net income}}{\text{Average total assets}}$$

Return on assets measures the return earned by the company on its assets.

- The higher the ROA, the greater the income generated by the company given its total assets.

ROA of ABC Company $= \dfrac{54,000}{(251,500 + 403,500)/2} = \textbf{16.5\%}$

The problem with this calculation of ROA (net income/average total assets) is that it uses only the return to equity holders (net income) in the numerator. Assets are financed by both equity holders and bond holders. Therefore, some analysts prefer to add interest expense back to net income in the numerator. However, interest expense must be adjusted for the tax shield that it provides. The adjusted ROA is computed as:

$$\textbf{Adjusted ROA} = \frac{\text{Net income} + \text{Interest expense} (1 - \text{Tax rate})}{\text{Average total assets}}$$

Some analysts choose to calculate ROA on a pre-interest and pre-tax basis as:

$$\text{Operating ROA} = \frac{\text{Operating income or EBIT}}{\text{Average total assets}}$$

- This ratio reflects the return on all assets used by the company, whether financed with debt or equity.

$$\text{Operating ROA of ABC Company} = \frac{79,000}{(251,500 + 403,500)/2} = 24.1\%$$

Note: Whichever formula is used to calculate ROA, the analyst must use it consistently in cross-sectional analysis and trend analysis.

$$\text{Return on total capital} = \frac{\text{EBIT}}{\text{Short-term debt} + \text{Long-term debt} + \text{Equity}}$$

This ratio measures the profits that a company earns on all sources of capital that it employs—short-term debt, long-term debt, and equity. Once again, returns are measured prior to deducting interest expense.

$$\text{Return on total capital of ABC Company} = \frac{79,000}{(83,000 + 283,500)} = 21.6\%$$

$$\text{Return on equity} = \frac{\text{Net income}}{\text{Average total equity}}$$

This ratio measures the rate of return earned by a company on its equity capital. Equity capital includes minority equity, preferred equity, and common equity. It measures a firm's efficiency in generating profits from every dollar of net assets (assets minus liabilities), and shows how well a company uses its investment dollars to generate earnings. ROE is commonly used to compare the profitability of a company to that of other firms in its industry.

ABC pays no preferred dividends.

$$\text{ROE of ABC Company} = \frac{54,000}{(190,000 + 283,500)/2} = 22.8\%$$

$$\text{Return on common equity} = \frac{\text{Net income} - \text{Preferred dividends}}{\text{Average common equity}}$$

This ratio measures the return earned by a company only on its common equity.

$$\text{Return on common equity of ABC Company} = \frac{54,000}{(120,000 + 180,000)/2} = 36\%$$

See Table 2-4.

Table 2-4: Definitions of Commonly Used Profitability Ratios[4]

Profitability Ratios	Numerator	Denominator
Return on Sales		
Gross profit margin	Gross profit	Revenue
Operating profit margin	Operating income	Revenue
Pre-tax margin	EBT (earnings before tax but after interest)	Revenue
Net profit margin	Net income	Revenue
Return on Investment		
Operating ROA	Operating income	Average total assets
ROA	Net income	Average total assets
Return on total capital	EBIT	Short- and long-term debt and equity
ROE	Net income	Average total equity
Return on common equity	Net income – Preferred dividends	Average common equity

4 - Exhibit 15, Volume 3, CFA Program Curriculum 2014

Example 2-1: Evaluating a Company Using a Combination of Ratios

An analyst obtains the following liquidity ratios of a Taiwanese manufacturing company:

	2008	2007	2006
Current ratio	2.2	2.0	1.7
Quick ratio	0.7	0.8	0.9

- The increase in the current ratio over the years, from 1.7 to 2.2, suggests that the company's liquidity position has strengthened.
- However, the decline in the quick ratio over the years, from 0.9 to 0.7, suggests that the liquidity position of the company has deteriorated.
- Both ratios have current liabilities as the denominator. Therefore, the difference must be due to the changes in certain current assets that are not included in the quick ratio (e.g., inventories).

To evaluate the disconnect between the suggestions offered by the trend in current and quick ratios regarding the company's liquidity position, the analyst obtains the following DOH and DSO figures for the company:

	2008	2007	2006
DOH	56	46	31
DSO	25	29	51

- The company's DOH has increased from 31 days to 56, which implies that the company is holding higher levels of inventory.
- The decrease in DSO indicates that the company is collecting on its receivables more quickly than before.
- Taking all these ratios together, we can reach the conclusion that although the company is collecting on its receivables more quickly than before, the proceeds from sales are being used to purchase inventory which is not being sold as quickly. Therefore, the company's quick ratio is suffering, but not its current ratio.

Example 2-2: Comparing Two Companies Using Ratios

An analyst is given the following information about two companies that operate in the same industry:

Company A	2008	2007	2006	2005
Inventory turnover	75.59	87.08	149.29	188.74
DOH	5.67	5.01	3.74	2.59
Receivables turnover	11.57	9.66	12.41	8.45
DSO	34.67	40.31	33.23	49.89
Accounts payable turnover	5.52	5.26	5.74	5.12
Days payable	79.87	84.88	76.29	87.78
Cash from operations/Total liabilities	41.31%	21.34%	9.89%	18.67%
ROE	7.56%	2.91%	2.82%	−0.54%
ROA	4.70%	2.05%	2.05%	−0.34%
Net profit margin	3.95%	2.47%	2.49%	−0.56%
Total asset turnover	1.19	0.83	0.82	0.60
Leverage (Average assets/Average equity)	1.61	1.42	1.38	1.61

Company B	2008	2007	2006	2005
Inventory turnover	11.29	11.07	9.23	16.18
DOH	40.12	41.23	49.11	26.45
Receivables turnover	7.98	6.76	5.34	4.21
DSO	44.32	53.26	60.98	70.59
Accounts payable turnover	6.78	6.98	7.45	6.81
Days payable	55.76	54.23	48.13	54.98
Cash from operations/Total liabilities	14.31%	17.34%	16.89%	12.67%
ROE	9.53%	6.85%	−4.07%	−6.60%
ROA	4.72%	3.55%	−1.95%	3.13%
Net profit margin	4.63%	3.45%	−1.43%	−2.63%
Total asset turnover	1.02	1.03	1.36	1.19
Leverage (Average assets/Average equity)	2.02	1.93	2.09	2.11

Which of the following choices best describes a reasonable conclusion that an analyst might make about the companies' efficiency levels?

A. Over the 4-year period, Company A has shown greater improvement in efficiency than Company B, as indicated by its total asset turnover ratio increasing from 0.60 to 1.19.

B. In 2007, Company A's DOH of only 5.01 indicates that it was less efficient at inventory management than Company B, which had a DOH of 41.23.

C. In 2008, Company B's receivables turnover of 7.98 indicates that it was more efficient at receivables management than Company A, which had a receivables turnover of 11.57.

D. Over the 4 years, Company B has shown greater improvement in efficiency than Company A, as indicated by its net profit margin of 4.62%.

Comments

- Choice A is correct because over the given period, Company A has shown greater improvement in efficiency than Company B. Company A's total asset turnover (a measure of operating efficiency) has almost doubled from 0.60 to 1.19. Over the same period, Company B total asset turnover has declined from 1.19 to 1.05.

- Choice B is incorrect because it misinterprets DOH. All other factors constant, a lower DOH indicates better inventory management.

- Choice C is incorrect because it misinterprets receivables turnover. All other factors constant, a higher receivables turnover indicates greater efficiency in receivables management.

- Choice D is incorrect because net profit margin is not an indicator of efficiency. It is an indicator of profitability.

LESSON 3: DUPONT ANALYSIS, EQUITY ANALYSIS, CREDIT ANALYSIS, AND BUSINESS AND GEOGRAPHIC SEGMENTS

LOS 28d: Demonstrate the application of DuPont analysis of return on equity, and calculate and interpret effects of changes in its components.
Vol 3, pp 361–366

ROE measures the return a company generates on its equity capital. Decomposing ROE into its components through DuPont analysis has the following uses:

- It facilitates a meaningful evaluation of the different aspects of the company's performance that affect reported ROE.
- It helps in determining the reasons for changes in ROE over time for a given company. It also helps us understand the reasons for differences in ROE for different companies over a given time period.
- It can direct management to areas that it should focus on to improve ROE.
- It shows the relationship between the various categories of ratios and how they all influence the return that owners realize on their investment.

Decomposition of ROE

$$\text{ROE} = \frac{\text{Net income}}{\text{Average total equity}}$$

Two-Way DuPont Decomposition

This decomposition breaks ROE down into two components.

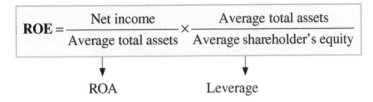

$$ROE = \frac{\text{Net income}}{\text{Average total assets}} \times \frac{\text{Average total assets}}{\text{Average shareholder's equity}}$$

$\downarrow$ ROA $\qquad$ $\downarrow$ Leverage

The two-way breakdown of ROE illustrates that ROE is a function of company's return on assets (ROA) and financial leverage ratio. A company can improve its ROE by improving ROA or by using leverage (debt) more extensively to finance its operations. As long as a company is able to borrow at a rate lower than the marginal rate it can earn by investing the borrowed money in its business, taking on more debt will result in an increase in ROE. However, if a company's borrowing costs exceed its marginal return, taking on more debt would depress ROA and ROE as well. Table 3-1 decomposes the ROE for Company A in Example 2 into two components:

Table 3-1: Company A 2-Way DuPont Decomposition

	ROE	=	ROA	×	Leverage
2008	7.56%		4.70%		1.61
2007	2.91%		2.05%		1.42
2006	2.82%		2.05%		1.38
2005	−0.54%		−0.34%		1.61

Analysis: Over the period, the company's financial leverage ratio was relatively stable. The increase in the company's ROE was primarily due to an increase in profitability (ROA).

Three-Way DuPont Decomposition

This decomposition expresses ROE as a product of three components.

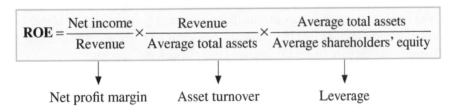

$$ROE = \frac{\text{Net income}}{\text{Revenue}} \times \frac{\text{Revenue}}{\text{Average total assets}} \times \frac{\text{Average total assets}}{\text{Average shareholders' equity}}$$

$\downarrow$ Net profit margin $\qquad$ $\downarrow$ Asset turnover $\qquad$ $\downarrow$ Leverage

This decomposition illustrates that a company's ROE is a function of its net profit margin, asset turnover ratio, and financial leverage ratio.

- Net profit margin is an indicator of profitability. It shows how much profit a company generates from each money unit of sales.
- Asset turnover is an indicator of efficiency. It tells us how much revenue a company generates from each money unit of assets.
- ROA is a function of its profitability (net profit [NP] margin) and efficiency (asset turnover [TO]).
- Financial leverage is an indicator of solvency. It reflects the total amount of a company's assets relative to its equity capital.

Table 3-2 breaks down the ROE for Company A from Example 2-1 into three components:

Table 3-2: Company A Three-Way DuPont Decomposition

	ROE	=	NP margin	×	Asset TO	×	Leverage
2008	7.56%		3.95%		1.19		1.61
2007	2.91%		2.47%		0.83		1.42
2006	2.82%		2.49%		0.82		1.38
2005	−0.54%		−0.56%		0.60		1.61

The increase in Company A's ROE is a result of better NP margins (improved profitability) *and* higher asset turnover (improved efficiency), which improved its ROA and its ROE.

Five-Way DuPont Decomposition

To separate the effects of taxes and interest, we can further decompose ROE into five components.

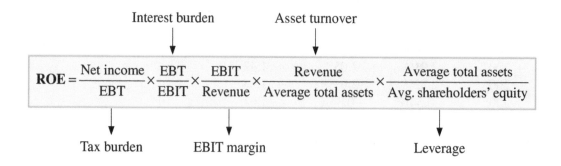

$$ROE = \frac{\text{Net income}}{\text{EBT}} \times \frac{\text{EBT}}{\text{EBIT}} \times \frac{\text{EBIT}}{\text{Revenue}} \times \frac{\text{Revenue}}{\text{Average total assets}} \times \frac{\text{Average total assets}}{\text{Avg. shareholders' equity}}$$

This decomposition shows that ROE is a function of the company's tax burden, interest burden, operating profitability, efficiency, and leverage. See Exhibit 3-1.

- The tax burden ratio equals one minus the average tax rate. It basically measures the proportion of its pretax profits that a company gets to keep. A *higher* tax burden ratio implies that the company can keep a *higher* percentage of its pretax profits. A decrease in the tax burden ratio implies the opposite.

- The interest burden ratio captures the effect of interest expense on ROE. High borrowing costs reduce ROE. As interest expense rises, EBT will fall as a percentage of EBIT, the interest burden ratio will fall, and ROE will also fall.

- The EBIT margin captures the effect of operating profitability on ROE.

- We already know that the asset turnover ratio is an indicator of the overall efficiency of the company, while the leverage ratio measures the total value of a company's assets relative to its equity capital.

Some candidates get confused as to how a higher tax or interest "burden" ratio can improve the ROE. The key is not to focus on the English. The ratios are just called burden ratios, but a higher ratio does not mean that there is literally more of a tax or interest "burden" on the company. In fact, it is the opposite. A higher tax and interest burden ratio is actually better for the company. Focus on the math behind the ratio, not the English behind its name.

Exhibit 3-1: Company A Five-Way DuPont Decomposition for 2008

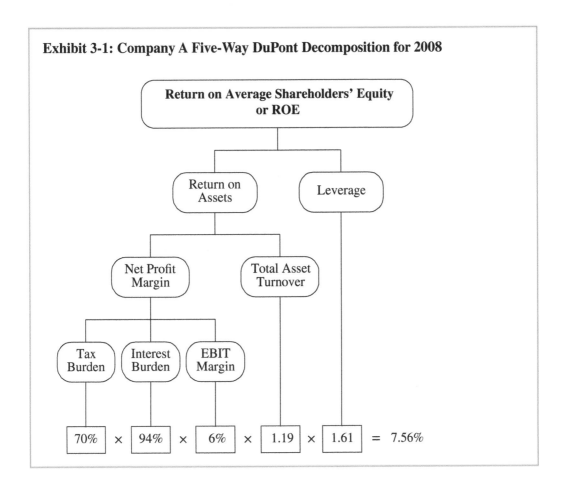

The calculated value for ROE will be the same under every kind of decomposition. DuPont analysis is a way of decomposing ROE to see more clearly the underlying changes in the company's operations that drive changes in its ROE.

In general, higher profit margins, asset turnover, and leverage will lead to higher ROE. However, the five-way decomposition shows that an increase in leverage will not always increase ROE. This is because as the company takes on more debt, its interest costs rise and the interest burden ratio falls. The reduction in interest burden ratio (as the difference between EBT and EBIT increases) offsets the effect of the increase in the financial leverage ratio.

Example 3-1: Five-Way Decomposition of ROE

Consider the following information:

	2011	2010	2009	2008	2007
ROE	9.47%	15.00%	24.31%	25.82%	24.07%
Tax burden	64.85%	59.37%	63.24%	58.20%	62.58%
Interest burden	92.58%	92.45%	92.74%	92.85%	92.61%
EBIT margin	8.63%	10.41%	13.24%	15.69%	14.35%
Asset turnover	0.85	1.21	1.47	1.44	1.58
Leverage	2.15	2.17	2.13	2.19	2.18

Based on this information, comment on the negative trend in the company's ROE.

Solution:

The following conclusions may be drawn from the given information:
- *The tax burden ratio has varied with no obvious trend over the years.* The recent increase in tax burden ratio (from 59.37% in 2010 to 64.85% in 2011) indicates that taxes declined as a percentage of pre-tax profits. Average tax rates may have declined as a result of (1) new legislation or (2) greater revenue generated in lower tax jurisdictions.
- *The interest burden ratio remained fairly constant over the period,* which suggests that the company's capital structure has remained fairly constant.
- *The EBIT margin declined over the period,* indicating that the company's operations were less profitable.
- *The company's asset turnover declined over the period,* which suggests that the company is becoming increasingly inefficient.
- *The financial leverage ratio remained fairly constant over the period,* which is consistent with the stable interest burden ratio.

Overall, the decline in the company's ROE is mainly caused by a decline in the EBIT margin (profitability) and asset turnover (efficiency).

LOS 28e: Calculate and interpret ratios used in equity analysis and credit analysis. Vol 3, pp 366–378

Equity Analysis

Analysts use a variety of methods to value a company's equity. One of the most common method involves the use of valuation ratios.

Valuation Ratios

Price-to-Earnings Ratio

$$P/E = \frac{\text{Price per share}}{\text{Earnings per share}}$$

The P/E ratio expresses the relationship between the price per share of common stock and the amount of earnings attributable to a single share. It basically tells us how much a share of common stock is currently worth per dollar of earnings of the company.

Other commonly used valuation ratios include:

Price to Cash Flow

$$P/CF = \frac{\text{Price per share}}{\text{Cash flow per share}}$$

Price to Sales

$$P/S = \frac{\text{Price per share}}{\text{Sales per share}}$$

Price to Book Value

$$P/BV = \frac{\text{Price per share}}{\text{Book value per share}}$$

Per Share Quantities that are Important in Equity Analysis

$$\text{Basic EPS} = \frac{\text{Net income} - \text{Preferred dividends}}{\text{Weighted average number of ordinary shares outstanding}}$$

Basic EPS are the earnings of a company attributable to each share of common stock. The weighted average number of shares consists of the number of ordinary shares outstanding at the beginning of the period, adjusted for those bought back or issued during the period, weighted by the length of time that they were outstanding during the relevant period.

$$\text{Diluted EPS} = \frac{\begin{array}{c}\text{Adjusted income available for ordinary shares}\\\text{reflecting conversion of dilutive securities}\end{array}}{\begin{array}{c}\text{Weighted average number of ordinary and potential}\\\text{ordinary shares outstanding}\end{array}}$$

Diluted EPS includes the effects of all outstanding securities whose conversion or exercise will result in a reduction in EPS. Dilutive securities include convertible debt, convertible preference shares, warrants, and options.

$$\text{Cash flow per share} = \frac{\text{Cash flow from operations}}{\text{Average number of shares outstanding}}$$

$$\text{EBITDA per share} = \frac{\text{EBITDA}}{\text{Average number of shares outstanding}}$$

$$\text{Dividends per share} = \frac{\text{Common dividends declared}}{\text{Weighted average number of ordinary shares}}$$

Dividend Related Quantities

$$\text{Dividend payout ratio} = \frac{\text{Common share dividends}}{\text{Net income attributable to common shares}}$$

The dividend payout ratio measures the percentage of earnings that a company pays out as dividends to shareholders. The per-share dividend paid by companies is typically fixed, so this ratio fluctuates as a percentage of earnings. Therefore, conclusions about a company's dividend payout policy should be based on examination of the payout ratio over a number of periods.

$$\text{Retention rate} = \frac{\text{Net income attributable to common shares} - \text{Common share dividends}}{\text{Net income attributable to common shares}}$$

This ratio measures the percentage of earnings that a company retains and reinvests in the business.

Retention rate = (1 − Dividend payout ratio)

$$\text{Sustainable growth rate} = \text{Retention rate} \times \text{ROE}$$

A company's sustainable growth rate is a function of its profitability (ROE) and its ability to finance its operations from internally generated funds (measured by the retention rate). Higher ROE and higher retention rates result in a higher sustainable growth rates.

EXAMPLE 3-2: Calculating the Sustainable Growth Rate

The following data is available for Sedag Inc. Calculate its sustainable growth rate

EPS	$3
Dividends per share	$1
Return on equity	10%

Solution

Dividend payout ratio = $1/$3 = 0.33
Retention Ratio = 1 − 0.33 = 0.67
Sustainable growth rate (g) = 0.67 × 10% = 6.7%

See Table 3-3 for definitions of selected valuation ratios and related quantities.

Table 3-3: Definitions of Selected Valuation Ratios and Related Quantities[5]

	Numerator	Denominator
Valuation ratios		
P/E	Price per share	Earnings per share
P/CF	Price per share	Cash flow per share
P/S	Price per share	Sales per share
P/BV	Price per share	Book value per share
Pre-share quantities		
Basic EPS	Net income minus preferred dividends	Weighted average number of ordinary shares outstanding
Diluted EPS	Adjusted income available for ordinary shares, reflecting conversion of dilutive securities	Weighted average number of ordinary and potential ordinary shares outstanding
Cash flow per share	Cash flow form operations	Average number of shares outstanding
EBITDA per share	EBITDA	Average number of shares outstanding
Dividends per share	Common dividends declared	Weighted average number of ordinary shares outstanding
Dividend-related quantities		
Dividend payout ratio	Common share dividends	Net income attributable to common shares
Retention rate (b)	Net income attributable to common shares – common share dividends	Net income attributable to common shares
Sustainable growth rate	b × ROE	

> Studies have shown that, in addition to being useful in evaluating the past performance of a company, ratios and comon-size metrics from accounting data are useful in forecasting earnings and stock returns.

Industry-Specific Ratios

Aspects of performance that are deemed relevant in one industry may be irrelevant in another. Industry-specific ratios reflect these differences.

- For companies in the retail industry, changes in same store sales should be tracked. This is because it is important to distinguish between sales growth generated from opening new stores and sales growth resulting from higher sales at existing stores.

- Regulated industries are required to adhere to specific regulatory ratios. The banking sector has liquidity and cash reserve ratio requirements. Banking capital adequacy requirements relate banks' solvency to their specific levels of risk exposure.

Table 3-4 lists some industry-specific ratios.

---

5 - Exhibit 18, Volume 3, CFA Program Curriculum 2014

Table 3-4: Definitions of Some Common Industry and Task-Specific Ratios[6]

Ratios	Numerator	Denominator
Business Risk		
Coefficient of variation of operating income	Standard deviation of operating income	Average operating income
Coefficient of variation of net income	Standard deviation of net income	Average net income
Coefficient of variation of revenues	Standard deviation of revenues	Average revenue
Financial Sector Ratios		
Capital adequacy—Banks	Various components of capital	Risk weighted assets, market risk exposure, and level of operational risk assumed
Monetary reserve requirement	Reserves held at central bank	Specified deposit liabilities
Liquid asset requirement	Approved "readily marketable securities"	Specified deposit liabilities
Net interest margin	Net interest income	Total interest-earning assets
Retail Ratios		
Same store sales	Average revenue growth year on year for stores open in both periods	Not applicable
Sales per square foot (meter)	Revenue	Total retail space in feet or meters
Service Companies		
Revenue per employee	Revenue	Total number of employees
Net income per employee	Net income	Total number of employees
Hotels		
Average daily rate	Room revenue	Number of rooms sold
Occupancy rate	Number of rooms sold	Number of rooms available

6 - Exhibit 19, Volume 3, CFA Program Curriculum 2014

Credit Analysis

Credit risk is the risk of loss that is caused by a debtor's failure to make a promised payment. Credit analysis is the evaluation of credit risk.

The Credit-Rating Process

The credit-rating process involves the analysis of a company's financial reports and a broad assessment of a company's operations. It includes the following procedures:[7]

- Meetings with management.
- Tours of major facilities, if time permits.
- Meetings of ratings committees where the analyst's recommendations are voted on, after considering factors that include:
    - **Business Risk**, including the evaluation of:
        - Operating environment.
        - Industry characteristics.
        - Success areas and areas of vulnerability.
        - Company's competitive position, including size and diversification.
    - **Financial risk**, including:
        - The evaluation of capital structure, interest coverage, and profitability using ratio analysis.
        - The examination of debt covenants.
    - **Evaluation of management**
- Monitoring of publicly distributed ratings, including reconsideration of ratings due to changing conditions.

In assigning credit ratings, rating agencies emphasize the importance of the relationship between a company's business risk profile and its financial risk.

---

7 - Based on Standard & Poor's Corporate Ratings Criteria (2006).

Table 3-5: Selected Credit Ratios Used by Standard & Poor's[7]

Credit Ratio	Numerator[a]	Denominator[b]
EBIT interest coverage	EBIT	Gross Interest (prior to deductions for capitalized interest or interest income)
EBITDA interest coverage	EBITDA	Gross Interest (prior to deductions for capitalized interest or interest income)
Funds from operations to total debt	FFO (net income adjusted for noncash items)[c]	Total debt
Free operating cash flow to total debt	CFO (adjusted) less capital expenditures[d]	Total debt
Return on capital	EBIT	Capital = Average equity (common and preferred equity) and short-term portions of debt, noncurrent deferred taxes, minority interest
Total debt to total debt plus equity	Total debt	Total debt plus equity

[a]Numerator: Emphasis is on earnings from continuing operations.
[b]Denominator: Both numerator and denominator definitions are adjusted from ratio to ratio and may not correspond to the definitions used in this reading.
[c]FFO: Funds from operations.
[d]CFO: Cash flow from operations.

Source: Based on data from Standard and Poor's Corporate Ratings Criteria 2006.

Segment Analysis

Analysts often need to analyze the performance of underlying business segments to understand the company as a whole. These segments may include subsidiary companies, operating units, or simply operations in different geographical areas.

A business segment is a separately identifiable component of a company that is engaged in providing an individual product or service or a group of related products or services. It is subject to risks and returns that are different from those of other business segments of the company.

A geographical segment is a distinguishable component of a company that is engaged in providing an individual product or service within a particular region.

7 - Exhibit 20, Volume 3, CFA Program Curriculum 2014

Table 3-6: Segment Ratios[8]

Segment Ratios	Numerator	Denominator	Measures
Segment margin	Segment profit (loss)	Segment revenue	Operating profitability relative to sales.
Segment turnover	Segment revenue	Segment assets	Overall efficiency—how much revenue is generated per dollar of assets.
Segment ROA	Segment profit (loss)	Segment assets	Operating profitability relative to assets.
Segment debt ratio	Segment liabilities	Segment assets	Solvency of the segment.

Example 3-3: Evaluation of Segment Ratios

Tiara Corp. divides its operations in three geographical segments. Selected financial information is provided in the following table:

(in $'000)	2011			2010		
	Revenue	Operating Income	Assets	Revenue	Operating Income	Assets
Australia	272,310	39,485	231,464	210,258	29,436	189,232
Asia Pacific	668,484	60,164	534,787	581,290	61,035	494,097
Europe	144,085	25,215	100,860	115,268	18,443	86,451
Total	1,084,879	124,863	867,110	906,816	108,914	769,780

Comment on the relative performance of the three segments.

Solution:

To compare the relative significance and performance of the three segments, we compute segment margin, segment ROA, and segment turnover in the table below:

(in $'000)	2011				2010			
	Segment Revenue as Percent of Total	Segment Margin	Segment ROA	Segment Turnover	Segment Revenue as Percent of Total	Segment Margin	Segment ROA	Segment Turnover
Australia	25.10%	14.50%	17.06%	1.2	23.19%	14.00%	15.56%	1.1
Asia-Pacific	61.62%	9.00%	11.25%	1.3	64.10%	10.50%	12.35%	1.2
Europe	13.28%	17.50%	25.00%	1.4	12.71%	16.00%	21.33%	1.3

8 - Exhibit 21, Volume 3, CFA Program Curriculum 2014

The following conclusions can be drawn from the table:
- Asia-Pacific is the company's largest segment, as highlighted by its share of total revenue (61.62%). However, the segment has the lowest profit margin (9%). Further, the relative size of the segment has decreased over the year (share of revenues down from 64.10% to 61.62%).
- Europe has the highest profit margin (17.5%) and is the most efficient segment as well (it has the highest ROA and asset turnover).
- Australia's profit margin is also relatively high.
- Europe and Australia have improved in terms of both profitability and efficiency. It bodes well for the company that the relative size of these two segments is increasing (in terms of the share of total revenue).

LOS 28g: Describe how ratio analysis and other techniques can be used to model and forecast earnings. Vol 3, pp 378–379

In forecasting future earnings of companies, analysts use data about the economy, industry, and company itself. The results of financial analysis, which includes common-size and ratio analysis, are integral to this process.

Analysts also develop models and pro forma financial statements to forecast future performance. They are constructed using past trends and relationships and also account for expected future events and changes. Pro forma income statements are usually prepared by using the historical relationship between a company's income statement items and sales to project the nature of the relationship going forward. Items that are not sales-driven can be assumed fixed, or assumed to vary with a balance sheet item (e.g., interest expense varies with the amount of long-term liabilities). Some balance sheet items also vary with sales, especially working capital accounts. As the company's scale of operations increases, the firm has to increase its investment in working capital to ensure the smooth running of day-to-day operations. Further, investments in long-lived assets will also be required to expand the scale of the business.

Some other techniques that are used in making forecasts are:

Sensitivity Analysis, which shows the range of possible outcomes as underlying assumptions are altered.

Scenario Analysis, which shows the changes in key financial quantities that result from given events such as a loss of supply of raw materials or a reduction in demand for the firm's products.

Simulations are computer-generated sensitivity or scenario analyses based on probability models for the factors that drive outcomes.

LESSON 1: COST OF INVENTORIES

LOS 29a: Distinguish between costs included in inventories and costs recognized as expenses in the period in which they are incurred. Vol 3, pp 395–396

IFRS and **U.S. GAAP** suggest a similar treatment of various expenses in the determination of inventory cost. The following items are capitalized inventory costs, which are included in the cost or carrying value of inventories on the balance sheet.

- Costs of purchase, which include the purchase price, import duties, taxes, insurance, and other costs that are directly attributable to the acquisition of finished goods, trade discounts, and other rebates that reduce costs of purchase.
- Costs of conversion, which include direct labor and other (fixed and variable) direct overheads.

Capitalization of these costs results in a buildup of asset balances and delays recognition of these costs (in COGS) until inventory is sold.

The following items are *not* capitalized as inventory costs; they are expensed on the income statement as incurred under **IFRS** and **U.S. GAAP**.

- Abnormal costs from material wastage.
- Abnormal costs of labor or wastage of other production inputs.
- Storage costs that are not a part of the normal production process.
- Administrative expenses.
- Selling and marketing costs.

Capitalization of costs that should be expensed results in **overstatement** of net income for the year (due to the deferral of recognition of costs) and an **overstatement** of inventory value on the balance sheet. See Example 1-1.

Example 1-1: Determination of Inventory Costs

ABC Company manufactures a single product. Various costs incurred during the year 2009 are listed below:

Cost of raw materials	$12,000,000
Direct labor conversion costs	$25,000,000
Production overheads	$5,000,000
Freight charges for raw materials	$2,000,000
Storage costs for finished goods	$800,000
Abnormal wastage	$80,000
Freight charges for finished goods	$100,000

Given that there is no work-in-progress inventory at the end of the year:

1. What costs should be included in inventory for 2009?
2. What costs should be expensed during 2009?

> **Solution**
>
> 1. Capitalized inventory costs include raw material costs, production overheads, labor conversion costs, and freight charges on raw materials.
>
> | | |
> |---|---|
> | Cost of raw materials | $12,000,000 |
> | Direct labor conversion costs | $25,000,000 |
> | Production overheads | $5,000,000 |
> | Freight-in charges | $2,000,000 |
> | **Total capitalized costs** | **$44,000,000** |
>
> 2. Costs that should be expensed on the income statement (and not included in the value of inventory on the balance sheet) include storage costs of finished goods, abnormal wastage, and freight on finished goods.
>
> | | |
> |---|---|
> | Storage costs of finished goods | $800,000 |
> | Abnormal wastage | $80,000 |
> | Freight on finished goods | $100,000 |
> | **Total expensed costs** | **$980,000** |

LESSON 2: INVENTORY VALUATION METHODS AND MEASUREMENT OF INVENTORY VALUE

LOS 29b: Describe different inventory valuation methods (cost formulas).
Vol 3, pp 396–398

LOS 29c: Calculate cost of sales and ending inventory using different inventory valuation methods and explain the effect of the inventory valuation method choice on gross profit. Vol 3, pp 398–400

LOS 29e: Compare cost of sales, ending inventory, and gross profit using different inventory valuation methods. Vol 3, pp 398–402

Let's work with an example of a trading company that purchases and retails coffee tables. At any point in time, the number of tables that the company has available for sale equals the total number of tables that it had in its inventory at the beginning of the period plus the number of tables it has purchased since then. In order to prepare its financial statements for the period, the company must allocate the cost of all units available for sale between ending inventory (EI) and costs of goods sold (COGS).

$$\text{Opening inventory} + \text{Purchases} = \text{Cost of goods sold} + \text{Ending inventory} \quad \text{... (Equation 1)}$$

Inventory Valuation Methods (Cost Formulas)

Separate Identification

- COGS reflects actual costs incurred to purchase or manufacture the specific units that have been sold over the period.
- EI reflects actual costs incurred to purchase or manufacture the specific units that still remain in inventory at the end of the period.
- This method is used for items that are not interchangeable and for goods produced for specific projects.

"Cost of sales" (**IFRS**) are also referred to as "cost of goods sold" (**U.S. GAAP**).

"Cost formulas" (**IFRS**) are also referred to as "cost flow assumptions" (**U.S. GAAP**).

- It is used for expensive goods that can be identified individually (e.g., precious gemstones).
- This method matches the physical flow of a particular inventory item with its actual cost.

First In, First Out (FIFO)

- Oldest units purchased or manufactured are assumed to be the *first* ones sold.
- Newest units purchased or manufactured are assumed to remain in ending inventory.
- COGS is composed of units valued at *oldest* prices.
- EI is composed of units valued at *most recent* prices.

Weighted Average Cost (AVCO)

This method allocates the total cost of goods available for sale (beginning inventory, purchases, and other inventory-related costs) evenly across all units available for sale.

- COGS is composed of units valued at average prices.
- EI is also composed of units valued at average prices.

Last In, First Out (LIFO)

- Newest units purchased or manufactured are assumed to be the *first* ones sold.
- Oldest units purchased or manufactured are assumed to remain in ending inventory.
- COGS is composed of units valued at *most recent* prices.
- EI is composed of units valued at *oldest* prices.

IFRS allows companies to use any of three valuation methods for inventory—separate identification, FIFO, and AVCO. **U.S. GAAP** allows companies to use the three methods allowed under **IFRS**, and also accepts the LIFO method.

The freedom to choose a particular inventory valuation method affords companies significant flexibility in how they apportion costs between EI (current assets on the balance sheet) and COGS (expenses on the income statement). Given the value of beginning inventory and purchases for the year, it is obvious (from Equation 1) that the **higher** the value of COGS, the **lower** the value allocated to EI and vice versa. Therefore, inventory valuation methods have a direct, material impact on financial statements and their comparability across companies.

If inventory purchase costs and manufacturing conversion costs were stable over time, it would be easy to apportion costs between EI and COGS. The number of units in inventory at the end of the year would be multiplied by the cost price per unit to compute EI, and the number of units sold multiplied by the cost price per unit to determine COGS. However, if prices fluctuate over the period (which is usually the case), the allocation of inventory costs becomes complicated because the valuation method used has significant implications on the value of EI and COGS for the period. In Example 2-1, we illustrate how the LIFO, FIFO, and AVCO cost flow assumptions work and demonstrate how they result in different values for EI and COGS when prices are not assumed constant over the period.

> Under separate identification, costs remain in inventory until the specific unit is sold.
>
> Under FIFO, LIFO, and AVCO companies make an assumption about which goods are sold and which ones remain in inventory. Therefore, the allocation of costs to units sold and those in inventory can be different from the physical movement of inventory units.

> A company must use the same inventory valuation method for all items of a similar nature and use.
>
> For items with a different nature or use, a different valuation method may be used.

Example 2-1: Illustration of Methods of Inventory Valuation

At the beginning of the year, Nakamura Inc. had 5 units of inventory, which cost $8 each. Over the year the company purchased 52 units and sold 50 units, leaving it with 7 unsold units at the end of the year. Nakamura purchased 10 (cost = $10/unit), 12 (cost = $11/unit), 14 (cost = $12/unit), and 16 (cost = $13/unit) units and sold 13, 13, 12, and 12 units in the four quarters respectively. All units were sold at $20 each. Determine the amounts that are allocated to EI and COGS for the year under the FIFO, LIFO, and AVCO cost flow assumptions.

Solution

First we must determine the total cost of goods available for sale that must be allocated between EI and COGS. This is done by summing the values of opening inventory (OI) and quarterly purchases:

Quarter	Units Held/ Purchased	Unit Cost $	Total Cost $
Opening inventory	5	8	40
1	10	10	100
2	12	11	132
3	14	12	168
4	16	13	208
Total	**57**		**648**

FIFO

Under this method:

- Older units are assumed to be the *first* ones sold.
- Units that are purchased *recently* are included in EI.
- COGS is composed of units valued at *older* prices.
- EI is composed of units valued at *recent* prices.

Under FIFO, in periods of **rising** prices the prices assigned to units in ending inventory are **higher** than the prices assigned to units sold.

COGS	$	EI	$
5 units at $8 from OI	40	7 units at $13 left over from Q4 purchases	91
10 units at $10 from Q1 purchases	100		
12 units at $11 from Q2 purchases	132		
14 units at $12 from Q3 purchases	168		
9 units at $13 from Q4 purchases	117		
50 units	**557**	**7 units**	**91**

LIFO

Under this method:

- Recently acquired units are assumed to be the *first* ones sold.
- Oldest units are included in EI.
- COGS is composed of units valued at *recent* prices.
- EI is composed of units valued at *older* prices.

COGS	$	EI	$
16 units at $13 from Q4 purchases	208	5 units at $8 from OI	40
14 units at $12 from Q3 purchases	168	2 units at 10 from Q1 purchases	20
12 units at $11 from Q2 purchases	132		
8 units at $10 from Q1 purchases	80		
50 units	588	**7 units**	60

> Under LIFO, in periods of **rising** prices the prices assigned to units in ending inventory are **lower** than the prices assigned to units sold.

AVCO

Under this method:

- COGS is composed of units valued at *average* prices.
- EI is also composed of units valued at *average* prices.

$$\text{Weighted average price} = \frac{\text{Value of goods available for sale}}{\text{Number of units available for sale}} = \$648/57 = \$11.37/\text{unit}$$

COGS	$	EI	$
50 units at $11.37	568.42	**7 units at $11.37**	79.58

> Under AVCO, regardless of whether prices are rising or falling the prices assigned to units in ending inventory are **the same as** the prices assigned to units sold.

The following table summarizes the costs allocated to EI and COGS under the three cost flow assumptions:

Method	BI	Purchases	Total	EI	COGS	Total
FIFO	$40	$608	$648	$91	$557	$648
AVCO	$40	$608	$648	$79.58	$568.42	$648
LIFO	$40	$608	$648	$60	$588	$648

> In the first year of operations, all four methods of inventory valuation will come up with the same value for cost of goods available for sale (OI + P).
>
> However, in subsequent years, the cost of goods available for sale under each method would typically differ because of the different amounts allocated to opening inventory (EI in the previous year).

	FIFO	AVCO	LIFO
Sales	1,000	1,000	1,000
COGS	557	568.42	588
Gross profit	**443**	**431.58**	**412**

> Notice that in periods with rising prices and stable inventory levels, FIFO results in the highest gross profit.

> The total cost allocated to COGS and EI is the same across the three different cost flow methods. If one method reports higher COGS, it must report lower EI.

Given constant or increasing inventory levels, if prices are **rising** over a given period (as in Example 2-1):

- $COGS_{LIFO} > COGS_{AVCO} > COGS_{FIFO}$
- $EI_{FIFO} > EI_{AVCO} > EI_{LIFO}$

Given constant or increasing inventory levels, if prices are **falling** over a given period:

- $COGS_{FIFO} > COGS_{AVCO} > COGS_{LIFO}$
- $EI_{LIFO} > EI_{AVCO} > EI_{FIFO}$

See Table 2-1.

Table 2-1: LIFO Versus FIFO with Rising Prices and Stable or Rising Inventory Levels

	LIFO	FIFO
COGS	Higher	Lower
Income before taxes	Lower	Higher
Income taxes	Lower	Higher
Gross profit & net income	Lower	Higher
Total cash flow	Higher	Lower
EI	Lower	Higher
Working capital	Lower	Higher

The difference in cash flows is the only direct economic difference that results from the choice of inventory valuation method.

Balance Sheet Information: Inventory Account

Nakamura (Example 2-1) has seven unsold units at the end of the year. If we were to measure the true economic value or the current replacement cost of these units, we would value them at $13 each (latest prices) for an EI value of $91. FIFO ending inventory therefore, reflects the replacement cost of inventory most accurately ($91), followed by AVCO ($79.58). The LIFO estimate for EI ($60) is farthest away from the true economic value of inventory.

It does not matter whether prices are rising (as in our example) or falling, **FIFO will always give a better reflection of the current economic value of inventory** because the units currently in stock are valued at the most *recent* prices.

The difference between the original cost of inventory and its current replacement cost is known as a holding gain or inventory profit.

- If prices are *rising*, LIFO and AVCO will *understate* ending inventory value.
- If prices are *falling*, LIFO and AVCO will *overstate* ending inventory value.
- When prices are stable, the three methods will value inventory at the same level.

Income Statement Information: Cost of Goods Sold

More information about inventory accounting methods is typically available in the footnotes to the financial statements.

COGS should ideally reflect the replacement cost of inventory. The 50 units sold should each be valued at $13 (latest prices) in calculating the true replacement cost of goods sold during the year, which equals $650 (50 units × $13). LIFO estimates of COGS capture current replacement costs fairly accurately ($588), followed by AVCO ($568.42). FIFO measures of COGS ($557) are farthest away from current replacement cost of inventory.

It does not matter whether prices are rising (as in our example) or falling, **LIFO will always offer a closer reflection of replacement costs in COGS** because it allocates *recent* prices to COGS. LIFO is the most economically accurate method for income statement purposes because it provides a better measure of current income and future profitability.

- If prices are *rising*, FIFO and AVCO will *understate* replacement costs in COGS and *overstate* profits.
- If prices are *falling*, FIFO and AVCO will *overstate* replacements costs in COGS and *understate* profits.
- When prices are stable, the three methods will value COGS at same level.

LOS 29d: Calculate and compare cost of sales, gross profit, and ending inventory using perpetual and periodic inventory systems. Vol 3, pp 400–402

Periodic Versus Perpetual Inventory Systems

Periodic inventory system: Under this system, the quantity of inventory on hand is calculated periodically. The cost of goods available for sale during the period is calculated as beginning inventory plus purchases over the period. The ending inventory amount is then deducted from cost of goods available for sale to determine COGS.

Perpetual inventory system: Under this system, changes in the inventory account are updated continuously. Purchases and sales are recorded directly in the inventory account as they occur. The best way to understand how the perpetual system works is through an example (see Example 2-2).

Example 2-2: Illustration of Periodic and Perpetual Inventory Systems

Use Nakamura's inventory information from the previous example and employ the LIFO cost flow assumption to determine COGS and EI under the periodic and perpetual inventory systems.

PERIODIC METHOD (Assuming LIFO)

	Units purchased	Cost /Unit ($)	Units Sold	Cost of Units Sold	Units of Inventory on Hand	Ending Inventory
Opening inventory	5	8			5	
Quarter 1	10	10	13		2	
Quarter 2	12	11	13		1	
Quarter 3	14	12	12		3	
Quarter 4	16	13	12	**588**	7	**60**
				16 units @ $13/unit		5 units @ $8/unit
				14 units @ $12/unit		2 units @ $10/unit
				12 units @ $11/unit		
				8 units @ $10/unit		

In the periodic system, the carrying value of EI and COGS is only determined at the end of the period (periodically).

PERPETUAL METHOD (Assuming LIFO)

	Units purchased	Cost/ Unit ($)	Units Sold	Cost of Units Sold	Description	Units of Inventory on Hand	Ending Inventory	Description
Opening inventory (OI)	5	8				5		
Quarter 1	10	10	13	$(10 \times \$10)+(3 \times \$8)$ =$124	10 units from Q1 purchases Note: Q1 purchases are now sold out 3 units from OI	2	$(2 \times \$8)=\$16$	2 units from OI remain Note: Q1 purchases are sold out
Quarter 2	12	11	13	$(12 \times \$11)+(1 \times \$8)$ =$140	12 units from Q2 purchases Note: Q2 purchases are now sold out Note: Q1 purchases are already sold out 1 unit from OI	1	$(1 \times \$8)=\$8$	1 unit from OI remains
Quarter 3	14	12	12	$(12 \times \$12)=\$144$	12 units from Q3 purchases Note: 2 units are left from Q3 purchases Note: 1 unit is still left from OI	3	$(2 \times \$12)+(1 \times \$8)$ =$32	2 units from Q3 purchases remain 1 unit from OI remains
Quarter 4	16	13	12	$(12 \times \$13)=\$156$	12 units from Q4 purchases Note: 4 units are left from Q4 purchases Note: 2 units are still left from Q3 purchases Note: 1 unit is still left from OI	7	$(4 \times \$13)+(2 \times \$12)$ $+(1 \times \$8)=\$84$	4 units from Q4 purchases remain 2 units from Q3 purchases remain 1 unit from OI remains Note: Q1 and Q2 purchases are sold out

COGS for the year = 564   **EI for the year = 84**

Conclusion

Under the **LIFO** cost flow assumption, in a period of **rising** prices, use of the periodic system for inventory results in a:

- **Lower** ($60 versus $84) value of ending inventory.
- **Higher** ($588 versus $564) value for COGS.

Therefore, gross profit would be **lower** under the periodic system.

Other important takeaways from Example 2-2:

- The value of sales and cost of goods available for sale are the same under the two systems in the first year of operations.
- In subsequent years, the amounts of cost of goods available for sale can be different under the two systems due to different values of opening inventory (previous periods' ending inventory).
- If a company uses FIFO or separate identification for inventory valuation, it would arrive at the same value for COGS and EI under the periodic and perpetual inventory systems. However, use of LIFO or AVCO may result in different values for COGS and EI under the periodic and perpetual inventory systems.

LESSON 3: PRESENTATION AND DISCLOSURE AND EVALUATION OF INVENTORY MANAGEMENT

LOS 29f: Describe the measurement of inventory at the lower of cost and net realizable value. Vol 3, pp 402–404

Under **IFRS**, inventory must be stated at the lower of cost or net realizable value (NRV). NRV is calculated as the estimated selling price minus estimated selling costs. If the NRV of inventory falls below the carrying value recorded on the balance sheet, inventory must be written down, and a loss must be recognized on the income statement. The company may record the decrease in value directly through the inventory account or through a valuation allowance (reserve) account. If it uses the valuation allowance, the net inventory value equals the cost of inventory minus the write-down.

> Inventory write-downs raise concerns regarding management's abilities to anticipate how much and what type of inventory was required. Furthermore they affect a company's future reported earnings.

A subsequent increase in NRV would require a reversal of the previous write-down, which would reduce inventory-related expenses on the income statement in the period that the increase in value occurs. However, the increase in value that can be recognized is limited to the total write-down that had previously been recorded. Typically, inventory value cannot exceed the amount originally recognized.

> **IFRS**
> Compare cost to NRV
> $NRV = SP - SC$

On the other hand, **U.S. GAAP** requires the application of the LCM (lower of cost or market) principle to value inventory. Market value is defined as current replacement cost, where current replacement cost must lie within a range of values from NRV minus normal profit margin to NRV. If replacement cost is higher than NRV it must be brought down to NRV, and if replacement cost is lower than NRV minus normal profit margin it must be brought up to NRV minus normal profit margin. This adjusted replacement cost is then compared to carrying value (cost) and the lower of the two is used to value inventory. Any write-down decreases the carrying value of inventory and is reflected on the income statement under COGS. An important thing to remember is that under **U.S. GAAP**, reversal of any write-down is prohibited.

> **U.S. GAAP**
> Compare cost to replacement cost (market) where:
> NRV – NP margin
> < Replacement cost
> < NRV

In certain industries like agriculture, forest products, and mining, both **U.S. GAAP** and **IFRS** allow companies to value inventory at NRV even when it exceeds historical cost. If an active market exists for the product, quoted market prices are used as NRV; otherwise the price of the most recent market transaction is used. Unrealized gains and losses on inventory resulting from fluctuating market prices are recognized on the income statement. See Example 3-1.

Example 3-1: Accounting for Declines and Recoveries in Inventory Value

1. XYZ Company manufactures watches and prepares its financial statements in accordance with **IFRS**. In 2008, its carrying value of inventory was $2,500,000 before a write-down of $220,000 was recorded. In 2009, the fair value of XYZ's inventory was $400,000 greater than its carrying value.

    a. What was the effect of the write-down on XYZ's 2008 financial statements?
    b. What is the effect of the recovery on XYZ's 2009 financial statements?
    c. What would be the effect of the recovery on XYZ's 2009 financial statements if XYZ's inventory were composed of agricultural products instead of watches?

    Solution

    a. In 2008, XYZ would have recorded a write-down of $220,000, which would decrease inventory asset and increase cost of goods sold to reduce net income.
    b. For 2009, only $220,000 of the total increase in value will be recorded as a gain, which would increase inventory asset and decrease COGS to increase net income.
    c. Had XYZ's inventory been composed of agricultural products, it would have been able to record an increase in inventory value of $400,000 in 2009.

2. Calculate the carrying value of a watch in XYZ's inventory under **IFRS** and **U.S. GAAP** given the following per-unit costs:

Original cost	$660
Estimated selling price	$700
Estimated selling costs	$55
Replacement cost	$640
Normal profit margin	$20

    Solution

    NRV = Selling price − Selling costs = $700 − $55 = $645
    NRV − Normal profit margin = $645 − $20 = $625

    Under **IFRS**, inventory is reported at the lower of cost or net realizable value. The original cost ($660) exceeds the NRV ($645). Therefore, inventory is written down to its NRV, and a loss of $15 ($660 − $645) is reported on the income statement.

    Under **U.S. GAAP**, inventory is reported at the lower of cost or market value (replacement cost). The carrying value of inventory ($660) is compared to replacement cost, where replacement cost must be adjusted so that it lies between NRV ($645) and NRV minus NP margin ($625). Since replacement cost ($640) already lies within the acceptable range, it does not have to be adjusted. Because replacement cost is lower than original cost, inventory is written down to replacement cost and a loss of $20 ($660 − $640) is recorded.

> If the NP margin is given in percent, apply the margin to the selling price to determine the NP margin in dollar terms.

3. Assume that in the year after the write-down, NRV and replacement cost both increase by $18. What is the impact of the recovery under **IFRS** and **U.S. GAAP**?

Solution

Under **IFRS**, the company will write-up inventory to $660 and recognize a gain of $15. The write-up (gain) is limited to the original write-down of $15. The carrying value cannot exceed original cost.

Under **U.S. GAAP**, reversal of a write-down is not allowed. The unit cost will remain at $640. XYZ will simply recognize a higher profit when inventory is sold.

LOS 29g: Describe the financial statement presentation of and disclosures relating to inventories. **Vol 3, pp 404–405**

Presentation and Disclosure

IFRS requires companies to make the following disclosures relating to inventory:

1. The accounting policies used to value inventory.
2. The cost formula used for inventory valuation.
3. The total carrying value of inventories and the carrying value of different classifications (e.g., merchandise, raw materials, work-in-progress, finished goods).
4. The value of inventories carried at fair value less selling costs.
5. Amount of inventory-related expenses for the period (cost of sales).
6. The amount of any write-downs recognized during the period.
7. The amount of reversal recognized on any previous write-down.
8. Description of the circumstances that led to the reversal.
9. The carrying amount of inventories pledged as collateral for liabilities.

> LIFO liquidation is a topic that has been moved to Level II.

U.S. GAAP does not permit the reversal of prior-year inventory write-downs. **U.S. GAAP** also requires disclosure of significant estimates applicable to inventories and of any material amount of income resulting from the liquidation of LIFO inventory.

Inventory Method Changes

Consistency in the inventory costing method used is required under **U.S. GAAP** and **IFRS**.

Under IFRS, a change in policy is acceptable only if the change results in the provision of more reliable and relevant information in the financial statements.

> This retrospective restatement requirement enhances the comparability of financial statements over time. An exemption to the retrospective restatement requirement applies when it is impractical to determine either the period-specific effects or the cumulative effect of the change.

- Changes in inventory accounting policy are applied retrospectively.
- Information for all periods presented in the financial report is restated.
- Adjustments for periods prior to the earliest year presented in the financial report are reflected in the beginning balance of retained earnings for the earliest year presented in the report.

U.S. GAAP has a similar requirement for changes in inventory accounting policies.

- However, a company must thoroughly explain how the newly adopted inventory accounting method is superior and preferable to the old one.
- The company may be required to seek permission from the Internal Revenue Service (IRS) before making any changes.
- If inventory-related accounting policies are modified, the changes to the financial statements must be made retrospectively, unless the LIFO method is being adopted (which is applied prospectively).

LOS 29h: Calculate and interpret ratios used to evaluate inventory management. Vol 3, pp 405–412

The three most important ratios used in the evaluation of a company's inventory management are the inventory turnover ratio, the number of days of inventory, and the gross profit margin:

$$\text{Inventory turnover} = \frac{\text{COGS}}{\text{Average inventory}}$$

$$\text{No. of days of inventory} = \frac{365}{\text{Inventory turnover}}$$

$$\text{Gross profit margin} = \frac{\text{Gross profit}}{\text{Sales revenue}}$$

Evaluation of inventory management is also covered in detail in Reading 39.

If a company has a *higher* inventory turnover ratio and a *lower* number of days of inventory than the industry average, it could mean one of three things:

- It could indicate that the company is more efficient in inventory management, as fewer resources are tied up in inventory.
- It could also suggest that the company does not carry enough inventory at any point in time, which could hurt sales.
- It could also mean that the company might have written-down the value of its inventory.

To determine which explanation holds true, analysts should compare the firm's revenue growth with that of the industry and examine the company's financial statement disclosures. A low sales growth compared to the industry would imply that the company is losing out on sales by holding low inventory quantities. A higher inventory turnover ratio combined with minimal write-downs and a sales growth rate similar to or higher than industry sales growth would suggest that the company manages inventory more efficiently than its peers. Frequent, significant write-downs of inventory value may indicate poor inventory management.

A firm whose inventory turnover is *lower* and number of days of inventory *higher* than industry average could have a problem with slow-moving or obsolete inventory. Again, a comparison with industry sales growth and an examination of financial statement disclosures would provide further information.

The gross profit margin indicates the percentage of sales that is contributing to net income as opposed to covering the cost of sales.

- Firms in relatively competitive industries have lower gross profit margins.
- Firms selling luxury products tend to have lower volumes and higher gross profit margins.
- Firms selling luxury products are likely to have lower inventory turnover ratios.

Remember that inventory ratios are directly affected by the cost flow assumption used by the company. When making comparisons across firms, analysts must understand the differences that arise from the use of different cost flow assumptions. See Example 3-2.

Example 3-2: Analysis of Inventories

The following information relates to Atlas Inc. for the years 2007 and 2008:

	2007	2008
Inventory turnover ratio	6.71	6.11
Number of days of inventory	54.4 days	59.7 days
Gross profit margin	24.8%	27.3%
Current ratio	1.11	1.12
Debt-to-equity ratio	0.24	0.83
Return on total assets	1.02%	−7.13%

Atlas uses the FIFO cost flow assumption to value inventory. Further, it kept stable inventory quantities during the year, while prices were gradually rising.

1. Comment on the changes in Atlas' financial statement ratios from 2007 to 2008.

2. If Atlas Inc. had used the LIFO cost flow assumption instead of FIFO, how would the carrying values of ending inventory and COGS be different? How would its financial statement ratios change?

Solutions

1. The inventory turnover ratio declined and the number of days of inventory increased. This implies that the company has been less efficient in managing its inventory in 2008 as compared to 2007.

   The gross profit margin improved by 2.5% from 24.8% in 2007 to 27.3% in 2008.

   The current ratio is relatively unchanged from 2007 to 2008.

   The debt-to-equity ratio had risen significantly in 2008. This could be a result of an increase in total debt, a decrease in shareholders' equity caused by a net loss for the period, or both.

   The return on assets declined significantly and was actually negative in 2008. This implies that the company made a net loss in 2008 despite the improvement in its gross profit margins over the year. This could be the result of a decrease in sales revenue, an increase in operating expenses, or both.

> 2. Given that prices have been rising over the period and that inventory quantities were relatively stable, COGS would have been higher and the gross profit margin would have been lower if Atlas had used the LIFO cost flow assumption. This is because LIFO allocates the most recent (in this case higher) prices to COGS. Consequently, the company's reported gross profit, net income, retained earnings, and taxes would be lower under LIFO. (See Table 3-1.)
>
> The carrying amount of ending inventory would be lower under LIFO because it allocates the oldest (in this case lower) prices to ending inventory.

Table 3-1: LIFO Versus FIFO with Rising Prices and Stable Inventory Levels

Type of Ratio	Effect on Numerator	Effect on Denominator	Effect on Ratio
Profitability ratios			
NP and GP margins	Income is lower under LIFO because COGS is higher	Sales are the same under both	Lower under LIFO
Solvency ratios			
Debt-to-equity and debt ratio	Same debt levels	Lower equity and assets under LIFO	Higher under LIFO
Liquidity ratios			
Current ratio	Current assets are lower under LIFO because EI is lower	Current liabilities are the same	Lower under LIFO
Quick ratio	Quick assets are higher under LIFO as a result of lower taxes paid	Current liabilites are the same	Higher under LIFO
Activity ratios			
Inventory turnover	COGS is higher under LIFO	Average inventory is lower under LIFO	Higher under LIFO
Total asset turnover	Sales are the same	Lower total assets under LIFO	Higher under LIFO

The values of these ratios under AVCO lie between their values under LIFO and under FIFO.

READING 30: LONG-LIVED ASSETS

LESSON 1: ACQUISITION OF LONG-LIVED ASSETS: PROPERTY, PLANT, AND EQUIPMENT, AND INTANGIBLE ASSETS

Long-lived assets are expected to provide economic benefits to a company over an extended period of time, typically longer than one year. There are three types of long-lived assets:

1. Tangible assets have physical substance, (e.g., land, plant, and equipment).
2. Intangible assets do not have physical substance (e.g., patents and trademarks).
3. Financial assets include securities issued by other companies.

The cost of most long-lived assets is allocated over the period of time that they are expected to provide economic benefits. The two types of long-lived assets whose costs are *not* expensed over time are **land** and **intangible assets with indefinite useful lives**.

LOS 30a: Distinguish between costs that are capitalized and costs that are expensed in the period in which they are incurred. **Vol 3, pp 426–431**

If an item is expected to provide benefits to the company for a period longer than one year, its cost is capitalized. If the item is only expected to provide economic benefits in the current period, its cost is expensed.

Capitalized Costs

A capitalized cost is recognized as a noncurrent asset on the balance sheet. The associated cash outflow is listed under *investing activities* on the statement of cash flows. In subsequent periods, the capitalized amount is allocated (expensed) over the asset's useful life as depreciation expense (for tangible assets) or amortization expense (for intangible assets with *finite* lives). These expenses reduce net income and decrease the book value of the asset. However, since they are noncash items, depreciation and amortization do not have an impact on future cash flows (apart from a possible reduction in taxes payable). See Table 1-1.

Table 1-1: Effects of Capitalization

	Effects on Financial Statements
Initially when the cost is capitalized	• Noncurrent assets *increase*. • Cash flow from investing activities *decreases*.
In future periods when the asset is depreciated or amortized	• Noncurrent assets *decrease*. • Net income *decreases*. • Retained earnings *decrease*. • Equity *decreases*.

Expensed Costs

A cost that is immediately expensed reduces net income for the current period by its *entire* after-tax amount. This hefty, one-off charge against revenues results in *lower* income and *lower* retained earnings for the related period. The associated cash outflow is classified under *operating activities* on the statement of cash flows. Crucially, no related asset is recognized on the balance sheet, so no related depreciation or amortization charges are incurred in future periods. See Table 1-2.

Table 1-2: Effects of Expensing

	Effects on Financial Statements
When the item is expensed	• Net income *decreases* by the entire after-tax amount of the cost. • No related asset is recorded on the balance sheet and therefore no depreciation or amortization expense is charged in future periods. • Operating cash flow *decreases.* • Expensed costs have no financial statement impact in future years.

All other factors remaining the same, the decision to expense an item as opposed to capitalizing it would give the impression of greater earnings growth (higher expenses in the current year followed by no related expenses in future years). On the other hand, the decision to capitalize an item as opposed to expensing it results in higher reported operating cash flow (as the related outflow is classified as cash flow from investing [CFI]). Companies may try to report higher cash flow from operations (CFO), as it is an important consideration in valuation. In making comparisons across companies, it is important to account for differences in the companies' expenditure capitalizing policies.

If an asset is acquired in a nonmonetary exchange (e.g., exchanges of mineral leases and real estate), the amount recognized on the balance sheet typically equals the fair value of the asset acquired. In accounting for such exchanges the carrying amount of the asset given up is removed from noncurrent assets on the balance sheet, the fair value of the asset acquired is added, and any difference between the two values is recognized on the income statement as a gain or a loss. If the fair value of the asset acquired is greater (lower) than the value of the asset given up, a gain (loss) is recorded on the income statement.

> In rare cases, if the fair value of the acquired asset cannot be determined, the amount recognized on the balance sheet equals the carrying amount of the asset given up. In this case, no gain or loss is recognized.

Costs Incurred at Acquisition

When a long-lived asset is acquired, expenses other than just the purchase price may be incurred (e.g., costs of shipping and installation and other costs necessary to prepare the asset for its intended use). These costs are also capitalized and included in the value of the asset on the balance sheet.

Subsequent expenses related to the long-lived asset may be capitalized if they are expected to provide economic benefits beyond one year, or expensed if they are not expected to provide economic benefits beyond one year. Expenditures that extend an asset's useful life are usually capitalized (see Example 1-1). See Table 1-3.

Table 1-3: Financial Statement Effects of Capitalizing Versus Expensing

	Capitalizing	Expensing
Net income (first year)	Higher	Lower
Net income (future years)	Lower	Higher
Total assets	Higher	Lower
Shareholders' equity	Higher	Lower
Cash flow from operations activities	Higher	Lower
Cash flow from investing activities	Lower	Higher
Income variability	Lower	Higher
Debt to equity ratio	Lower	Higher

Example 1-1: Capitalizing Versus Expensing

Katayama Inc. incurred the following expenses to purchase a piece of manufacturing equipment:

Purchase price (including taxes)	$15,000
Delivery charges	55
Installation charges	200
Cost of training machine maintenance staff	300
Reinforcement of factory floor to support machine	150
Cost of repairing factory roof	500
Cost of painting factory walls	325

Note: Factory roof repairs are expected to extend the life of the factory by 3 years.

1. Which of these expenses will be capitalized and which ones will be expensed?
2. How will the treatment of these items affect the company's financial statements?

Solution

1. All costs that are undertaken to ready the machine for its intended use must be capitalized. Therefore, the following expenses will be capitalized by the company:

Purchase price (including taxes)	$15,000
Delivery charges	55
Installation charges	200
Reinforcement of factory floor to support machine	150
Cost of repairing factory roof	500
Total	$15,905

   The expenditure incurred to repair the factory roof is capitalized because it extends the useful life of the factory.

   The following items will be expensed by the company:

Cost of training machine maintenance staff	$300
Cost of painting factory walls	325
Total	$625

   The funds spent on training maintenance staff are not necessary to ready the asset for its intended use. Further, the money spent on painting factory walls is also expensed, as it does not enhance the productive capacity of the asset.

2. The equipment-related costs that are capitalized (i.e., the purchase price, delivery charges, installation charges, and floor reinforcement costs) will be included in the carrying amount of equipment under noncurrent assets on the balance sheet. The related cash outflows will be listed under investing activities on the cash flow statement.

The factory related cost that is capitalized (i.e., the cost of repairing the factory roof), which extends the useful life of the factory, is included in the carrying amount of factory asset on the balance sheet. The related cash outflow will be listed under investing activities.

The expenses incurred to train the equipment maintenance staff and to paint the factory walls will be expensed on the income statement in the current period. The related cash outflows will be listed under operating activities on the cash flow statement.

Capitalization of Interest Costs

Companies must capitalize interest costs associated with financing the acquisition or construction of an asset that requires a long period of time to ready for its intended use. For example, if a company constructs a building for its own use, interest expense incurred to finance construction must be capitalized along with the costs of constructing the building. The interest rate used to determine the amount of interest capitalized depends on the company's existing borrowings or, if applicable, on borrowings specifically incurred to finance the cost of the asset. Under **IFRS**, but not **U.S. GAAP**, income earned from temporarily investing borrowed funds that were acquired to finance the cost of the asset must be subtracted from interest expense on the borrowed funds to determine the amount that can be capitalized. Capitalized interest costs are included in the cost of the asset and depreciated once the asset is brought into use. This results in a better "matching" of costs with associated revenues.

If construction and sale of buildings is the core business activity of the firm, and a building is constructed with the intention of selling it, capitalized interest costs are included along with costs of construction in inventory as a part of current assets. The capitalized interest is also included in COGS in the period that the building is sold.

As a result of this accounting treatment, a company's interest costs can appear on the balance sheet (when capitalized) or on the income statement (when expensed).

Analytical Issues Relating to Capitalization of Interest Costs

1. Capitalized interest costs reduce investing cash flow, while expensed interest costs reduce operating cash flow under **U.S. GAAP** and operating or financing cash flow under **IFRS**. Therefore, analysts must examine the impact of classification on reported cash flow.

2. To provide a true picture of a company's **interest coverage ratio**, the entire amount of interest expense, whether capitalized or expensed, should be used in the denominator.

$$\text{Interest coverage ratio} = (\text{EBIT} / \text{Interest expense})$$

The interest coverage ratio measures the number of times that a company's operating profits (EBIT) cover its interest expense. A higher ratio indicates that the company can comfortably service its debt through operating earnings. See Example 1-2.

> **Example 1-2: Capitalized Interest**
>
> A company borrows $10 million to finance the construction of an office building where it expects to base its headquarters for the next 50 years. The interest rate on the loan is 6%. Construction takes 3 years, and over this period the company earns $65,000 from investing the borrowed funds in money-market instruments.
>
> 1. What amount of interest cost would the company capitalize under **IFRS** and under **U.S. GAAP**?
> 2. Where will the capitalized interest costs appear on the company's financial statements?
>
> **Solution**
>
> 1. Under **U.S. GAAP**, the company would capitalize the amount of interest paid on the loan during construction. This amount equals ($10m × 0.06 × 3) = $1,800,000.
>
>   Under **IFRS**, the amount that can be capitalized must be adjusted for income earned from temporarily investing borrowed funds. Therefore, capitalized interest would equal $1,800,000 − $65,000 = $1,735,000
> 2. • Capitalized interest will be included in the carrying amount of the asset (building) under noncurrent assets on the balance sheet.
>   • The amount of interest that is capitalized will appear on the cash flow statement under investing activities (during the 3 years of construction).
>   • Once construction is complete and the asset is in use, capitalized interest will be depreciated as a part of depreciation on office building on the income statement.
>   • Once construction is complete, depreciation of capitalized interest (as a part of total depreciation) will appear on the company's cash flow statement each year if prepared using the indirect method (added to net income in the calculation of CFO).

LOS 30b: Compare the financial reporting of the following types of intangible assets: purchased, internally developed, acquired in a business combination. Vol 3, pp 431–435

Intangible assets lack physical substance and include items that involve exclusive rights such as patents, copyrights, and trademarks. Some intangible assets have finite lives, while others have indefinite lives.
- The cost of an intangible assets with a finite life is amortized over its useful life.
- The cost of an intangible asset with an indefinite life is not amortized; instead, the asset is tested (at least annually) for impairment. If deemed impaired, the asset's balance sheet value is reduced and a loss is recognized on the income statement.

Intangible assets can also be classified as identifiable or unidentifiable intangible assets.

Under **IFRS**, identifiable intangible assets must meet three definitional criteria and two recognition criteria.

Definitional criteria:
- They must be identifiable. This means that they should either be separable from the entity or must arise from legal rights.
- They must be under the company's control.
- They must be expected to earn future economic benefits.

Recognition criteria:
- It is probable that their expected future economic benefits will flow to the entity.
- The cost of the asset can be reliably measured.

An unidentifiable intangible asset is one that cannot be purchased separately and may have an indefinite life. The best example of such an asset is goodwill, which arises when one company purchases another and the acquisition price exceeds the fair value of the identifiable (tangible and intangible) assets acquired.

Accounting for an intangible asset depends on the manner of its acquisition, as described in the sections that follow.

1. Intangible Assets Acquired in Situations Other than Business Combinations (e.g., Buying a Patent)

These assets are recorded at their fair value when acquired, where the fair value is assumed to equal the purchase price. They are recognized on the balance sheet, and costs of acquisition are classified as investing activities on the cash flow statement. If several intangible assets are acquired as a group, the purchase price is allocated to each individual asset based on its fair value.

Companies use a significant degree of judgment to determine fair values of individual intangible assets purchased. Therefore, analysts focus more on the types of intangible assets purchased as opposed to the value assigned to each individual asset. Understanding the types of intangible assets the company is acquiring can offer valuable insight into the company's overall strategy and future potential.

2. Intangible Assets Developed Internally

These are generally expensed when incurred, but may be capitalized in certain situations. A firm that chooses to grow via internal development of intangible assets will have significantly different financial ratios from a firm that chooses to acquire intangible assets from other companies
- A company that internally develops intangible assets will expense costs of development and recognize no related assets, while a firm that acquires intangible assets will recognize them as assets.
- A company that develops intangible assets internally will classify development-related cash outflows as operating activities on the cash flow statement, while an acquiring firm will classify these costs as investing activities.

Research and Development Costs (R&D)

Generally, **U.S. accounting standards** require that R&D costs be expensed when incurred. However, they require that certain costs related to *software development* be *capitalized*.

- Costs incurred to develop software for sale are *expensed* until the product's technological feasibility has been established. Once feasibility has been established, associated development costs are *capitalized*.
- Costs related directly to the development of software for internal use are also *expensed* until it is probable that the project will be completed and that the software will be used as intended. After that, related development costs are *capitalized*.

Note that the probability of the project being completed is easier to establish than technological feasibility.

Expensing rather than capitalizing development costs results in:
- *Lower* net income in the current period.
- *Lower* operating cash flow and *higher* investing cash flow in the current period.

The capitalized costs related directly to developing software for sale or internal use include the cost of employees who help build and test the software. If current period software development costs *exceed* amortization of prior periods' capitalized development costs, net income would be *lower* under expensing. If, however, software development expenditures were to slow down such that current year expenses are *lower* than amortization of prior periods' capitalized costs, net income would be *higher* under expensing.

IFRS requires that expenditures on **research** or during the research phase of an internal project be expensed rather than capitalized as an intangible asset. The "research phase of an internal project" refers to the period during which the company cannot demonstrate that an intangible asset is being created.

> The treatment of software development costs under **U.S. GAAP** is similar to the treatment of all costs of internally developed intangible assets under **IFRS**.

IFRS allows companies to recognize an internal asset from **development** or the development phase of an internal project if certain criteria are met, including a demonstration of the technical feasibility of completing the intangible asset and the intent to use or sell the asset. See Example 1-3.

> Even though standards require companies to capitalize software development costs after a product's feasibility is established, judgment in determining feasibility means that companies' capitalization practices differ.

Example 1-3: Software Development Costs

A company spends $3,000 each month during the year 2009 developing software for internal use.

1. Assuming that the company follows **IFRS**, how will these expenses be treated if the company is able to meet the recognition criteria on (i) May 1, 2009 and (ii) October 1, 2009?
2. Assuming that the company follows **U.S. GAAP**, how would these expenses be classified if the company established in late 2008 that the project was going to be completed?

Solution

1. Under **IFRS**, the company must expense these costs until the recognition criteria are met, and capitalize them thereafter.
   i. If the recognition criteria are met on May 1, $12,000 worth of development expenses will be expensed on the income statement and expenses worth $24,000 will be capitalized.

> ii. If the recognition criteria are met on October 1, $27,000 worth of development expenses will be expensed on the income statement and expenses worth $9,000 will be capitalized.
>
> 2. Under **U.S. GAAP**, expenses incurred for the development of software for internal use can be capitalized once it has been demonstrated that it is probable that the project will be completed. Therefore, all related expenses that were incurred in 2009 ($36,000) will be capitalized.

Both **IFRS** and **U.S. GAAP** require the use of the acquisition method in accounting for business combinations (**IFRS 3 and ASC 805**).

3. Intangible Assets Acquired in a Business Combination

When a company acquires another company, the transaction is accounted for using the acquisition method. Under this method, if the purchase price paid by the acquirer to buy a company exceeds the fair value of its net assets, the excess is recorded as goodwill. Goodwill is an intangible asset that cannot be identified separately from the business as a whole. Only goodwill created in a business acquisition can be recognized on the balance sheet; internally generated goodwill cannot be capitalized.

Under **IFRS**, acquired intangible assets are classified as identifiable intangible assets if they meet the definitional and recognition criteria that we listed earlier. If an item acquired does not meet these criteria and cannot be recognized as a tangible asset, it is recognized as goodwill.

Under **U.S. GAAP**, an intangible asset acquired in a business combination should be recognized separately from goodwill if:
- The asset arises from legal or contractual rights; or
- The item can be separated from the acquired company.

LESSON 2: DEPRECIATION AND AMORTIZATION OF LONG-LIVED ASSETS, AND THE REVALUATION MODEL

LOS 30c: Describe the different depreciation methods for property, plant, and equipment, the effect of the choice of depreciation method on the financial statements, and the effects of assumptions concerning useful life and residual value on depreciation expense. Vol 3, pp 435–443

LOS 30d: Calculate depreciation expense. Vol 3, pp 435–443

Depreciation and amortization are effectively the same concept, with the term depreciation referring to the process of allocating costs of tangible assets and the term amortization referring to the process of allocating costs of intangible assets.

There are two primary models for reporting long-lived assets.

The cost model is required under **U.S. GAAP** and permitted under **IFRS**. Under this model, the cost of long-lived tangible assets (except land) and intangible assets with finite useful lives is allocated over their useful lives as depreciation and amortization expense. Under the cost model, an asset's carrying value equals its historical cost minus accumulated depreciation/amortization (as long as the asset has not been impaired).

The revaluation model is permitted under **IFRS**, but not under **U.S. GAAP**. Under this model, long-lived assets are reported at fair value (not at historical cost minus accumulated depreciation/amortization).

Depreciation methods include the straight-line method, accelerated methods, and the units-of-production method.

Straight-Line Depreciation

$$\text{Depreciation expense} = \frac{\text{Original cost} - \text{Salvage value}}{\text{Depreciable life}}$$

Regardless of the depreciation method used, the carrying amount of the asset is not reduced below the estimated residual value. Example 1-3 provides an example of these depreciation methods.

Accelerated Depreciation

$$\text{DDB depreciation in Year X} = \frac{2}{\text{Depreciable life}} \times \text{Book value at the beginning of Year X}$$

Units-of-Production Method

In this method depreciation expense is based on the actual use of an asset over the period.

Example 2-1 illustrates the three depreciation methods.

MACRS (Modified Accelerated Cost Recovery System) depreciation is an accelerated depreciation method that is popular in the United States.

Example 2-1: Depreciation Methods

Three companies, Company A, Company B, and Company C, purchase an identical piece of manufacturing equipment for use in their operations. The cost of the equipment is $3,000, the estimated salvage value is $200, and the useful life of the equipment is 4 years. Further, the total production capacity of the equipment over its useful life equals 1,000 units. Each company earns $3,500 in revenues and incurs expenses of $1,500 (excluding depreciation) every year. The companies are subject to a tax rate of 30%. Actual output levels of each of the companies over the 4 years are:

Year	1	2	3	4
Production (units)	300	400	200	100

- Company A uses the straight-line method of depreciation.
- Company B uses the double-declining balance (DDB) method for the first year. In the remaining years, it uses the straight-line method.
- Company C uses the units-of-production method.

1. Calculate each company's beginning net book value, annual depreciation expense, end of year accumulated depreciation, and ending net book value for each year.
2. Explain the differences in the timing of recognition of depreciation expense between the companies.

Solution

1. **Company A** uses straight-line depreciation. Therefore, its annual depreciation expense equals $700 [($3,000 – $200) / 4 years].

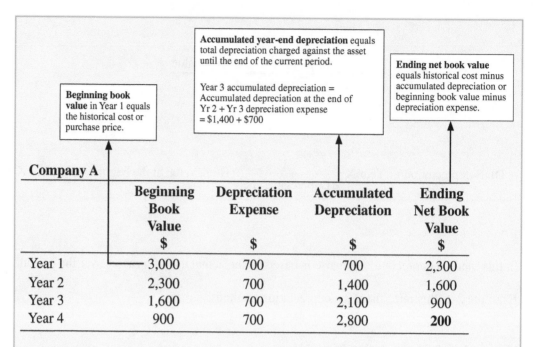

Company A

	Beginning Book Value $	Depreciation Expense $	Accumulated Depreciation $	Ending Net Book Value $
Year 1	3,000	700	700	2,300
Year 2	2,300	700	1,400	1,600
Year 3	1,600	700	2,100	900
Year 4	900	700	2,800	**200**

Company B

For the first year, we calculate depreciation expense using the DDB method.

Depreciation in Year 1 = (2/4) × $3,000 = $1,500

Depreciation expense in Years 2, 3, and 4 is calculated using the straight-line method.

$$\text{Therefore, annual depreciation} = \frac{(\text{Year 1 ending book value} - \text{Salvage value})}{\text{Remaining use ful life}}$$

$$= \frac{(\$1,500 - \$200)}{3 \text{ years}} = \$433.33/ \text{ year}$$

Company B

	Beginning Net Book Value $	Depreciation Expense $	Accumulated Depreciation $	Ending Net Book Value $
Year 1	3,000	1,500	1,500	1,500
Year 2	1,500	433	1,933	1,067
Year 3	1,067	433	2,366	634
Year 4	634	434	2,800	**200**

Company C

$$\text{Depreciation expense per unit} = \frac{(\$3,000 - \$200)}{1,000 \text{ units}} = \$2.80/\text{unit}$$

	Yr 1	Yr 2	Yr 3	Yr 4
Production (units)	300	400	200	100
Depreciation expense	**840**	**1,120**	**560**	**280**

Company C				
	Beginning Net Book Value	Depreciation Expense	Accumulated Depreciation	Ending Net Book Value
	$	$	$	$
Year 1	3,000	840	840	2,160
Year 2	2,160	1,120	1,960	1,040
Year 3	1,040	560	2,520	480
Year 4	480	280	2,800	**200**

All three methods result in the same *total depreciation expense* over the life of the equipment ($2,800). The difference between the methods lies in the timing of recognition of total depreciation expense across the years. The straight-line method recognizes the expense evenly over the asset's life, the DDB method recognizes most of the expense in the first year, and the units-of-production method recognizes depreciation expense based on actual usage over each period. Under all 3 methods, the book value of equipment at the end of its useful life equals $200.

Comparison Between Straight-Line and Accelerated Depreciation Methods

All other factors remaining the same, a company that uses the straight-line method to depreciate its assets will report:

- A lower asset turnover ratio during the early years of the asset's use (due to higher net assets).
- Higher operating profit margin in the early years of the asset's use (due to lower depreciation expense).
- Higher operating return on assets (ROA) in the early years of the asset's use (due to lower depreciation expense) and lower ROA in later years.

Further, a company that uses an accelerated depreciation method will report an improving asset turnover ratio, operating profit margin, and ROA over time. Therefore, it is important to understand that the different depreciation methods used by companies in the same industry can influence their trends in ratios over time and result in significant differences in their reported financial performance.

On the balance sheet, companies may present the total net amount of property, plant, and equipment and the total net amount of intangible assets. More details are usually disclosed in the notes to the financial statements. These details typically include:

- Acquisition costs.
- Depreciation and amortization expenses.
- Accumulated depreciation and amortization.
- Depreciation and amortization methods used.
- Information on assumptions used to depreciate and amortize long-lived assets.

Estimates Used for Calculating Depreciation

Assumptions of a *longer* useful life and a *higher* expected residual value result in *lower* annual depreciation expense compared to assumptions of a *shorter* useful life and a *lower* salvage value. The subjective nature of these assumptions allows management to manipulate earnings.

Management could significantly write-down the value of long-lived assets and recognize a hefty charge against net income in the current period. While this would depress earnings in the current year, it would allow management to recognize lower annual depreciation expense going forward, inflate profits, and report impressive growth in profitability.

Management could also overstate the useful life and the salvage value of an asset to show impressive profits over the near term, and recognize a significant loss at a later point in time when the asset is eventually retired.

Additional assumptions are required to allocate depreciation expense between cost of goods sold (COGS) and selling, general, and administrative expenses (SG&A). Including a higher proportion of total depreciation expense in COGS lowers the gross profit margin and lowers operation expenses. However, it does not effect the net profit margin.

There are no significant differences between **IFRS** and **U.S. GAAP** regarding the definition of depreciation and acceptable depreciation methods. However, **IFRS** requires companies to use the component method of depreciation. Under this method, companies depreciate different components of assets separately (using estimates for each component). Under **U.S. GAAP**, this method is allowed but not widely used. See Example 2-2.

Example 2-2: Component Method of Depreciation

A company purchases a machine with an expected useful life of 10 years and an estimated salvage value of $2,000 for $10,000. $4,000 of the cost of the machine represents the cost of the wheel, which is a significant component of the machine. The company estimates that the wheel will need to be replaced every 2 years. Answer the following questions assuming that the wheel has zero salvage value and that the company uses straight-line depreciation for all assets.

1. How much depreciation would the company record for Year 1 if it uses the component method, and if it does not use the component method?
2. Assuming that a new wheel is purchased at the end of Year 2, how much depreciation would the company record (in Year 3) if it uses the component method, and if it does not use the component method?
3. Assuming that wheel is replaced every 2 years for $4,000, what is the total amount of depreciation charged over the 10 years if the company uses the component method, and if it does not use the component method?
4. Which additional estimates must be made if the company chooses to use the component method instead of depreciating the machine as a whole?

Solution

1. If the company does not use the component method, it would charge depreciation of $800 in Year 1.

    Calculation: ($10,000 − $2,000) / 10 = $800

    Under the component method, depreciation expense for Year 1 would be calculated as:

    [($6,000 − $2,000) / 10] + ($4,000 / 2) = $2,400

2. If a new wheel is purchased at the end of Year 2, depreciation expense for Year 3 if the component method were not used is calculated as:

    [($10,000 − $2,000) / 10] + ($4,000 / 2) = $2,800

    Depreciation expense under the component method would be calculated as:

    [($6,000 − $2,000) / 10] + ($4,000 / 2) = $2,400

3. If the company does not use the component method, total depreciation charged over the 10 years, assuming that the wheel is replaced every 2 years, is calculated as:

    ($800 × 2) + ($2,800 × 8) = $24,000

    Under the component method, total depreciation charged over the 10 years is calculated as:

    $2,400 × 10 = $24,000

    Note that the same amount of total depreciation is charged over the entire life of the asset under both methods.

    > Total depreciation over the life of the asset under both methods equals total expenditure on assets adjusted for any salvage value.

4. If the company elects to depreciate the asset using the component method (as opposed to depreciating it as a whole), it must make the following assumptions in addition to the useful life and residual value of the machine:

    i.   Portion of machine cost attributable to the wheel.
    ii. Portion of residual value attributable to the wheel.
    iii. Useful life of wheel.

Intangible assets *with finite useful lives* are amortized over their useful lives. This results in the cost of these assets being "matched" with the benefits that accrue from them. Examples of intangible assets with finite useful lives include:

- An acquired patent or copyright with a specific expiration date.
- Customer lists acquired by a direct mail marketing company that are expected to provide future economic benefits.
- An acquired license with a specific expiration date with no associated right to renew the license.
- An acquired trademark for a product that a company plans to phase out over a specific number of years.

Acceptable amortization methods are the same as acceptable depreciation methods. Similar to the estimates required to calculate depreciation expense of tangible fixed assets, the estimates required to calculate yearly amortization expense for an intangible fixed asset with a finite life are:

- The original value of the intangible asset.
- The residual value at the end of its useful life.
- The length of its useful life. See Example 2-3.

Example 2-3: Calculation of Amortization Expense

Gluco Pharmaceuticals acquired another company during 2011 and reported the following intangible assets at the end of the year:

Patent = $950,000
Operating license = $500,000
Copyright = $500,000
Goodwill = $1,200,000

The following information is also available:
- The patent will expire in 10 years.
- The company expects to sell the copyright in 5 years for an estimated amount of $100,000.
- The license will expire in 5 years, but can be renewed at no cost.

Given that the company uses the straight-line method for amortizing its intangible assets, calculate the total value of intangible assets on the company's 2012 balance sheet.

Solution:

- Goodwill is not amortized. It must be checked for impairment (at least annually).

- The operating license is an intangible asset with an indefinite life, as the company retains the right to renew the license at little or no cost. If the license had a specific expiration date, or if the company did not have the right to renew the license, Gluco would have to amortize the value of the license over its useful life.

- Amortization of patent = 950,000 / 10 = $95,000
  - The patent is an identifiable intangible asset with a finite life. It is amortized over its useful life.

- Amortization of copyright = [(500,000 – 100,000) / 5] = $80,000
  - The copyright is an identifiable intangible asset with a finite life. Its "amortizable value" is amortized over its useful life.

Therefore, Gluco's 2012 balance sheet will reflect the following values for its intangible assets:

- Patent = 950,000 – 95,000 = $855,000
- Copyright = 500,000 – 80,000 = $420,000
- Goodwill = $1,200,000
- Operating license = $500,000

LOS 30g: Describe the revaluation model. **Vol 3, pp 445–448**

The Revaluation Model

IFRS allows companies to use the revaluation model or the cost model (where the carrying amount of an asset equals its historical cost minus accumulated depreciation/ amortization) to report the carrying amounts of noncurrent assets on the balance sheet. Revaluation results in the carrying amount of an asset reflecting its fair value (as long as it can be measured reliably). Under the revaluation model, the carrying amount of an asset is reported at its fair value on the date of revaluation minus any subsequent accumulated depreciation or amortization. Under **U.S. GAAP** only use of the cost model is permitted.

> For practical purposes, the revaluation model is rarely used for either tangible or intangible asses, but its use is especially rare for intangible assets.

A key difference between the revaluation and the cost model is that revaluation allows for the reported value of the asset to be higher than its historical cost. Under the cost model on the other hand, the reported value of an asset can never exceed its historical cost.

IFRS allows the revaluation model to be used for certain classes of assets and for the cost model to be used for others as long as:

1. The company applies the same model to assets in a particular class (e.g., land and buildings, machinery, factory equipment, etc.)
2. Whenever a revaluation is performed, all assets in the particular class must be revalued (to avoid selective revaluation).

The revaluation model may also be used to value intangible assets, but only if an active market for the asset exists where its fair value can be determined.

The effects of an asset revaluation on the financial statements depend on whether a revaluation *initially* increases or decreases the asset's carrying value.

Under the revaluation model, whether a revaluation affects earnings (net income) depends on whether the revaluation initially increases or decreases the carrying amount of the asset class (see Examples 2-4 and 2-5):

If a revaluation initially decreases the carrying amount of an asset:
- The decrease in value is recognized as a loss on the income statement.
- Later, if the value of the asset class increases:
  - The increase is recognized as a gain on the income statement to the extent that it reverses a revaluation loss previously recognized on the income statement against the same asset class.
  - Any increase in value beyond the reversal amount will not be recognized on the income statement, but adjusted directly to equity through the revaluation surplus account.

If a revaluation initially increases the carrying amount of an asset:
- The increase in value bypasses the income statement and goes directly to equity through the revaluation surplus account.
- Later, if the value of the asset class decreases:
  - The decrease reduces the revaluation surplus to the extent of the gain previously recognized in the revaluation surplus against the same asset class.
  - Any decrease in value beyond the reversal amount will be recognized as a loss on the income statement.

Example 2-4: Asset Revaluation

A company purchases an asset for $10,000. After one year, it determines that the value of the asset is $8,000 and another year later it determines that the fair value of the asset is $15,000. Assuming that the company follows the revaluation model to report this asset, describe the financial statement impact of the revaluation in Year 1 and Year 2.

Solution

At the end of Year 1, the company will report the asset at its fair value ($8,000). The decrease in its value ($2,000) will be charged as a loss on the income statement.

At the end of Year 2, the company will report the asset at its fair value ($15,000). The increase in value from the Year 1 value ($8,000) to the historical cost ($10,000) will essentially be reversing the previously recognized write-down (in Year 1). Therefore, a gain of $2,000 will flow through the income statement in Year 2. The remaining increase in value ($5,000) from the historical cost to the current fair value (end of Year 2) will bypass the income statement and will be recorded directly on the balance sheet under shareholders' equity in the revaluation surplus.

Example 2-5: Asset Revaluation

A company purchases an asset for $5,000. After one year, it determines that the value of the asset is $7,700 and another year later it determines that the fair value of the asset is $2,400. Assuming that the company follows the revaluation model to report this asset, describe the financial statement impact of the revaluation in Year 1 and Year 2.

Solution

At the end of Year 1, the company will report the asset at its fair value ($7,700). The increase in its value ($2,700) will be recorded directly on the balance sheet under shareholders' equity in the revaluation surplus.

At the end of Year 2, the company will report the asset at its fair value ($2,400). The decrease in value from the Year 1 value ($7,700) to the historical cost ($5,000) will essentially be reversing the previously recognized increase in value (in Year 1). Therefore, the revaluation surplus (shareholders' equity) will be reduced by $2,700. The remaining decrease in value ($2,600) from the historical cost to the current fair value (end of Year 2) will be recorded as a loss on the income statement.

> Clearly, the use of the revaluation model as opposed to the cost model can have a significant impact on the financial statements of companies. This has potential consequences for comparing financial performance using financial ratios of companies that use different models.

LESSON 3: IMPAIRMENT OF ASSETS, DERECOGNITION OF ASSETS, PRESENTATION AND DISCLOSURES AND INVESTMENT PROPERTY

LOS 30h: Explain the impairment of property, plant, and equipment and intangible assets. Vol 3, pp 448–450

An impairment charge is made to reflect the unexpected decline in the fair value of an asset. Impairment recognition has the following effects on a company's financial statements:

- The carrying value of the asset decreases.
- The impairment charge reduces net income.
- Impairment does not affect cash flows because it is a noncash charge.

> Both **IFRS** and **U.S. GAAP** require companies to write down the carrying amount of impaired assets. Impairment reversals are permitted under **IFRS** but not under **U.S. GAAP**.

Impairment of Property, Plant, and Equipment

Companies are required to assess whether there are indications of impairment of property, plant, and equipment at the end of each financial year. If there are no suggestions of impairment, the asset is not tested for impairment. However, if there are indications of impairment, the recoverable amount of the asset must be measured in order to test the asset for impairment. Indications of impairment include evidence of obsolescence, decrease in demand for the asset's output, and technological advancements.

A company must recognize an impairment loss when the asset's carrying value is higher than its recoverable amount. Impairment losses reduce the carrying amount of the asset on the balance sheet and reduce net income (and shareholders' equity). Note that impairment does not affect cash flows.

Under **IFRS**, an asset is considered impaired when its carrying amount exceeds its recoverable amount. The recoverable amount equals the higher of "fair value less costs to sell" and "value in use," where value in use refers to the discounted value of future cash flows expected from the asset. The impairment loss that must be recognized equals the carrying amount minus the recoverable amount.

Under **U.S. GAAP**, determing whether an asset is impaired is different from measuring the impairment loss. An asset is considered impaired when its carrying value exceeds the total value of its *undiscounted* expected future cash flows (recoverable amount). Once the carrying value is determined to be nonrecoverable, the impairment loss is measured as the difference between the asset's carrying amount and its fair value (or the *discounted* value of future cash flows, if fair value is not known). See Example 3-1.

Example 3-1: Impairment of Property, Plant, and Equipment

Susan Inc. owns a piece of equipment that has a carrying value of $3,000. The demand for the products manufactured by this piece of equipment has fallen drastically. The company estimates that the total expected future cash flows from this piece of equipment would amount to $3,200, and the present value of these expected cash flows is $2,700. The company estimates that the fair value of the asset is $2,800 and selling costs would amount to $200.

1. Under **IFRS**, what would be the carrying amount of the machine and how much impairment would be charged against it?
2. Under **U.S. GAAP**, what would be the carrying amount of the machine and how much impairment would be charged against it?

Solution

1. The carrying amount of the machine must be compared to the higher of fair value less costs to sell ($2,600) and value in use ($2,700). The carrying amount ($3,000) is greater than the asset's value in use ($2,700), so the asset's value is written down to $2,700 and an impairment charge worth $300 is recognized on the income statement. Depreciation for future years would be based on the new carrying value of $2,700.

2. The carrying amount of the machine ($3,000) is less than the total undiscounted cash flows expected from the asset in the future ($3,200). Therefore, the asset is not considered impaired and no impairment charge is made on the income statement for the period.

Impairment of Intangible Assets with a Finite Life

Intangible assets with finite lives are amortized. These assets are not tested for impairment annually (unlike intangible assets with infinite lives); they are only tested for impairment upon the occurrence of significant adverse events (e.g., a significant decrease in market price or adverse changes in legal and economic factors). Accounting for impairment of these assets is essentially the same as accounting for impairment of property, plant, and equipment.

Impairment of Intangibles with Indefinite Lives

Goodwill and other intangible assets with indefinite lives are not amortized. They are carried on the balance sheet at historical cost and tested at least annually for impairment. Impairment must be recognized when carrying value exceeds fair value.

Impairment of Long-Lived Assets Held for Sale

A noncurrent asset is reclassified (from being an asset "held-for-use") to an asset "held-for-sale" when it is no longer in use and management intends to sell it. These assets are tested for impairment when they are categorized as held-for-sale. If it is found that the carrying value exceeds their fair value less selling costs, an impairment loss is recorded and their carrying value is brought down to fair value less selling costs. Once classified as held-for-sale, these assets are no longer depreciated or amortized by the company.

Reversals of Impairments of Long-Lived Assets

Under **U.S. GAAP**, once an impairment loss is recorded for assets held-for-use, it cannot be reversed. The value of these assets cannot be revised upward. However, for assets held-for-sale, if the fair value of the asset increases subsequent to impairment recognition, the loss can be reversed and the asset's value can be revised upward.

IFRS allows reversal of impairment losses if the value of the asset increases regardless of classification of the asset. Reversal of a previously recognized impairment charge increases reported profits. Note that **IFRS** only allows reversals of impairment losses. It does not allow the value of the asset to be written up to a value greater than the previous carrying amount even if the new recoverable amount is greater than the previous carrying value.

A significant degree of subjective judgment is involved in projecting future cash flows from assets, and in assessing fair values. This affords management considerable discretion relating to the amount and timing of impairment recognition. Therefore, analysts must carefully consider how impairment charges should be considered in analyzing past performance of companies and in projecting performance going forward.

LOS 30i: Explain the derecognition of property, plant, and equipment and intangible assets. Vol 3, pp 451–453

A company derecognizes or removes an asset from its financial statements when the asset is disposed of or is not expected to provide any future economic benefits from use or disposal. A company can dispose of a long-lived operating asset by selling it, exchanging it for another asset, or by abandoning it.

Sale of Long-Lived Assets

The gain or loss on sale of a long-lived asset is computed as:

Gain/(loss) on asset disposal = Selling price – Carrying/book value of asset

Carrying or book value = Historical cost – Accumulated depreciation

A gain or loss on the sale of a fixed asset is disclosed on the income statement either as a component of other gains and losses (if the amount is insignificant) or as a separate line item (if the amount is significant). Gains and losses on disposal of fixed assets can also be found on the cash flow statement if prepared using the indirect method. Recall that the effect of fixed asset disposal-related gains and losses are removed from net income to compute cash flow from operating activities under the indirect method. A company may disclose further details about the sale of long-lived assets in the management discussion and analysis (MD&A) section and/or financial statement footnotes.

Long-Lived Assets Disposed of Other than by a Sale

Long-lived assets intended to be disposed of other than by a sale (e.g., abandoned, exchanged for another asset, or distributed to owners in a spin-off) are classified as held for use until disposal. Just like other noncurrent assets held by the company, they continue to be depreciated and tested for impairment until they are disposed off.

When an asset is retired or abandoned, the company does not receive any cash for it. Assets are reduced by the carrying value of the asset at the time of retirement or abandonment, and a loss equal to the asset's carrying amount is recorded on the income statement.

When an asset is exchanged for another asset, the gain or loss on the transaction is calculated by comparing the carrying value of the asset given up to the fair value of the asset acquired. The carrying value of the disposed asset is removed from the balance sheet and replaced by the fair value of the new asset.

LOS 30j: Describe the financial statement presentation of and disclosures relating to property, plant, and equipment and intangible assets.
Vol 3, pp 453–460

Disclosures: Tangible Assets

A comprehensive example discussing the financial statement presentation and disclosures relating to PP&E and intangible assets is included in the practice questions.

IFRS	U.S. GAAP
• The measurement bases used.	• Depreciation expense for the period.
• The depreciation method used.	• The balances of major classes of depreciable assets.
• Useful lives (or depreciation rate).	• Accumulated depreciation by major classes or in total.
• Accumulated depreciation at the beginning and end of the period.	• General description of depreciation methods used for major classes of depreciable assets.
• Restrictions on title.	
• Pledges of property as security.	
• Contractual agreements to acquire PP&E.	
• If the revaluation model is used, the company must disclose:	
○ The date of revaluation.	
○ Details of fair value determination.	
○ The carrying amount under the cost model.	
○ Amount of revaluation surplus.	

Disclosures: Intangible Assets

IFRS

- For each class of intangible assets whether they have a finite or indefinite life.
  - If finite, for each class disclose:
    - The useful life (or amortization rate).
    - The amortization methods used.
    - The gross carrying amount.
    - Accumulated amortization at the beginning and end of the period.
    - Where amortization is included on the income statement.
    - Reconciliation of carrying amounts at the beginning and end of the period.
  - If indefinite:
    - Carrying amount of the asset.
    - Why it is considered to have an indefinite life.
- Restrictions on title.
- Pledges as security.
- Contractual agreement to purchase any intangible assets.
- If the revaluation model is used, the company must disclose:
  - The date of revaluation.
  - Details of fair value determination.
  - The carrying amount under the cost model.
  - Amount of revaluation surplus.

U.S. GAAP

- Gross carrying amounts in total and by major classes of intangible assets.
- Accumulated amortization in total and by major classes of intangible assets.
- Aggregate amortization expense for the period.
- Estimated amortization expense for the next 5 fiscal years.

Disclosures: Impairment

IFRS

- The amounts of impairment losses and reversal of impairment losses recognized in the period.
- Where these impairment losses and reversals are recognized on the financial statements.
- Main classes of assets affected by impairment losses and reversals.
- Events and circumstances that led to these impairment losses and reversals.

U.S. GAAP

- Description of the impaired asset.
- Circumstances that led to impairment.
- The method of fair value determination.
- The amount of impairment loss.
- Where the loss is recognized on the financial statements.

The above disclosures help an analyst to understand a company's investments in tangible and intangible assets, how these investments changed during the reporting period, how the changes affected current performance, and what those changes might indicate about future performance.

LOS 30k: Compare the financial reporting of investment property with that of property, plant, and equipment. Vol 3, pp 460–462

Investment Property

IFRS defines investment property as property that is owned (or leased under a finance lease) for the purpose of earning rentals or capital appreciation or both.[1] Investment property differs from long-lived tangible assets (e.g., PP&E) in that investment property is not owner occupied, nor is it used for producing the company's products and services. Long-lived tangible assets that are held for sale in a company's normal course of business (e.g., houses made by a construction company) are also not classified as investment property. These assets would be included in the company's inventory.

Under **IFRS**, investment property may be valued using the cost model or fair value model.

- Cost model: This is identical to the cost model used for property, plant, and equipment.

- Fair value model: This differs from the revaluation model used for PP&E in the way net income is affected.
    - Under the revaluation model, the impact of the revaluation on net income depends on a previously recognised increase or decrease in the carrying amount of the asset.
    - Under the fair value model, all changes in the fair value of an asset impact net income.

> Note that valuation gains/losses on investment properties are different from gains/losses on disposal of investment property. Valuation gains/losses are related to changes in fair values of properties (those that are accounted for using the fair value model) that are still held by the company at the end of the year. Gains/losses on disposal of investment property relate to properties that have been disposed of (sold or exchanged) by the company during the year at a price different from their carrying amount.

A company is required to use one model (cost or fair value) for all of its investment properties. Further, the fair value model may only be used if the company is able to reliably estimate the property's fair value on a continuing basis.

If a company chooses the fair value model, it must continue to do so until it disposes of it or changes its use such that it is no longer classified as investment property. The fair value model must be applied consistently even if it becomes difficult to estimate fair value (e.g., due to infrequent comparable-property transactions).

The following valuation issues arise when the classification of investment property changes to or from owner-occupied property or inventory:

- If investment property is valued using the cost model, a move to owner-occupied property or inventory will not lead to a change in the carrying amount of the property.

---

1 - IAS 40 Investment Property prescribes the accounting treatment for investment property.

- If investment property is valued using the fair value model, a move to owner-occupied property or inventory will be made at fair value. The property's fair value will become its new cost for the purpose of ongoing accounting for the property.

- If owner-occupied property is reclassified as investment property (and the owner prefers to use the fair value model), the change in the value from depreciated cost to fair value at the time of transfer is treated like a revaluation.

- If inventory is reclassified as investment property (and the owner prefers to use the fair value model), the difference between the carrying amount and fair value at the time of transfer is recognized as a profit or loss.

Investment property is reported as a separate line item on the balance sheet. Further, companies must disclose which model they have used (cost or fair value) to value the property.

- If the company uses the fair value model, it must make additional disclosures regarding how it has determined fair value and reconcile beginning and ending carrying amounts of investment property.

- If the company uses the cost model, it must make additional disclosures similar to those required for PP&E (e.g., the depreciation method used and useful life). Further, the fair value of the property should also be disclosed.

U.S. GAAP does not specifically define investment property. It does not distinguish between investment property and other types of long-lived assets. U.S. companies that hold investment-type property use the historical cost model.

READING 31: INCOME TAXES

LESSON 1: KEY DEFINITIONS AND CALCULATING THE TAX BASE OF ASSETS AND LIABILITIES

LOS 31a: Describe the differences between accounting profit and taxable income, and define key terms, including deferred tax assets, deferred tax liabilities, valuation allowance, taxes payable, and income tax expense. Vol 3, pp 474–475

> We have reorganized the order of the LOS in this reading to make the concepts flow in a more structured manner.

The tax return is prepared to calculate taxes payable to the authorities. Taxes payable result in an outflow of cash from the firm, so firms try to minimize taxes payable and retain cash. This objective is achieved by recognizing *higher* expenses on the tax return, which leads to *lower* taxable income and consequently, *lower* taxes payable.

Financial statements are prepared to report the company's operating performance over the year to shareholders, financial institutions, and other stakeholders. For financial reporting purposes, companies try to show healthy performance and profitability. This objective is achieved by recognizing *lower* expenses on the income statement, which lead to *higher* pretax income, and (despite *higher* income tax expense) *higher* net income than on the tax return.

In Exhibit 1-1, we illustrate the differences between the tax return and the financial statements of ABC Company for 2009. ABC makes sales worth $100, incurs cost of goods sold of $60, and recognizes other gains of $10. On the tax return, it recognizes depreciation of $40 for the year, while on the income statement it recognizes depreciation of $30 only. Depreciation is the only expense incurred by ABC in 2009. The company pays taxes at the rate of 40%.

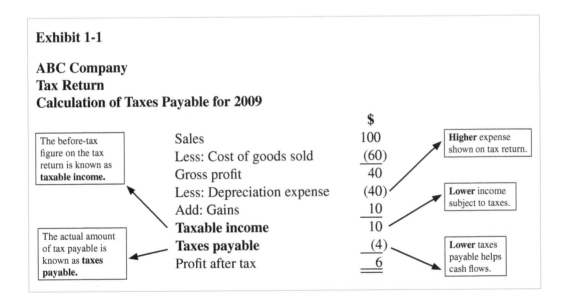

Exhibit 1-1

ABC Company
Tax Return
Calculation of Taxes Payable for 2009

	$	
The before-tax figure on the tax return is known as **taxable income.**		
Sales	100	**Higher** expense shown on tax return.
Less: Cost of goods sold	(60)	
Gross profit	40	
Less: Depreciation expense	(40)	**Lower** income subject to taxes.
Add: Gains	10	
Taxable income	10	
The actual amount of tax payable is known as **taxes payable.**		
Taxes payable	(4)	**Lower** taxes payable helps cash flows.
Profit after tax	6	

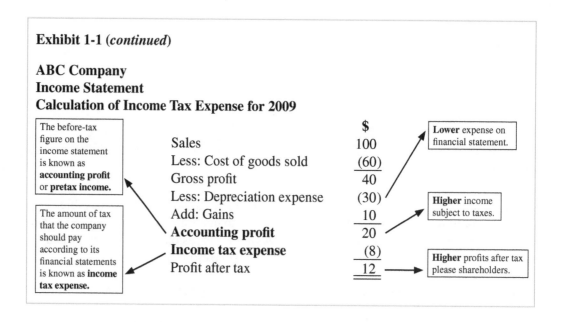

Exhibit 1-1 (*continued*)

ABC Company
Income Statement
Calculation of Income Tax Expense for 2009

	$
Sales	100
Less: Cost of goods sold	(60)
Gross profit	40
Less: Depreciation expense	(30)
Add: Gains	10
Accounting profit	20
Income tax expense	(8)
Profit after tax	12

The before-tax figure on the income statement is known as **accounting profit** or **pretax income**.

The amount of tax that the company should pay according to its financial statements is known as **income tax expense**.

Lower expense on financial statement.

Higher income subject to taxes.

Higher profits after tax please shareholders.

Depreciation expense is the source of discrepancy between taxable income and pretax income in Exhibit 1-1. This difference in the amount of depreciation recognized on the two sets of statements for 2009 also drives a difference in the tax base of the asset and the carrying value on the balance sheet (financial statements).

Assuming that 2009 is the year of fixed asset purchase, accumulated depreciation consists only of depreciation for 2009. There is no accumulated depreciation on the asset from previous years. Exhibit 1-2 illustrates the computation of the asset's tax base and carrying value, assuming that the asset was purchased for $100.

Exhibit 1-2

Tax Base

	$
Equipment	100
Accumulated depreciation for tax purposes	(40)
Tax base of equipment	60

Financial Statements
Balance Sheet Extract

Noncurrent Assets	$
Equipment	100
Accumulated depreciation	(30)
Carrying value of equipment	70

From Exhibit 1-2, notice that:

- The gross amount of equipment recognized on the two statements is the same ($100).
- *Higher* accumulated depreciation is subtracted from gross equipment on the tax return because *higher* depreciation was charged on the asset for tax purposes ($40) compared to financial reporting purposes ($30).
- Therefore, the tax base of the asset is lower ($60) than its carrying value ($70).

LOS 31c: Calculate the tax base of a company's assets and liabilities.
Vol 3, pp 480–483

The tax base of an asset or liability is the amount at which the asset or liability is valued for tax purposes, while the carrying value is the amount recognized on the balance sheet for financial reporting purposes.

Determining the Tax Base of an Asset

An asset's tax base is the amount that will be expensed on the tax return in the future as economic benefits are realized from the asset. For example, if the historical cost of an asset is $10,000, and $4,000 accumulated depreciation has already been charged against it on *tax returns* over previous years, the asset's tax base currently equals $6,000. The tax base is the amount that will be depreciated in future periods (expensed on the tax return) as the asset is utilized over its remaining life (economic benefits of the asset are realized).

The carrying value of an asset is simply the historical cost of the asset minus the accumulated depreciation charged against it in previous years on the company's *financial statements*.

Example 1-1: Determining the Tax Base of an Asset

Calculate the tax base and the carrying amount for the following assets:

1. A company has dividends of $1 million receivable from another company. Assume that dividends are not taxable.

2. A company capitalized $2 million in development costs. It amortized $500,000 over the year, but for tax purposes amortization of 30% is allowed each year.

3. A company incurred $1 million in research costs. All of these were expensed for financial reporting, but for tax purposes these costs must be written off over 5 years.

4. A company shows $200,000 as a provision for bad debts. The balance sheet amount for accounts receivable after providing for the doubtful debts is $2 million. Tax authorities allow a maximum of 30% of the gross amount of accounts receivable to be provided for doubtful debts for a given period.

Solution

1. Dividends receivable are an asset of the company. Assets that are not taxable have a tax base that equals their carrying value. Therefore, the carrying amount and the tax base of the dividends receivable asset equal $1 million.

2. The company amortized $500,000 of development costs for financial reporting purposes, so the asset's carrying value is $1.5 million ($2 million – $500,000). Tax authorities allow 30% amortization per year, so on the tax return, $600,000 (30% of $2 million) will be amortized and the tax base will equal $1.4 million ($2 million – 600,000).

3. The company expensed the entire amount of the research costs on its financial statements, so no asset is recognized (carrying value equals zero). On the tax return, the company must write these costs off over 5 years, so the amount expensed on the tax return for the year will be $200,000 and the asset's tax base will equal $800,000 ($1 million – 200,000).

4. The company has expensed $200,000 and shown the carrying value of accounts receivable as $2 million *after* deducting the expensed amount. On the tax return, the company can expense $660,000 (30% of $2.2 million). Therefore, the tax base of accounts receivable will equal $1.54 million ($2.2 million – 660,000).

	Carrying Amount ($)	Tax Base ($)
Dividends receivable	1,000,000	1,000,000
Development costs	1,500,000	1,400,000
Research costs	0	800,000
Accounts receivable	2,000,000	1,540,000

Determining the Tax Base of a Liability

Pay very careful attention to the wording here. The best way to deal with these problems is to commit the exact wording of the two formulas/rules to memory and then determine whether the question concerns an accrued expense liability or an unearned revenue liability.

In Reading 23, we learned that two types of liabilities can result from accrual accounting—unearned revenues and accrued expenses. The *carrying value* of these liabilities is the amount recognized on the balance sheet in the financial statements. The rules for calculating the *tax base* of these liabilities are given below.

1. Tax base of accrued *expense* liability = Carrying amount of the liability (financial reporting) minus amounts that have **not** been expensed for tax purposes yet, but **can** be expensed (are tax-deductible) in the future.

2. The tax base of unearned *revenue* liability = Carrying value of the liability minus the amount of revenue that **has already been taxed**, and therefore, will **not** be taxed in the future.

Basically, the tax base of a liability is its carrying amount, less any amount that will be deductible for tax purposes in respect to that liability in future periods. For revenue received in advance, the tax base of the resulting liability is its carrying amount, less any amount of that revenue that will not be taxable in future periods.

Example 1-2: Determining the Tax Base of a Liability

Calculate the tax base and the carrying amount of the following liabilities:

1. During the year, a company made a donation of $1 million that it expensed for financial reporting purposes. Donations are not tax deductible.

2. The company received interest in advance of $500,000. Tax authorities recognize interest received as income on the date of receipt and consider it taxable.

3. The company recognized rent received in advance of $1 million. Rent received in advance is deferred for accounting purposes, but taxed when cash is received.

4. The company has to pay interest of $500,000 on its long-term loan of $8 million. The interest is payable at the end of each fiscal year.

5. A company estimates that $200,000 of warranty expenses will be incurred on television units sold. However, for tax purposes no deductions are allowed for warranty expense until they are actually incurred. The company does not receive any warranty claims during the period.

Solution

1. The company expensed the entire amount of the donation so the carrying value of the liability equals zero. This liability is related to expenses so we use the first of the rules that we stated earlier to determine its tax base. The donation has **not** been deducted for tax purposes yet, but it is also **not** deductible in the future. Therefore, the amount that must be subtracted from the carrying value to determine its tax base equals zero.

   Tax base of the liability = Carrying value − Amount tax deductible in the future

   $= 0 - 0 = 0$

> The donation has not been deducted for tax purposes, and is *never* going to be deducted on the tax return. It has already been recognized on the financial statements.
>
> This difference in the treatment of donations for tax and accounting purposes is a **permanent** difference that will not reverse in the future. We will discuss these differences in detail in LOS 31f.

2. The carrying value of the liability related to interest received in advance is $500,000. This liability is related to unearned revenue, so we use the second rule to determine its tax base. For tax purposes, the entire amount of $500,000 has **already been** taxed in the current year as cash has been received. Consequently, these revenues will **not** be taxed in the future, so they are subtracted from the carrying value to determine the tax base of the liability.

   Tax base of unearned revenue liability = $500,000 − $500,000 = 0

3. The carrying value of the liability related to rent received in advance (unearned revenue) is $1 million. For tax purposes, this entire amount **has already been** taxed in the current year as cash has been received, and will **not** be taxed in the future.

   Tax base of unearned revenue liability = $1 million − $1 million = 0

---

4. Taking a loan or repaying it has no tax or income statement implications. The total amount of the loan ($8 million) is a long-term liability. Interest paid ($500,000) is expensed on the income statement and on the tax return, so there is no liability relating to interest payments.

5. The actual warranty expense will be incurred when claims are made in subsequent years. Therefore, the company shows a carrying value of warranty liability of $200,000 on the financial statements. This liability is related to expenses so we use the first rule to determine its tax base. The amount of $200,000 has **not** been deducted from revenues for tax purposes yet, but **will** eventually be deducted when actual expenses are borne.

Tax base of the warranty liability = $200,000 − $200,000 = Zero

	Carrying Amount ($)	Tax Base ($)
Donations (Permanent difference)	0	0
Interest received in advance	500,000	0
Rent received in advance	1,000,000	0
Loan (capital)	8,000,000	8,000,000
Interest paid	0	0
Warranty liability	200,000	0

LESSON 2: CREATION OF DEFERRED TAX ASSETS AND LIABILITIES, RELATED CALCULATIONS AND CHANGES IN DEFERRED TAXES

LOS 31b: Explain how deferred tax liabilities and assets are created and the factors that determine how a company's deferred tax liabilities and assets should be treated for the purposes of financial analysis. **Vol 3, pp 475–479**

LOS 31d: Calculate income tax expense, income taxes payable, deferred tax assets, and deferred tax liabilities, and calculate and interpret the adjustment to the financial statements related to a change in the income tax rate. **Vol 3, pp 483–484**

Under **U.S. GAAP**, a company can use a different depreciation method on its financial statements from the one it uses on its tax return. Taking advantage of this facility, firms try to record *higher* depreciation expense on their tax returns to minimize taxes payable, and recognize *lower* depreciation expense on their financial reports to maximize reported profits. Let's see how this works through a comprehensive example.

Bestwear Inc. has only one fixed asset, which generates revenues of $10,000 every year. The only expense that Bestwear incurs is depreciation on this asset, whose original cost was $12,000. The firm decides to completely write off this asset over *four* years for financial reporting, and over *three* years for tax reporting. The applicable tax rate is 40%.

Exhibit 2-1 illustrates the computation of taxes payable and income tax expense for Bestwear Inc.

Exhibit 2-1: Income Statements of Bestwear Inc.

Tax Reporting

	Year 1	Year 2	Year 3	Year 4	Total
	$	$	$	$	$
Revenue	10,000	10,000	10,000	10,000	40,000
Dep exp (3 yrs. st. line)	4,000	4,000	4,000	0	12,000
Taxable income	6,000	6,000	6,000	10,000	28,000
Taxes payable	2,400	2,400	2,400	4,000	11,200
(40% of taxable income)					
Profit after tax	3,600	3,600	3,600	6,000	16,800

Financial Reporting

	Year 1	Year 2	Year 3	Year 4	Total
	$	$	$	$	$
Revenue	10,000	10,000	10,000	10,000	40,000
Dep exp (4 yrs. st. line)	3,000	3,000	3,000	3,000	12,000
Pretax income	7,000	7,000	7,000	7,000	28,000
Income tax expense	2,800	2,800	2,800	2,800	11,200
(40% of pretax income)					
Profit after tax	4,200	4,200	4,200	4,200	16,800

Notice the following important things from Exhibit 2-1 before moving ahead:

1. Total depreciation charged on the asset over its entire life is the same across both statements ($12,000).

2. Total taxes payable and income tax expense over the life of the asset are the same across both statements ($11,200).

3. Total profit after tax over the life of the asset is the same across both statements ($16,800).

Essentially, the differences across the two sets of statements lie in the *distribution* of total depreciation expense ($12,000) over the four years.

- Depreciation expense on the tax return is *higher* in Years 1 through 3 by $1,000 each year ($4,000 – $3,000), so a difference of $3,000 accumulates over these three years.

- This cumulative difference is entirely offset, or *reversed* in Year 4 when depreciation on the tax return is *lower* than depreciation on financial statements by $3,000 (0 – $3,000).

A difference in expense recognition across the two statements that reverses in this manner is known as a temporary difference.

Exhibit 2-2 reproduces Bestwear's taxes payable and income tax expense for the four years (calculated in Exhibit 2-1).

Exhibit 2-2

	Year 1 $	Year 2 $	Year 3 $	Year 4 $
Taxes payable	2,400	2,400	2,400	2,400
Income tax expense	2,800	2,800	2,800	2,800
Increase in deferred tax liability (DTL)	400	400	400	−1,200
DTL cumulative	400	800	1,200	0

The cumulative DTL amount shows up on the balance sheet under liabilities.

The key here is to recognize that although *total* taxes payable and *total* income tax expense are the same ($11,200), their distribution over the years is not identical. Think of taxes payable as taxes that a company pays to the authorities. Think of income tax expense as the taxes that the company *should* pay according to its financial statements. In Years 1, 2, and 3 the company pays lower taxes on the tax return ($2,400 per year) than what it should according to its financial statements ($2,800 per year). Because the company actually pays less tax than it should, it creates a deferred tax liability (DTL) in Year 1, whose balance increases in Years 2 and 3 as the annual shortfall persists.

If expense recognition for tax purposes is relatively aggressive, it will give rise to a DTL.

The company will:
Pay less taxes now.
Pay more taxes in the future.

In Year 4 however, the company pays out more taxes (taxes payable of $4,000) than it should according to its financial statements (ITE of $2,800). It pays an *excess* tax of $1,200. This $1,200 serves to retire the liability that the company had accumulated over the first three years when it was paying less tax than it should have (paying $400 less every year resulting in a cumulative liability of $1,200 by the end of Year 3). Even though by the end of Year 4, the company has paid off its entire tax liability, it gained a cash flow advantage by *deferring* the payment of a portion of total yearly taxes to Year 4.

One way to calculate the value of the DTL balance sheet account is by adding the change in DTL over the period to the previous year's balance sheet value. An easier way is to simply use the following formula:

$$\text{DTL (cumulative)} = (\text{Carrying value of asset} - \text{Tax base}) \times \text{Tax rate}$$

We illustrate the computation of the tax base and carrying value of the asset and the calculation of the DTL balance for Bestwear in Exhibit 2-3.

Exhibit 2-3

Tax Return
Balance Sheet Extract

	Year 1 $	Year 2 $	Year 3 $	Year 4 $
Equipment	12,000	12,000	12,000	12,000
Accumulated depreciation	(4,000)	(8,000)	(12,000)	(12,000)
Tax base	**8,000**	**4,000**	**0**	**0**

Financial Statements
Balance Sheet Extract

	Year 1 $	Year 2 $	Year 3 $	Year 4 $
Equipment	12,000	12,000	12,000	12,000
Accumulated depreciation	(3,000)	(6,000)	(9,000)	(12,000)
Carrying Value	**9,000**	**6,000**	**3,000**	**0**

Using the formula on the previous page, Bestwear's DTL balance for each year is calculated as:

Year 1: $(9,000 - 8,000) \times 40\% = \$400$
Year 2: $(6,000 - 4,000) \times 40\% = \$800$
Year 3: $(3,000 - \text{Zero}) \times 40\% = \$1,200$
Year 4: $(\text{Zero} - \text{Zero}) \times 40\% = 0$

Once the balance sheet DTL value has been calculated, the change in DTL over a given period can be calculated using the following formula:

> Change in deferred tax liability = Closing DTL balance − Opening DTL balance

Bestwear's change in DTL over each of the four years can be calculated as:

Year 1: $400 - 0 = \$400$
Year 2: $800 - 400 = \$400$ ⟶ In Years 1–3 there is an increase in DTL.
Year 3: $1,200 - 800 = \$400$
Year 4: $0 - 1,200 = -\$1,200$ ⟶ In Year 4, there is a decrease in DTL.

The relationship between taxes payable (TP), change in deferred tax liabilities (DTL), and income tax expense (ITE) is driven by the following formula:

$$ITE = TP + \text{Change in DTL}$$

Once the tax returns of the company are ready and the amount of taxes payable is known, a company can compute income tax expense for the year simply by using the formula above. Bestwear's income tax expense for each of the four years is calculated as:

$ITE = TP + \text{Change in DTL}$

Year 1: 2,400 + 400 = $2,800
Year 2: 2,400 + 400 = $2,800
Year 3: 2,400 + 400 = $2,800
Year 4: 4,000 + (−1,200) = $2,800

To summarize, a deferred tax liability usually arises when:

- *Higher* expenses are charged on the tax return compared to the financial statements.
- Taxable income is *lower* than pretax or accounting profit.
- Taxes payable are *lower* than income tax expense.
- An asset's tax base is *lower* than its carrying value.

Note that deferred tax liabilities can also arise due to temporary differences resulting from revenues (or gains) being recognized on the income statement before they are included on the tax return.

Accounting Entries for an Increase in Deferred Tax Liabilities

- An *increase* in deferred tax liabilities **increases total liabilities** on the balance sheet.

- The increase in deferred tax liabilities is added to taxes payable in the calculation of income tax expense, so it decreases net income, retained earnings, and **owners' equity.**

Deferred Tax Assets

Deferred tax assets (DTA) usually arise when a company's taxes payable exceed its income tax expense. The company pays more taxes based on its tax return than it should pay according to its financial statements. This is a sort of a prepayment, and therefore counts as an asset.

Clearvision Inc. is a distributor of television sets, and has revenues of $10,000 every year. It offers a two-year warranty on its TV screens, and assumes that it will receive warranty claims of 5% of sales over each of the two years for financial statement purposes. For tax purposes, the company can recognize warranty expenses only when claims are actually made. Clearvision receives no claims in Year 1, but receives claims worth $1,000 in Year 2. Clearvision is taxed 40% of its profits.

Exhibit 2-4 demonstrates the calculation of income tax expense and taxes payable for Clearvision for the two years.

Exhibit 2-4

Clearvision Inc.
Tax Return

	Year 1 $	Year 2 $
Revenue	10,000	10,000
Warranty expense (actual expenses incurred)	0	1,000
Taxable income	10,000	9,000
Taxes payable (40% of taxable income)	4,000	3,600
Profit after tax	6,000	5,400

Clearvision Inc.
Income Statement

	Year 1 $	Year 2 $
Revenue	10,000	10,000
Warranty expense (5% of sales)	500	500
Pretax income	9,500	9,500
Income tax expense (40% of pretax income)	3,800	3,800
Profit after tax	5,700	5,700

Comparison of taxes payable and income tax expense:

	Year 1 $	Year 2 $	Total
Taxes payable	4,000	3,600	7,600
Income tax expense	3,800	3,800	7,600
Increase in DTA	200	−200	0
DTA cumulative	200	0	

> If expense recognition for accounting purposes is relatively aggressive, it will give rise to a DTA.

> The company will: Pay more taxes now. Pay less taxes in the future.

- In Year 1, taxes payable ($4,000) exceed income tax expense ($3,800), giving rise to a deferred tax asset. The company pays more taxes than it should according to its financial statements.

- In Year 2, this temporary difference of $200 is entirely offset or reversed.

> Recall that the tax base of an expense-related liability equals its carrying value minus amounts that have not been recognized on the tax return yet, but will be expensed on the tax return in the future.

The carrying value of warranty expense liability on the balance sheet after Year 1 equals $500. Warranty claims are only expensed on the tax return when they are received, and no claims are received in Year 1. At the end of Year 1, the total value of expenses that have not been recognized on the tax return **yet**, but **will** be recognized in the future (when claims are actually received) is $500. Therefore, the tax base of the liability equals zero ($500 − $500).

In Year 2, the carrying value and the tax base of the warranty-related liability equal zero.

Deferred tax asset balances at a given balance sheet date can be calculated using the following formula:

$$(\text{Carrying value of liability} - \text{Tax base of liability}) \times \text{Tax rate}$$

Therefore, the deferred tax asset balances for Clearvision can be calculated as:

Year 1: (500 – 0) × 40% = $200
Year 2: (0 – 0) × 40% = 0

There is an increase in deferred tax assets of $200 in Year 1. However, in Year 2, the temporary difference in warranty expense recognition that gave rise to the deferred tax asset reverses. This results in a reduction in DTA of $200 and leaves the cumulative DTA balance at zero.

The relationship between taxes payable, the change in deferred tax assets, and income tax expense is captured by the following formula:

$$\text{ITE} = \text{TP} - \text{Change in DTA}$$

Therefore, once the company has prepared its tax return and determined the amount of taxes payable, it can easily calculate income tax expense by subtracting any increase in DTA over the period from taxes payable. Clearvision's income tax expense for the two years can be calculated as:

Year 1: $4,000 – $200 = $3,800
Year 2: $3,600 – (–$200) = $3,800

To summarize, a deferred tax asset arises when:

- *Higher* expenses are charged on the financial statements than on the tax return.
- Taxable income is *higher* than pretax or accounting profit.
- Taxes payable are *greater* than income tax expense.
- A liability's tax base is *lower* than its carrying value.

Note that a deferred tax asset may also result from a temporary difference arising due to revenues (or gains) being recognized on the tax return before being recognized on the income statement.

Accounting Entries for an Increase in Deferred Tax Assets

- An *increase* in deferred tax assets **increases total assets** on the balance sheet.
- The increase in deferred tax assets is subtracted from taxes payable in the calculation of income tax expense, so it **increases net income, retained earnings, and equity**.

LOS 31e: Evaluate the impact of tax rate changes on a company's financial statements and ratios. **Vol 3, pp 483–484**

When income tax rates change, the balances of deferred tax assets and liabilities on the balance sheet must be adjusted for the new tax rates. When tax rates *rise*, the balances of both deferred tax assets and liabilities *rise*. When tax rates *fall*, the balances of both deferred tax assets and liabilities *fall*.

Let's work with the financial numbers of Bestwear Inc. that we introduced earlier, and now assume that in Year 3, tax rates are brought down to 30%. The information in Exhibit 2-5 is reproduced from Exhibits 2-1 and 2-3 to facilitate our analysis.

Exhibit 2-5

	Year 1 $	Year 2 $	Year 3 $	Year 4 $
Tax Base	8,000	4,000	0	0
Carrying value	9,000	6,000	3,000	0
DTL cumulative	400	800	1,200	0

Depreciation expense

	Yr 3
Tax reporting	4,000
Financial reporting	3,000

Deferred tax liability (BS value) = (Carrying value − Tax base) × New tax rate

Therefore, the DTL balance at the end of Year 3 = (3,000 − 0) × 30% = $900

Although the difference between the carrying amount and the tax base of the asset is the same as before ($3,000), the deferred tax liability is lower because this difference is now multiplied by a lower tax rate to determine the end-of-year DTL amount on the balance sheet.

Compared to the scenario where tax rates were 40%, Year 3 deferred tax liabilities fall by $300 ($1,200 − $900) when tax rates are lowered to 30%.

This reduction can be broken down into two components:

1. The temporary difference of $1,000 ($4,000−$3,000) in additional depreciation on the tax return in Year 3 will now result in a tax shield of only $300 ($1,000 × 30%) as compared to $400 ($1,000 × 40%) earlier. This reduces DTL by $100.

   > Step 1: Calculate the change in DTL in the year of change in tax rates using the new tax rate.

2. The cumulative deferred tax liability at the end of Year 2 will now be valued at the new tax rate and reduce DTL by 25%. [(40% − 30%) / 40%] 25% of the Year 2 DTL balance ($800) equals $200.

   > Step 2: Adjust the value of the cumulative DTL balance from previous years for the change in tax rates.

Therefore DTL decreases by $100 + $200 = $300.

Income tax expense for Year 3 will be calculated using the following formula:

Income tax expense = Taxes payable + Change in DTL − Change in DTA

> Bestwear's taxable income in Year 3 was $6,000. (Exhibit 2-1)
>
> Bestwear had no deferred tax assets.

Taxes payable equal taxable income multiplied by the new tax rate.

TP = $6,000 × 30% = $1,800

Therefore:

$$ITE = \$1,800 + (-300) = \$1,500$$

Our analysis allows us to reach the following important conclusions:

- If a company has a net DTL (excess of DTL over DTA), a reduction in tax rates would *reduce* liabilities, *reduce* income tax expense, and *increase* equity.
- If the company has a net DTA (excess of DTA over DTL), a reduction in tax rates will *reduce* assets, *increase* income tax expense, and *decrease* equity.
- If a company has a net DTL, an increase in tax rates would *increase* liabilities, *increase* income tax expense, and *reduce* equity.
- If the company has a net DTA, an increase in tax rates will *increase* assets, *decrease* income tax expense, and *increase* equity.

LOS 31f: Distinguish between temporary and permanent differences in pre-tax accounting income and taxable income. Vol 3, pp 484–488

Temporary differences arise because of differences between the tax base and carrying amounts of assets and liabilities. Permanent differences, on the other hand, arise as a result of expense or income items that can be recognized on one statement (tax return or income statement), but not the other. They are differences in tax and financial reporting of revenues and expenses that *will not* reverse at any point in the future. Examples of the items that give rise to permanent differences include:

1. Revenue items that are not taxable. For example, government grants are tax exempted, thus they are not accounted for in the tax returns but are still included in the financial statements.
2. Expense items that are not tax deductible. For example, fines and penalties in many jurisdictions are not tax-allowable expenses, but are still written off in the financial statements.
3. Tax credits for some expenses that directly reduce taxes.

The important thing to remember is that permanent differences do not result in deferred taxes. They result in differences between effective and statutory tax rates and should be considered in the analysis of effective tax rates. A firm's reported effective tax rate is calculated as:

$$\text{Effective tax rate} = \frac{\text{Income tax expense}}{\text{Pretax income}}$$

The comprehensive examples in this relating to Bestwear and Clearvision were illustrations of temporary differences between the recognition of expenses on the tax return and on the income statement. Temporary differences can be divided into two categories:

1. Taxable Temporary Differences

Taxable temporary differences result in *deferred tax liabilities*. They are expected to result in future taxable income. Deferred tax liabilities arise when:

- The carrying amount of an asset *exceeds* its tax base; or
- The carrying amount of a liability is *less* than its tax base.

Bestwear offered an example of taxable temporary differences. In Years 1 through 3, the carrying amount of the asset exceeded its tax base and resulted in a deferred tax liability.

2. Deductible Temporary Differences

Deductible temporary differences result in *deferred tax assets*. They are expected to provide tax deductions in the future. Deferred tax assets arise when:

- The tax base of an asset *exceeds* its carrying amount; or
- The tax base of a liability is *less* than its carrying amount.

Clearvision offered an example of deductible temporary differences. In Year 1, the carrying value of the warranty liability exceeded its tax base and resulted in a deferred tax asset.

Bear in mind that the recognition of a deferred tax asset is only allowed when there is a reasonable expectation of future profits against which these assets can provide tax deductions.

As long as the difference is temporary, the rules in Table 2-1 will help you ascertain the nature of the deferred tax items created.

Table 2-1

Balance Sheet Item	Carrying Value vs. Tax Base	Results in...	
Asset	Carrying amount is greater.	DTL	→ Bestwear example
Asset	Tax base is greater.	DTA	
Liability	Carrying amount is greater.	DTA	→ Clearvision example
Liability	Tax base is greater.	DTL	

For each of the entries listed in Table 2-2, indicate whether the difference between the tax base and the carrying amount of the asset or liability is temporary or permanent and whether a deferred tax asset or liability will be created. The related transactions were discussed earlier when we calculated the tax bases of assets and liabilities under LOS 31c.

Table 2-2

		Carrying Value	Tax Base
1.	Dividends receivable	1,000,000	1,000,000
2.	Development costs	1,500,000	1,400,000
3.	Research costs	0	800,000
4.	Accounts receivable	2,000,000	1,540,000
5.	Donations	0	0
6.	Interest received in advance	500,000	0
7.	Rent received in advance	1,000,000	0
8.	Loan (capital)	8,000,000	8,000,000
	Interest paid	0	0
9.	Warranty expense	200,000	0

1. We stated earlier that dividends receivable were not taxable. The related income will *never* be included on the tax return to calculate taxable income. The difference in income recognition between the tax return and the financial statements will *never* reverse, so taxable income and accounting profit will *permanently* differ.

2. The carrying value of capitalized development costs (asset) *exceeds* the tax base. This is a temporary difference, so a deferred tax liability will be created (see Table 2-1). Taxable income will be *higher* in future years when reversal occurs.

3. The carrying value of capitalized research costs is *lower* than their tax base. This is a temporary difference, so a deferred tax asset will be created. Taxable income will be *lower* in the future as these costs are written off for tax purposes.

4. The difference between the carrying amount and the tax base is a temporary difference that will result in a deferred tax liability.

5. Legislation does not allow donations to be deducted for tax purposes. This constitutes a *permanent* difference that will not have any impact on deferred taxes.

6. Interest received in advance results in a temporary difference that gives rise to a deferred tax asset. The carrying value of the liability *exceeds* the tax base.

7. Rent received in advance also causes a temporary difference that gives rise to a deferred tax asset.

8. No temporary differences result from loan or interest payments. Therefore, *no* deferred tax items are recognized.

9. The carrying value of the liability *exceeds* its tax base. This difference is temporary and gives rise to a deferred tax asset.

Temporary Differences at Initial Recognition of Assets and Liabilities

In some situations, the carrying value and tax base of certain assets and liabilities may not be equal at initial recognition. For example, a company may deduct a government grant from the initial carrying amount of an asset or liability on the balance sheet. In such circumstances (even though the tax base and the carrying amount of the item are different) a company cannot recognize deferred tax assets or liabilities.

Basically, deferred tax assets or liabilities should not be recognized in cases that would arise from the initial recognition of an asset or a liability in transactions that are not a business combination and when, at the time of transaction, there is no impact on either accounting or taxable profit.

Goodwill may be treated differently across different tax jurisdictions, which may lead to differences in the carrying amount and tax base of goodwill. However, accounting standards do not permit the recognition of a deferred tax liability (due to differences between the tax base and carrying amount of goodwill) upon its **initial** recognition. Subsequently, deferred taxes may be recognized due to differences between the carrying amount and tax base of goodwill that arise from impairment charges.

Business Combinations and Deferred Taxes

In a business combination, if the fair value of acquired intangible assets (including goodwill) is different from their carrying amounts, deferred taxes can be recognized.

With regard to investments in subsidiaries, branches, associates, and interests in joint ventures, **deferred tax liabilities** (arising from temporary differences on the consolidated versus the parent's financial statements) can be recognized unless:
- The parent is in a position to control the timing of the future reversal of the temporary difference, and
- It is probable that the temporary difference will not reverse in the future.

Deferred tax assets will only be recognized if:
- The temporary difference will reverse in the future, and
- Sufficient taxable profits exist against which the temporary difference can be used.

Under **IFRS**, unused tax losses and credits may only be recognized to the extent of probable future taxable income against which these can be applied. On the other hand, under **U.S. GAAP**, deferred tax assets are recognized in full and then reduced through a valuation allowance if they are unlikely to be realized. A company that has a history of tax losses may be unlikely to earn taxable profits in the future against which it can apply deferred tax assets.

Current taxes are based on the tax rates applicable at the balance sheet date. Deferred taxes on the other hand are measured at the rate that is expected to apply when they are realized (when the temporary differences that gave rise to them are expected to reverse).

Even though deferred tax assets and liabilities arise from temporary differences that are expected to reverse at some point in the future, present values are not used in determining the amounts to be recognized. Deferred taxes as well as income taxes should always be recognized unless they pertain to:
- Taxes or deferred taxes charged directly to equity.
- A possible provision for deferred taxes related to a business combination.

Even if there has been no change in temporary differences during the current period, the carrying amount of DTA and DTL may change due to:
- Changes in tax rates.
- Reassessments of recoverability of DTA.
- Change in expectations as to how the DTA or DTL will be realized.

Although DTL and DTA are created from temporary differences that are expected to reverse *in the future*, they are *not discounted* to their present values to ascertain book values. However, deferred tax assets must be evaluated at each balance sheet date to ensure that they will be recovered. If there are any doubts as to whether they will be realized, their carrying value should be reduced to the expected recoverable amount. Doubts regarding the actual realization of deferred tax assets can stem from the expectation of insufficient future taxable income to recover the tax assets (prepaid taxes).

Under **U.S. GAAP**, DTA are reduced by creating a contra-asset account known as the valuation allowance. An increase in the valuation allowance *reduces* deferred tax assets. The negative change in deferred tax assets results in an *increase* in income tax expense, which in turn translates into *lower* net income, retained earnings, and equity. Should circumstances subsequently change, and the likelihood of realizing deferred tax assets increase, the previous reduction in DTA can be reversed by reducing the valuation allowance.

Since the timing and amount of any reduction in value of DTA is rather subjective in nature, analysts should carefully scrutinize these changes. Analysts should also forecast a company's financial performance and gauge whether any deferred tax assets are likely to be realized.

Recognition of Current and Deferred Tax Charged Directly to Equity

Under both **IFRS** and **U.S. GAAP**, deferred tax assets and liabilities should generally have the same accounting treatment as the assets and liabilities that give rise to them. If the item that gave rise to the deferred tax asset/liability is taken directly to equity, the resulting deferred tax item should also be taken directly to equity.

If a deferred tax liability is not expected to reverse it should be reduced, and the amount by which it is reduced should be taken directly to equity. Any deferred taxes related to business combinations should also be recognized in equity. See Example 3-1.

Example 3-1: Taxes Charged Directly to Equity

On January 1, 2005, Jeremy Builders purchased a piece of equipment for $2,000,000. For accounting purposes, it is depreciated at a rate of 5% a year on a straight-line basis. However, for tax purposes it is depreciated at a rate of 10% a year on a straight-line basis. On January 1, 2007, the equipment is revalued at $2,400,000 and it is estimated that the machinery will be in use for a further 20 years after revaluation. For tax purposes, the revaluation is not recognized. Assume that the tax rate is 40% and the asset has zero salvage value for tax and financial reporting purposes.

1. Calculate the depreciation expense for the machinery for 2005 for accounting and tax purposes.
2. What is the tax base of equipment on December 31, 2005?
3. Calculate the deferred tax asset or liability on December 31, 2006.
4. Calculate the deferred tax asset or liability on December 31, 2007.

Solution

1. Depreciation expense for accounting purposes = 5% × 2,000,000 = $100,000

   Depreciation expense for tax purposes = 10% × 2,000,000 = $200,000

2.

Tax base on January 1, 2005	$2,000,000
Depreciation expense (tax purposes)	$200,000
Tax base on December 31, 2005	$1,800,000

---

3. Carrying amount on December 31, 2006 = 2,000,000 − (100,000 × 2) = $1,800,000

   Tax base on December 31, 2006 = 2,000,000 − (200,000 × 2) = $1,600,000

   Since the carrying amount of the equipment is greater than its tax base, it gives rise to a deferred tax liability.

   Deferred tax liability = (1,800,000 − 1,600,000) × 40% = $80,000

4. Carrying amount on December 31, 2007 = 2,400,000 − 120,000 = $2,280,000 (The asset was revalued upward to $2,400,000 at the beginning of 2007 and is expected to be in use for a further 20 years. Therefore, annual depreciation for financial reporting purposes is $120,000 (= $2,400,000/20).

   Tax base on December 31, 2007 = 1,600,000 − 200,000 = $1,400,000

   It may seem that deferred tax liability on December 31, 2007 would amount to $352,000 (calculated as [($2,280,000 − $1,400,000) × 40%]), but this is NOT the case. Only the portion of the difference between the tax base and the carrying amount that is not caused by the revaluation gives rise to a deferred tax liability.

   The $600,000 revaluation is only recognized on the financial statements, not for tax purposes. The revaluation surplus and the associated tax effects are accounted for as a direct adjustment to equity. The $600,000 revaluation surplus is reduced by the tax provision associated with the excess of fair value over carrying value (600,000 × 40%) = $240,000 and it affects retained earnings.

   The deferred liability that should be reported on the balance sheet for 2007 is therefore not $352,000, but only $112,000 (= $352,000 − $240,000). The change in deferred tax liability over the year is $32,000 (= $112,000 − $80,000).

   Finally, note that each year after the revaluation, an amount equal to depreciation arising from the revaluation minus the deferred tax effect will be transferred from the revaluation reserve to retained earnings. In 2007 for example, this amount will be calculated as the portion of annual depreciation arising from the revaluation, $30,000 (= $600,000 / 20) minus the deferred tax effect of $12,000 (= $30,000 × 0.40), which comes to $18,000.

LOS 31h: Compare a company's deferred tax items. **Vol 3, pp 494–499**

LOS 31i: Analyze disclosures relating to deferred tax items and the effective tax rate reconciliation, and explain how information included in these disclosures affects a company's financial statements and financial ratios. **Vol 3, pp 493–499**

This LOS is best understood through a comprehensive example. In Exhibit 3-1, we have included ABC Company's income statement, balance sheet, and income tax disclosures. The questions following the financials illustrate the importance of deferred tax items.

Exhibit 3-1a

ABC Company

Income Statement

	Dec. 31, 2008	Dec. 31, 2007	Dec. 31, 2006
	($)	($)	($)
Sales	5,000	4,500	4,000
Cost of goods sold	3,500	3,300	3,000
Gross profit	1,500	1,200	1,000
Total expenses	(1,000)	(800)	(650)
Interest income	200	180	165
Income before taxes	700	580	515
Income tax expense	(23)	(15)	(54)
Net income after tax	677	565	461

The tax provision of $23 million is only 3.3% of income before taxes (23/700) × 100.

Exhibit 3-1b

ABC Company

Balance Sheet

		Dec. 31, 2008	Dec. 31, 2007
		($)	($)
Assets			
Cash		525	425
Receivables		80	65
Inventories		75	55
Deferred income taxes		25	35
Total current assets	1	705	580
Noncurrent Assets			
Net fixed assets		1,200	1,000
Goodwill		500	400
Deferred income taxes	1	59	35
Total Assets		2,464	2,015
Liabilities and Shareholders' Equity			
Accounts payable		59	102
Current portion of long-term debt		75	165
Total current liabilities		134	267
Long-term debt		1,125	1,225
Deferred income taxes	1	40	35
Total liabilities		1,165	1,260
Common stock		300	300
Retained earnings		865	188
Total Liabilities and Shareholders' Equity		2,464	2,015

Current deferred tax assets.

Noncurrent deferred tax assets

Noncurrent deferred tax liabilities

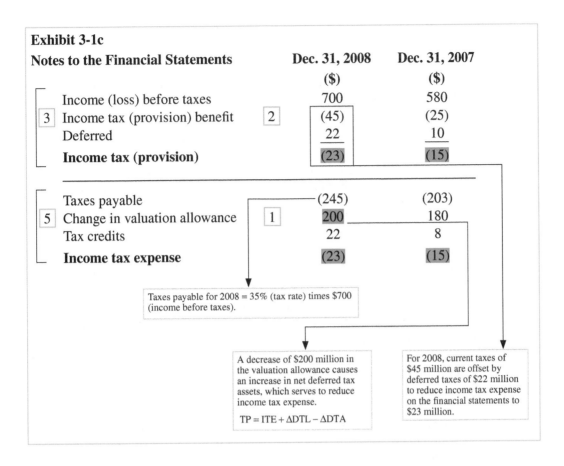

Exhibit 3-1c

Notes to the Financial Statements

	Dec. 31, 2008 ($)	Dec. 31, 2007 ($)
Income (loss) before taxes	700	580
[3] Income tax (provision) benefit [2]	(45)	(25)
Deferred	22	10
Income tax (provision)	(23)	(15)
Taxes payable	(245)	(203)
[5] Change in valuation allowance [1]	200	180
Tax credits	22	8
Income tax expense	(23)	(15)

Taxes payable for 2008 = 35% (tax rate) times $700 (income before taxes).

A decrease of $200 million in the valuation allowance causes an increase in net deferred tax assets, which serves to reduce income tax expense.

$$TP = ITE + \Delta DTL - \Delta DTA$$

For 2008, current taxes of $45 million are offset by deferred taxes of $22 million to reduce income tax expense on the financial statements to $23 million.

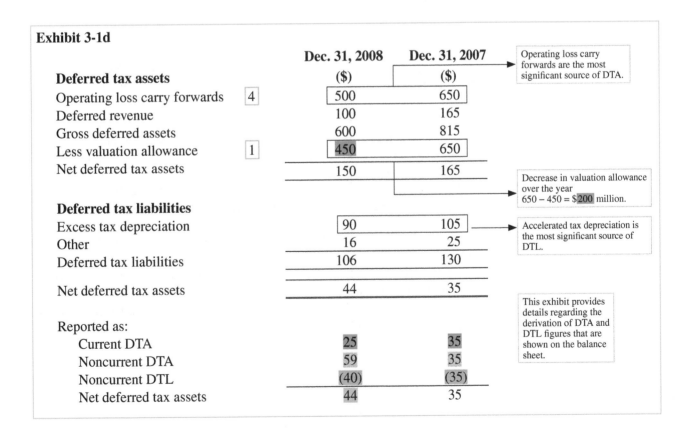

Exhibit 3-1d

	Dec. 31, 2008 ($)	Dec. 31, 2007 ($)
Deferred tax assets		
Operating loss carry forwards [4]	500	650
Deferred revenue	100	165
Gross deferred assets	600	815
Less valuation allowance [1]	450	650
Net deferred tax assets	150	165
Deferred tax liabilities		
Excess tax depreciation	90	105
Other	16	25
Deferred tax liabilities	106	130
Net deferred tax assets	44	35
Reported as:		
Current DTA	25	35
Noncurrent DTA	59	35
Noncurrent DTL	(40)	(35)
Net deferred tax assets	44	35

Operating loss carry forwards are the most significant source of DTA.

Decrease in valuation allowance over the year 650 – 450 = $200 million.

Accelerated tax depreciation is the most significant source of DTL.

This exhibit provides details regarding the derivation of DTA and DTL figures that are shown on the balance sheet.

1. What implications does the valuation allowance of $450 million against grossed deferred assets of $600 million in 2008 (Exhibit 3-1d) have on the company's future earning prospects?
2. How would the company's DTL and DTA be affected by a reduction in tax rates to 32% from 35%. Would this change benefit the company?
3. How would the company's earnings be different if it did not use a valuation allowance?
4. How would the operating loss carryforwards of $500 million (Exhibit 3-1d) affect the value a prospective buyer might pay for the company?
5. Under what circumstances should an analyst consider DTL as debt or as equity? When should an analyst exclude deferred taxes entirely from the calculation of leverage ratios?

Solution

1. The company has a valuation allowance against a significant portion of its deferred tax assets, which implies that the company does not think that it will have sufficient future earnings against which it can realize its deferred tax assets. However, it is clear from the income statement that the company is generating profits, and if this trend in profitability were to continue, it would be able to realize its deferred tax assets. In 2008, the valuation allowance decreased by $200 million. The decrease in the valuation allowance increased net deferred tax assets, and reduced income tax expense by $200m to $23 million. (See Exhibit 3-1c.)

2. The company currently has net deferred tax assets of $44 million (see Exhibit 3-1d). A reduction in tax rates will reduce the value of these assets and hurt the company. Further, there is a possibility that there will be further downward adjustments in the valuation allowance to the extent of $450 million, which will increase net deferred tax assets. In that case, the negative effect of the reduction in tax rates will be magnified.

3. The reduction in valuation allowance lowered income tax expense by $200 million in 2008. If there were no reduction in the valuation allowance in 2008, income tax expense would have been higher, and reported income lower.

4. If the acquiring company is profitable, it could use the company's significant operating loss carryforwards to offset its own deferred tax liabilities. The acquirer would be willing to pay the present value of the tax savings (based on its own tax rate) that it could realize against ABC's loss carryforwards. The higher the acquirer's tax rate, and the more profitable the acquirer, the sooner it will be able to benefit.

5. If the deferred tax liability will reverse with an eventual tax payment, it should be treated as a liability. However, if reversal is not expected, and there is no expectation of an eventual cash outflow, the liability should be treated as equity. This could happen because of a reduction in tax rates in the future or expected future losses. When the amount and timing of reversal of temporary differences is uncertain, analysts should exclude DTL from both debt and equity in their analysis.

Example 3-2: Statuary U.S. Federal Income Tax Rate Reconciliation

Winterfell Inc. is a U.S.-based telecom company. The company faces a statutory tax rate of 35%. Its reconciliation between statutory and effective income taxes is provided below.

Income Tax Reconciliation

	2012	2011	2010
Taxable income	$2,080	$2,360	$2,940
U.S. federal income tax (provision) benefit at statutory rate	728	826	1,029
State taxes, net of federal benefit	40	50	70
Benefits and taxes related to foreign operations	(165)	(150)	(125)
Tax credits	4	16	8
Export sales benefit	3	(15)	11
Other	(5)	23	(17)
Effective income taxes	**557**	**750**	**976**

Calculate the effective tax rates for Winterfell for each of the three years. Also comment on the trend in effective tax rates over the period.

Solution

The analysis of effective tax rates can be based on absolute amounts and/or on percentages. We present percentage numbers as well as effective income tax rates in the table below:

	2012	2011	2010
U.S. federal income tax (provision) benefit at 35%	35.00%	35.00%	35.00%
State taxes, net of federal benefit	1.92%	2.12%	2.38%
Foreign operations	(7.93%)	(6.36%)	(4.25%)
Tax credits	0.19%	0.68%	0.27%
Export sales benefit	0.14%	(0.64%)	0.37%
Other	(0.24%)	0.97%	(0.58%)
Effective income tax rates	**26.78%**	**31.78%**	**33.20%**

The effective tax rate exhibits a downward trend over the 3-year period.
- The (1) decrease in the state income tax rate and (2) increase in benefits related to foreign income contribute to the downward trend.
- During each of the three years benefits from export sales and other items partially offset each other. The volatility in these two items makes it difficult to forecast the effective tax rate for Winterfell going forward and reduces the comparability of its financial statements with peer companies.

LOS 31j: Identify the key provisions of and differences between income tax accounting under IFRS and U.S. GAAP. **Vol 3, pp 499–502**

	IFRS	U.S. GAAP
Issue Specific Treatments		
Revaluation of fixed assets and intangible assets.	Recognized in equity as deferred taxes.	Revaluation is prohibited.
Treatment of undistributed profits from investment in subsidiaries.	Recognized as deferred taxes except when the parent company is able to control the distribution of profits and it is probable that temporary differences will not reverse in the future.	No recognition of deferred taxes for foreign subsidiaries that fulfill the indefinite reversal criteria. No recognition of deferred taxes for domestic subsidiaries when amounts are tax free.
Treatment of undistributed profits from investments in joint ventures.	Recognized as deferred taxes except when the investor controls the sharing of profits and it is probable that there will be no reversal of temporary differences in the future.	No recognition of deferred taxes for foreign corporate joint ventures that fulfill the indefinite reversal criteria.
Treatment of undistributed profits from investments in associates.	Recognized as deferred taxes except when the investor controls the sharing of profits and it is probable that there will be no reversal of temporary differences in the future.	Deferred taxes are recognized from temporary differences.
Deferred Tax Measurement		
Tax rates.	Tax rates and tax laws enacted or substantively enacted.	Only enacted tax rates and tax laws are used.
Deferred tax asset recognition.	Recognized if it is probable that sufficient taxable profit will be available in the future.	Deferred tax assets are recognized in full and then reduced by a valuation allowance if it is likely that they will not be realized.
Deferred Tax Presentation		
Offsetting of deferred tax assets and liabilities.	Offsetting allowed only if the entity has right to legally enforce it and the balance is related to tax levied by the same authority.	Similar to **IFRS**.
Balance sheet classification.	Classified on the balance sheet as net noncurrent with supplementary disclosures.	Classified as either current or noncurrent based on classification of underlying asset and liability.

READING 32: NON-CURRENT (LONG-TERM) LIABILITIES

LESSON 1: BONDS PAYABLE

Financing Liabilities: Terminology

A bond is a contract between a borrower and a lender that obligates the borrower to make payments to the lender over the term of the bond. Two types of payments are usually involved—periodic interest payments and principal repayments. Before we get into the analysis of financing liabilities, we must understand the following terms:

Par or face value: This is the amount that the borrower must pay back investors at maturity. The par value is not necessarily the amount that the borrower receives upon issuing debt.

Coupon rate (nominal or stated rate): This is multiplied by the par value of the bond to determine the periodic coupon payment.

Market interest rates are used to value bonds. These rates incorporate various types of risks inherent in the bond, and must not be confused with coupon rates. Market interest rates change from day to day.

The value of a company's debt obligations at any point in time, t, equals the present value of all remaining payments discounted at current market interest rates (mi_t). However, for accounting purposes, the book value of the liability recognized on the issuer's balance sheet equals the present value of its obligations discounted at market interest rates at issuance (mi_0). Market interest rates at issuance determine how much the company receives in bond proceeds from the issuance of bonds. The market rate at the time of issuance is the effective interest rate on the loan.

At issuance, the market rate can be the same as or different than the coupon rate.

- If the market interest rate is the *same* as the bond's coupon rate, the bond will be issued at *par.*
- If the market interest rate is *greater* than the coupon rate, the bond will be issued at a *discount.* Since the coupon rate on offer is *less* than the compensation required by market participants, the bond will sell for less than its face value.
- If the market interest rate is *lower* than the coupon rate, the bond will be issued at a *premium.* Since the coupon rate on offer *exceeds* the compensation required by the market, the bond will sell for more than its face value.

Finally, interest expense (recognized on the income statement) under the effective interest method for a given period is calculated as the book value of the liability at the beginning of the period multiplied by the market interest rate at issuance (mi_0). It is **not** the coupon payment (actual periodic cash outflow) that is recognized as interest expense on the income statement.

> The market rate of interest at the time of issue often differs from the coupon rate because of interest rate fluctuations that occur between the time the issuer establishes the coupon rate and the day the bonds are actually available to the investors.

> **Formulas**
>
> **Bond proceeds at issuance (t = 0):**
> $BV_0 = PV$ (cash flows) discounted at mi_0
>
> **Market value of bonds at time, t:**
> PV (cash flows) discounted at mi_t
>
> **Coupon payment:**
> Periodic coupon rate × Par value
>
> **Interest expense:**
> mi_0 × Book value of liability at the beginning of the period.

LOS 32a: Determine the initial recognition, initial measurement, and subsequent measurement of bonds. **Vol 3, pp 512–523**

LOS 32b: Describe the effective interest method and calculate interest expense, amortization of bond discounts/premiums, and interest payments. **Vol 3, pp 512–523**

There are two methods of accounting for noncurrent liabilities.

The effective interest method results in a constant rate of interest over the life of the bond. It is required under **IFRS** and preferred under **U.S. GAAP**. Under this method, the market interest rate at issuance is applied to the carrying amount of the bonds to determine periodic interest expense. Further, the difference between interest expense and the actual coupon payment equals the amount of discount/premium amortized over the period.

The straight-line method, which is also permitted under **U.S. GAAP**, evenly amortizes the premium or discount over the life of the bond (similar to straight-line depreciation).

The financial statement effects of bond issuance, as well as the effective interest and straight-line methods of amortizing bond premiums and discounts are illustrated in Example 1-1.

Example 1-1: Accounting for Financing Liabilities

Alan Company plans to issue bonds worth $100,000 par with a 10% annual coupon and a 4-year maturity. The amount of bond proceeds received by the company depends on market interest rates at issuance. We will work with three scenarios to illustrate the differences in accounting and analysis of par bonds, premium bonds, and discount bonds under the effective interest method.

Scenario A: Market Interest Rates at Issuance = 10%

The amount of bond proceeds equals the present value of the bond's cash flows discounted at market interest rates at issuance (10%).

FV = $100,000; N = 4; I/Y = 10; PMT = $10,000; CPT PV; PV → −$100,000

Cash flows from bonds:
- Alan will receive $100,000 for these bonds today.
- Alan will pay an annual coupon of $10,000 for 4 years.
- At the end of Year 4, Alan will return the par value ($100,000) to investors.

Interest Expense and Book Value of Par Bond (Effective Interest Method)

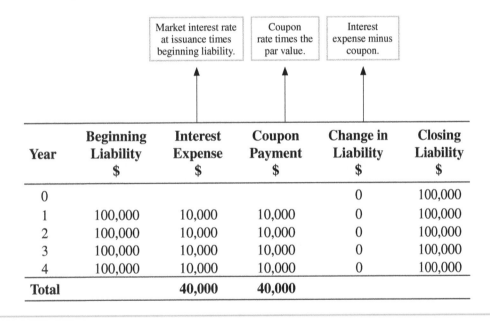

Year	Beginning Liability $	Interest Expense $	Coupon Payment $	Change in Liability $	Closing Liability $
0				0	100,000
1	100,000	10,000	10,000	0	100,000
2	100,000	10,000	10,000	0	100,000
3	100,000	10,000	10,000	0	100,000
4	100,000	10,000	10,000	0	100,000
Total		**40,000**	**40,000**		

Effects on Financial Statements

Balance sheet: The year-end value of the liability is listed on the balance sheet. For bonds issued at par, the liability balance remains at par throughout the life of the bond ($100,000 every year).

Income statement: Interest expense is deducted from operating income. For bonds issued at par, interest expense *equals* the coupon payment, and is constant over the life of the bond ($10,000 every year).

Statement of cash flows:
- At issuance, bond proceeds are reported as inflows from *financing activities.*
- During the tenure of the bond, coupon payments (not interest expense) are deducted from *cash flow from operating (CFO) activities.*
- At maturity, cash used to repay the principal amount (par value) is deducted from *cash flow from financing (CFF) activities.*

For bonds issued at par, the inflows recorded at issuance under CFF equal the outflows from CFF at maturity. Coupon payments are deducted from CFO every year.

Scenario B: Market Interest Rates at Issuance = 11%

Calculation of bond proceeds:

FV = $100,000; N = 4; I/Y = 11; PMT = $10,000; CPT PV; PV → –$96,897.55

Cash flows from bonds:
- Alan will receive $96,898 for these bonds today.
- Alan will pay an annual coupon of $10,000 for 4 years.
- At the end of the Year 4, Alan will return the par value ($100,000) to investors; **not** the issuance proceeds ($96,898).

Interest Expense and Book Value of Discount Bond (Effective Interest Method)

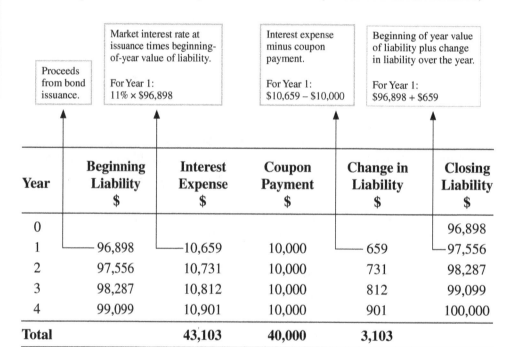

	Proceeds from bond issuance.	Market interest rate at issuance times beginning-of-year value of liability. For Year 1: 11% × $96,898	Interest expense minus coupon payment. For Year 1: $10,659 – $10,000	Beginning of year value of liability plus change in liability over the year. For Year 1: $96,898 + $659

Year	Beginning Liability $	Interest Expense $	Coupon Payment $	Change in Liability $	Closing Liability $
0					96,898
1	96,898	10,659	10,000	659	97,556
2	97,556	10,731	10,000	731	98,287
3	98,287	10,812	10,000	812	99,099
4	99,099	10,901	10,000	901	100,000
Total		**43,103**	**40,000**	**3,103**	

Every year, Alan pays out *less* in the form of coupon (cash outflow of $10,000) than it owes in interest expense (e.g., $10,659 in Year 1). This *shortfall* serves to *increase* the value of the liability over the period (e.g., the liability increases by $659 over Year 1).

Important Shortcut 1:

Interest expense over the term of the bond can be calculated as all the issuer's outflows over the life of the bond (coupon payments plus principal repayment) minus the inflows received at issuance (bond proceeds). Total interest expense over the 4 years:

$100,000 + $40,000 – $96,898 = $43,102

Year 2 beginning liability equals Year 1 closing liability.

If the straight-line method were used, the discount would be evenly amortized over the term of the bonds. In this scenario, the discount of $3,102 would be amortized by $775.50 each year. Annual interest expense under the straight-line method would be $10,000 + $775.50 = $10,775.50.

Effects on Financial Statements

Balance sheet: For bonds issued at a discount, the book value of the liability increases over the life of the bond. The entire discount ($3,102) is amortized over the 4 years. The value of the liability at the end of Year 4 equals par value, which is the amount that must be paid to investors at maturity.

Income statement: Interest expense rises from year to year in line with the increasing book value of the liability.

Statement of cash flows: For bonds issued at a discount, the inflow recorded at issuance under CFF ($96,898) is *lower* than the outflow from CFF at maturity ($100,000). Coupon payments ($10,000) are deducted from CFO every year.

Scenario C: Market Interest Rates at Issuance = 9%

Calculation of bond proceeds:

FV = $100,000; N = 4; I/Y = 9; PMT = $10,000; CPT PV; PV → -$103,239.71

Cash flows from bonds:

- Alan will receive $103,240 for these bonds today.
- Alan will pay an annual coupon of $10,000 for 4 years.
- At the end of Year 4, Alan will return the par value ($100,000) to investors; **not** the initial proceeds from sale ($103,239.71).

Interest Expense and Book Value of Premium Bond (Effective Interest Method)

| | | Market interest rate at issuance times beginning of year liability. | Interest expense minus coupon payment. | Beginning of year value of liability plus change in liability. | |
| | Proceeds from bond issuance. | For Year 1: 9% × $103,240 | For Year 1: $9,292 – $10,000 | For Year 1: $103,240 + (–$708) | |

Year	Beginning Liability $	Interest Expense $	Coupon Payment $	Change in Liability $	Closing Liability $
0					103,240
1	103,240	9,292	10,000	–708	102,531
2	102,531	9,228	10,000	–772	101,759
3	101,759	9,158	10,000	–842	100,917
4	100,917	9,083	10,000	–917	100,000
Total		**36,760**	**40,000**	**–3,240**	

Every year, Alan pays out more in the form of coupon (cash outflow of $10,000) than it owes in interest expense (e.g., $9,292 in Year 1). This *excess* payment serves to *decrease* the book value of the liability each year (e.g., by $708 in Year 1).

> **Important Shortcut 2**
>
> To determine the book value of the liability at any point in time, simply compute the present value of the bond's remaining cash flows, discounting them at market interest rates at issuance.
>
> Closing Liability (Year 2): FV = $100,000; PMT = $10,000; N = 2; I/Y = 9 CPT PV; PV = $101,759

> If the straight-line method were used, the premium would be evenly amortized over the term of the bonds. In this scenario, the premium of $3,240 would be amortized by $810 each year. Annual interest expense under the straight-line method would be $10,000 – $810 = $9,190.

Effect on Financial Statements

Balance sheet: For bonds issued at a premium, the book value of the liability decreases over the life of the bond. The entire premium ($3,240) is amortized over the 4 years. The value of the liability at the end of Year 4 equals the par value, which is the amount that must be paid to investors at maturity.

Income statement: Interest expense declines every year in line with the decreasing book value of the liability.

Statement of cash flows: For bonds issued at a premium, the inflow recorded at issuance under CFF ($103,240) is *greater* than the outflow from CFF at maturity ($100,000). Coupon payments ($10,000) are deducted from CFO every year.

Zero-Coupon Bonds

Zero-coupon bonds accrue interest over their terms. No coupon payments are made and the lump sum payment at maturity includes repayment of principal and interest. Zero-coupon bonds are steeply discounted instruments because coupon rates (zero) fall significantly short of the compensation required by the market (market interest rate at issuance) for investing in them.

Example 1-2: Zero-Coupon Bonds

A company issues a 4-year, $100,000 par, zero-coupon bond when market interest rates equal 10%. Calculate the proceeds from bond issuance, the periodic interest expense, and the closing value of the liability at the end of each year.

Solution

The amount that the company receives upon bond issuance equals $68,301 (FV = –$100,000: N = 4; I/Y = 10%; PMT = 0; CPT PV; PV → $68,301). Annual interest expense and the closing values of the liability are calculated below:

Year	Beginning Liability	Interest Expense	Coupon Payment	Change in Liability	Closing Liability
0					68,301
1	68,301	6,830	0	6,830	75,131
2	75,131	7,513	0	7,513	82,645
3	82,645	8,265	0	8,265	90,909
4	90,910	9,091	0	9,091	100,000
Total		**31,699**	**0**	**31,699**	

> Notice that for zero coupon bonds, interest expense each year equals the amount of discount amortized each year.

Treatment of Noncurrent Liabilities under U.S. GAAP and IFRS

Costs like printing, legal fees, and other charges are incurred when debt is issued. Under **IFRS**, these costs are included in the measurement of the liability. Under **U.S. GAAP** on the other hand, companies usually capitalize these costs and write them off over the bond's term. Therefore, the liability value recognized on the balance sheet equals the amount of sales proceeds.

Under **IFRS** and **U.S. GAAP**, cash outflows related to bond issuance costs are usually netted against bond proceeds and reported as financing cash flows.

U.S. GAAP requires interest payments on bonds to be classified under CFO. **IFRS** allows more flexibility in that classification of interest payments as CFO or CFF is permitted. Typically cash interest payments are not disclosed on the face of the cash flow statement, but companies are required to disclose interest paid separately.

Amortization of the bond discount/premium is a noncash item so it has no effect on cash flows (aside from the effect on taxable income). In the reconciliation of net income to operating cash flow, amortization of a discount (premium) is added back to (deducted from) net income.

Fair Value Reporting Option

When a company uses the effective interest method to amortize bond discounts and premiums, the book value of debt is based on market interest rates at issuance. Over the life of the bonds, as market interest rates fluctuate the actual value of the firm's debt deviates from its reported book value. For example, if interest rates rise, the current market value of debt would fall. The reported book value of debt (based on the market interest rates at issuance) would be *higher* than the true economic value of the firm's obligations. In this case, using the book value will *overstate* leverage levels as the firm is actually better off than its financial statements indicate.

Two companies with identical book values of debt could have issued debt in very different circumstances. One could have issued debt at lower and older interest rates, while the other may have issued debt at higher current rates. The former is in the better economic position because the true economic value of its obligations is *lower.*

Recently, companies have been allowed to report financing liabilities at fair value. Companies that choose to report their financing liabilities at fair value report gains (losses) on their profit and loss statements (P&Ls) when market interest rates increase (decrease) as the carrying value of their obligations (liabilities) falls (rises).

If fair values are not explicitly reported on the financial statements, **IFRS** and **U.S. GAAP** both require companies to disclose the fair value of their financing liabilities. An analysis of a company could be materially affected if the company's reported carrying amount of debt (based on amortized cost) is significantly different from the fair value of its liabilities.

> Reporting standards for financial investments and derivatives require companies to report a significant portion of their assets at fair values. Measuring financial liabilities at other than fair value, when financial assets are measured at fair value, results in earnings volatility. This volatility is the result of using different bases of measurement for financial assets and financial liabilities.

LOS 32c: Explain the derecognition of debt. **Vol 3, pp 523–525**

> Few companies opt to report debt at fair values on the balance sheet.
>
> Most companies report the fair values of financial liabilities in disclosures.
>
> The primary exception to the disclosure occurs when fair value cannot be reliably measured.

Derecognition of Debt

A company may leave the bonds that it issues outstanding until maturity or retire them prior to maturity by either purchasing them from the open market or calling them (if a call provision exists). If the company leaves the bonds outstanding until maturity, it pays investors the par value of the bonds at maturity.

However, if the company decides to retire the bonds prior to maturity, the book value of the liability is reduced to zero and a gain or loss on extinguishment is computed by subtracting the amount paid to retire the bonds from their book value. For example, if a liability with a book value of $5 million is retired before maturity for $5.25 million, there is a loss on extinguishment of $0.25 million.

- Under **U.S. GAAP**, because issuance costs are capitalized any unamortized issuance costs must also be subtracted from gains on extinguishment.
- Under **IFRS**, issuance costs are included in the book value of the liability so there is no need to adjust the gain on extinguishment for these expenses.

The gain or loss on extinguishment is reported as a separate line item on the income statement if significant, and more details regarding the redemption are discussed in the management discussion & analysis (MD&A) section. Cash paid to redeem the bond is classified as a financing cash outflow.

If the indirect method is used to report cash flow from operating activities, net income is adjusted for the gain (loss) on extinguishment by subtracting (adding) it as it arises from nonoperating activities.

LOS 32d: Describe the role of debt covenants in protecting creditors. Vol 3, pp 525–527

Debt contracts often include clauses that protect bondholders by limiting the issuer's ability to invest, pay dividends, or make other strategic and operating decisions. These restrictions or covenants also benefit borrowers (issuers) in that they reduce default risk and lower the cost of borrowing. Common covenants include:

- Maintenance of pledged collateral.
- Restrictions on dividend payments.
- Requirements to meet certain working capital levels.
- Maximum levels of leverage.

When a company violates a covenant it is said to be in default. In the event of default, bondholders can choose to waive the covenant, renegotiate, or call for repayment. Covenants are discussed in more detail in the Fixed Income section.

LOS 32e: Describe the financial statement presentation of and disclosures relating to debt. Vol 3, pp 527–530

A comprehensive example discussing the financial statement presentation and disclosures relating to debt is included in our practice questions.

On the balance sheet, long-term liabilities are listed as one aggregate figure for all liabilities due after one year. Liabilities due within one year are included in short-term liabilities (current liabilities). Financial statement footnotes provide more information on the nature and types of long-term debt issued by the company. They usually include:

- Stated and effective interest rates.
- Maturity dates.
- Restrictions imposed by creditors (covenants).
- Pledged collateral.
- Scheduled repayments over the next 5 years.

More information regarding a firm's debt and off balance-sheet financing sources can be found in the MD&A section. The information in the footnotes and MD&A section can be used to forecast patterns and levels of future cash flows.

LOS 32f: Explain the motivations for leasing assets instead of purchasing them. Vol 3, pp 530–531

A lease is a contract between the owner of the asset (lessor) and another party that wants to use the asset (lessee). The lessee gains the right to use the asset for a period of time in return for periodic lease payments. Leasing an asset holds the following advantages over purchasing the asset:

- Leases often have fixed interest rates.
- They require no down payment so they conserve cash.
- At the end of the lease, the asset can be returned to the lessor so the lessee escapes the risk of obsolescence and is not burdened with having to find a buyer for the asset.
- The lessor may be in a better position to value and dispose of the asset.
- Negotiated lease contracts usually have less restrictions than borrowing contracts.
- The lessor can take advantage of the tax benefits of ownership such as depreciation and interest.
- In the United States, leases can be structured as synthetic leases, where the company can gain tax benefits of ownership while not reflecting the asset on its financial statements.

LOS 32g: Distinguish between a finance lease and an operating lease from the perspectives of the lessor and the lessee. Vol 3, pp 531–548

LOS 32h: Determine the initial recognition, initial measurement, and subsequent measurement of finance leases. Vol 3, pp 531–548

Lessee's Perspective

U.S. GAAP requires a lessee to classify a lease as a capital lease if **any** of the following conditions hold:

> Finance lease is **IFRS** terminology and capital lease is **U.S. GAAP** terminology.

1. The lease transfers ownership of the asset to the lessee at the end of the term.
2. A bargain purchase option exists.
3. The lease term is greater than 75% of the asset's useful economic life.
4. The present value of the lease payments at inception exceeds 90% of the fair value of the leased asset.

If none of these conditions hold, the lessee may treat the lease as an operating lease.

Under **IFRS**, classification of a lease depends on whether all the risks and rewards of ownership are transferred to the lessee. If they are, the lease is classified as a finance lease; if they are not, the lease is classified as an operating lease.

Operating Lease (Lessee's Perspective)

The accounting treatment for an operating lease is similar to that of simply renting an asset for a period of time. The asset is not purchased; instead, payments are made for using it.

Under an operating lease, no lease-related entries are made on the balance sheet. The firm has effectively rented a piece of equipment. It has not purchased the asset so there is no addition to fixed assets, and it has not borrowed any money to finance the purchase, so there are no related liabilities.

Accounting Entries at Inception

Balance sheet: None, because no asset or liability is recognized.
Income statement: None, because the asset has not been used yet.
Cash flow statement: None, because there has been no cash transaction.

Accounting Entries Every Year During the Term of the Lease

Balance sheet: None, because no lease-related assets and liabilities are recognized.
Income statement: Leasehold (rental) expense is charged every year.
Cash flow statement: The lease payment is classified as a cash outflow from operating activities.

Capital or Finance Lease (Lessee's Perspective)

A finance lease requires the company to recognize a lease-related asset and liability on its balance sheet at inception of the lease. The accounting treatment for a finance lease is similar to that of purchasing an asset and financing the purchase with a long-term loan.

Accounting Entries at Inception

Balance sheet: The present value of lease payments is recognized as a long-lived asset. The same amount is also recognized as a noncurrent liability.
Income statement: None because the asset has not been used yet.
Cash flow statement: None because no cash transaction has occurred. Disclosure of lease inception is required as a "significant noncash financing and investing activity."

Accounting Entries Every Year During the Term of the Lease

Balance sheet: The value of the asset falls every year as it is depreciated. Interest is charged on the liability as the appropriate discount rate times the beginning-of-year value of the liability. The excess of the lease payment over the year's interest expense reduces the liability.
Income statement: Depreciation expense (against the asset) and interest expense (on the liability) are charged every year.
Cashflow statement: The portion of the lease payment equal to the interest expense is subtracted from CFO, while the remainder that serves to reduce the liability is subtracted from CFF.

Example 2-1: Lease Classification by Lessees

ABC Company leases an asset for 4 years, making annual payments of $10,000. The appropriate discount rate is 7%. Illustrate the effects on the financial statements if the lease is classified as a finance lease and an operating lease.

Solution

First let us work through the effects on the financial statements of the lessee if the lease is classified as a **finance lease**.

The present value of the lease payments is recognized as an asset and a liability. The PV of the lease payments equals $33,872 (PMT = $10,000; N = 4; I/Y = 7; CPT PV).

The table below illustrates the calculation of periodic interest expense and the ending value of the liability for a finance lease:

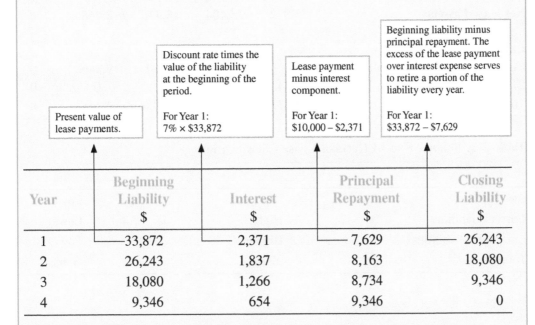

Year	Beginning Liability $	Interest $	Principal Repayment $	Closing Liability $
1	33,872	2,371	7,629	26,243
2	26,243	1,837	8,163	18,080
3	18,080	1,266	8,734	9,346
4	9,346	654	9,346	0

There are two ways to calculate the ending value of the liability for any period:

1. Opening liability minus the excess of the lease payment over the period's interest expense.
   For Year 1: 33,872 − (10,000 − 2,371) = $26,243

2. Present value of remaining lease payments.
   For Year 1: N = 3, I/Y = 7, PMT = $10,000, CPT PV; PV = $26,243

In an **operating** lease, no lease-related asset or liability is recognized on the balance sheet of the lessee. The lease payments are classified as operating expenses on the income statement.

Now let us compare the effects on the lessee's financial statements of classifying a lease as an operating or finance lease (see Tables 2-1–2-6):

Balance Sheet

Value of asset recognized at inception = $33,872 (Present value of lease payments). Annual depreciation (Straight-line) = $8,468

	Year 0 $	Year 1 $	Year 2 $	Year 3 $	Year 4 $
Assets					
Leased assets	33,872	33,872	33,872	33,872	33,872
Accumulated depreciation	0	8,468	16,936	25,404	33,872
Net leased assets	**33,872**	**25,404**	**16,936**	**8,468**	**0**
Liabilities					
Current portion of lease obligation	7,629	8,163	8,734	9,346	0
LT debt: Lease obligation	26,243	18,080	9,346	0	0
Total liabilities	**33,872**	**26,243**	**18,080**	**9,346**	**0**

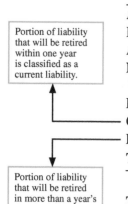

Portion of liability that will be retired within one year is classified as a current liability.

Portion of liability that will be retired in more than a year's time is classified as a long-term liability.

Table 2-1: Balance Sheet Effects of Lease Classification

Balance Sheet Item	Finance Lease	Operating Lease
Assets	Higher	Lower
Current liabilities	Higher	Lower
Long-term liabilities	Higher	Lower
Total cash	Same	Same

Income Statement

In an operating lease, the annual lease payment is recognized as an operating expense, while in a finance lease, the asset is depreciated and interest expense is charged against operating income (EBIT).

	Finance Lease			Operating Lease	
Year	Depreciation Expense $	Interest Expense $	Total Expense $	Rent Expense $	Total Expense $
1	8,468	2,371	10,839	10,000	10,000
2	8,468	1,837	10,305	10,000	10,000
3	8,468	1,266	9,734	10,000	10,000
4	8,468	654	9,122	10,000	10,000
TOTAL	**33,872**	**6,128**	**40,000**	**40,000**	**40,000**

Table 2-2: Income Statement Effects of Lease Classification

Income Statement Item	Finance Lease	Operating Lease
Operating expenses	Lower (Depreciation)	Higher (Lease payment)
Nonoperating expenses	Higher (Interest expense)	Lower (None)
EBIT (operating income)	Higher	Lower
Total expenses: early years	Higher	Lower
Total expenses: later years	Lower	Higher
Net income: early years	Lower	Higher
Net income: later years	Higher	Lower

Statement of Cash Flows

Under an operating lease, the lease payments are deducted from CFO, while for a finance lease the interest expense portion of the lease payment is deducted from CFO and the remainder that serves to decrease the value of the liability is deducted from CFF.

	Finance Lease			Operating Lease
Year	CFO $	CFF $	Total $	CFO $
1	–2,371	–7,629	–10,000	–10,000
2	–1,837	–8,163	–10,000	–10,000
3	–1,266	–8,734	–10,000	–10,000
4	–654	–9,346	–10,000	–10,000

Table 2-3: Cash Flow Effects of Lease Classification

CF Item	Finance Lease	Operating Lease
CFO	Higher	Lower
CFF	Lower	Higher
Total cash flow	Same	Same

Table 2-4: Impact of Lease Classification on Financial Ratios

Ratio	Numerator Under Finance Lease	Denominator Under Finance Lease	Effect on Ratio	Ratio Better or Worse Under Finance Lease
Asset turnover	Sales–same	Assets–higher	Lower	Worse
Return on assets (ROA)*	Net income–lower	Assets–higher	Lower	Worse
Current ratio	Current assets–same	Current liabilities–higher	Lower	Worse
Leverage ratios (D/E and D/A**)	Debt–higher	Equity–same Assets–higher	Higher	Worse
Return on equity (ROE)*	Net income–lower	Equity–same	Lower	Worse

> * In early years of the lease agreement.
>
> Note: Lower ROE under a finance lease is due to lower net income (numerator effect), while lower ROA is primarily due to higher assets (denominator effect).

**Notice that both the numerator and the denominator for the D/A ratio are higher when classifying the lease as a finance lease. Beware of such exam questions. When the numerator and the denominator of any ratio are heading in the same direction (either increasing or decreasing), determine which of the two is changing more in percentage terms. If the percentage change in the numerator is greater than the percentage change in the denominator, the numerator effect will dominate.

Firms usually have lower levels of total debt compared to total assets. The increase in both debt and assets by classifying the lease as a finance lease will lead to an increase in the debt to asset ratio because the percentage increase in the numerator is greater.

Lessor's Perspective

Under **IFRS**, the lessor must classify the lease as a finance lease if all the risks and rewards of ownership are transferred to the lessee.

Under **U.S. GAAP**, lessors are required to recognize capital leases when any one of the four previously mentioned criteria for recognition of a capital lease by the lessee hold, and the following two criteria also hold:

> When the lease is classified as an operating lease, the asset is listed on the balance sheet of the lessor, who continues to depreciate it. No lease-related asset shows up on the lessee's balance sheet.

1. Collectability of the lease payments is predictable.
2. There are no significant uncertainties regarding the amount of costs still to be incurred by the lessor under the provisions of the lease agreement.

Leases not meeting these criteria must be classified as operating leases because the earning process is not complete.

> When the lease is classified as a finance lease, the lessor removes the long-lived asset from its balance sheet, and instead records a receivable in its books. The lessee records the long-lived asset on its balance sheet and depreciates it.

If the lessor classifies the lease as an operating lease, it records lease revenue when earned, continues to list the asset on its balance sheet, and depreciates it every year on its income statement. If the lessor classifies the lease as a finance lease, it records a receivable equal to the present value of lease payments on its balance sheet and removes the asset from long-lived assets in its books.

Finance Leases

Under **U.S. GAAP**, lessors can classify finance leases into two types:

1. Some manufacturers offer their customers financing options to purchase their products. These sales-type leases result in a gross profit (the normal selling price of the product minus its cost), which is recognized at inception of the lease, and interest income as payments are received over the lease term. In a sales-type lease, the present value of lease payments equals the *selling price* of the asset.

2. Financial institutions and leasing companies offer financial leases that generate interest income only. These are known as direct financing leases, where the present value of lease payments equals the *carrying value* of the asset. Further, there is no gross profit recognition at lease inception.

Example 2-2: Operating Lease Versus Direct Financing Lease—Lessor's Perspective

A company leases out a piece of equipment for 4 years in return for a lease payment of $10,000 every year. At the end of the lease term the asset will have no salvage value. The discount rate applicable is 6% and the carrying value of the leased asset is $34,651.

Solution

We must calculate the present value of lease payments to determine whether the lease should be classified as a sales-type lease or a direct financing lease.

The present value of lease payments equals $34,651 (PMT = $10,000; I/Y = 6; N = 4; FV = 0; CPT PV), which equals the carrying value of the asset on the lessor's books. Therefore, this is a direct financing lease.

At inception, the lessor removes the carrying value of the equipment from long-lived assets in its books (derecognizes the asset). Instead, the lessor recognizes a lease receivable asset equal to the present value of lease payments.

Lease Amortization Schedule

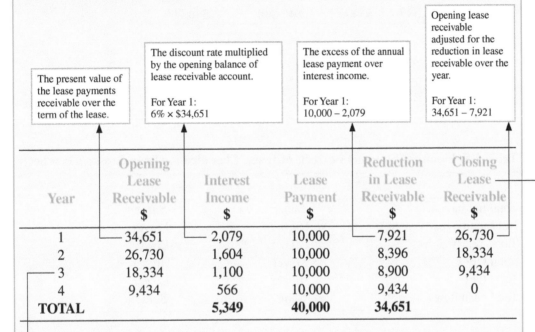

	The present value of the lease payments receivable over the term of the lease.	The discount rate multiplied by the opening balance of lease receivable account. For Year 1: 6% × $34,651	The excess of the annual lease payment over interest income. For Year 1: 10,000 – 2,079	Opening lease receivable adjusted for the reduction in lease receivable over the year. For Year 1: 34,651 – 7,921	This asset is reported on the balance sheet.

Year	Opening Lease Receivable $	Interest Income $	Lease Payment $	Reduction in Lease Receivable $	Closing Lease Receivable $
1	34,651	2,079	10,000	7,921	26,730
2	26,730	1,604	10,000	8,396	18,334
3	18,334	1,100	10,000	8,900	9,434
4	9,434	566	10,000	9,434	0
TOTAL		5,349	40,000	34,651	

For Year 3, the lessee owed the company interest of $1,100. However, the total payment made by the lessee in Year 3 was $10,000. The excess ($10,000–$1,100) reduced the total receivable amount.

Effects on Income Statement

Depreciable value = $34,651
Life of asset = 4 years
Annual depreciation = $8662.75

In an operating lease, the lessor realizes rental income every year, and charges depreciation expense on the asset leased out.

		Direct Financing Lease	Operating Lease		
Year		**Income ($)**	**Revenue ($)**	**Depreciation ($)**	**Income ($)**
1	Interest income	2,079	10,000	8,662.75	1,337.25
2	Interest income	1,604	10,000	8,662.75	1,337.25
3	Interest income	1,100	10,000	8,662.75	1,337.25
4	Interest income	566	10,000	8,662.75	1,337.25
TOTAL		**$5,349**			**$5,349**

In the early years, higher income is recognized under a direct financing lease. This results in more taxes being paid out sooner.

Total income over the term of the lease is the same across both classifications.

Higher income is recognized in later years under an operating lease. Payment of taxes is therefore, delayed for a period.

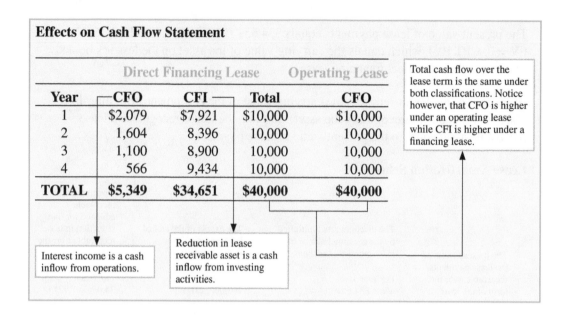

Effects on Cash Flow Statement

	Direct Financing Lease			Operating Lease
Year	CFO	CFI	Total	CFO
1	$2,079	$7,921	$10,000	$10,000
2	1,604	8,396	10,000	10,000
3	1,100	8,900	10,000	10,000
4	566	9,434	10,000	10,000
TOTAL	$5,349	$34,651	$40,000	$40,000

Total cash flow over the lease term is the same under both classifications. Notice however, that CFO is higher under an operating lease while CFI is higher under a financing lease.

Interest income is a cash inflow from operations.

Reduction in lease receivable asset is a cash inflow from investing activities.

Table 2-5: Financial Statement Effects of Lease Classification from Lessor's Perspective

	Financing Lease	Operating Lease
Total net income	Same	Same
Net income (early years)	Higher	Lower
Taxes (early years)	Higher	Lower
Total CFO	Lower	Higher
Total CFI	Higher	Lower
Total cash flow	Same	Same

Sales-Type Leases

In a sales-type lease, the present value of lease payments is greater than the carrying value of the asset in the lessor's books. Consequently, the lessor recognized a gross profit equal to the difference between the two in the year of inception, and recognizes interest income over the term of the lease.

Example 2-3: Sales-Type Leases

A company leases out a piece of equipment for 4 years in return for a lease payment of $10,000 every year. At the end of the lease term, the asset will have no salvage value. The discount rate applicable is 6% and the carrying value of the asset is $30,000.

Solution

Notice that we are working with similar numbers as in Example 2-2. We have only changed the carrying value of the asset on the lessor's books to $30,000 in this example.

Since the present value of lease payments (which we have previously calculated as $34,651) is *greater* than the carrying value of the asset, this is a sales-type lease.

At the inception, the lessor will recognize a gross profit of $4,651 (34,651 − 30,000).

The lessor also recognizes interest income over the term of the lease. Notice that interest income is the same as we had calculated in the direct financing lease in Example 2-2. We only changed the carrying value of the asset in this example to illustrate that under a sales-type lease, in addition to interest income the lessor also recognizes a gross profit on sale that increases total income over the lease, and results in a significant contribution to profits at inception.

Lease Amortization Schedule

Year	Opening Lease Receivable	Interest Income	Lease Payment	Reduction in Lease Receivable	Closing Lease Receivable
1	$34,651	$2,079	$10,000	$7,921	$26,730
2	26,730	1,604	10,000	8,396	18,334
3	18,334	1,100	10,000	8,900	9,434
4	9,434	566	10,000	9,434	0
TOTAL		$5,349	$40,000	$34,651	

Under **IFRS**, the present value of the lease payments receivable is recognized as a net investment in the lease asset. The leased asset is derecognized and removed from noncurrent assets.

For lessors that are manufacturers or dealers, initial direct costs are expensed when the selling profit is recognized (typically at inception of the lease).

- Sales revenue equals the lower of fair value and the present value of minimum lease payments.
- The cost of sale equals the carrying amount of the leased asset minus the present value of the expected salvage value.

> A comprehensive example discussing the financial statement presentation and disclosures relating to finance and operating leases is included in our practice questions.

LOS 32i: Compare the disclosures relating to finance and operating leases. Vol 3, pp 531–548

Disclosures

Under **U.S. GAAP**, given the explicit standards required to classify a lease as a capital lease, companies can easily structure the terms of a lease in a manner that allows them to report it as an operating lease (it must simply ensure that none of the four capital lease-classifying criteria are met in the terms of the lease).

Lease disclosures require a company to list the lease obligations of the firm for the next 5 years under all operating and finance leases. These disclosures allow analysts to evaluate the extent of off-balance sheet financing used by the company. They can also be used to determine the effects on the financial statements if all the operating leases were capitalized and brought "onto" the balance sheet. See Table 2-6.

Under **IFRS**, companies are required to:
- Present finance lease obligations as a part of debt on the balance sheet.
- Disclose the amount of total debt attributable to obligations under finance leases.
- Present information about all lease obligations (operating and finance leases).

Table 2-6: Summary of Financial Statement Impact of Leases on the Lessee and Lessor[1]

Lessee	Balance Sheet	Income Statement	Statement of Cash Flows
Operating Lease	No effect	Reports rent expense	Rent payment is an operating cash outflow.
Finance Lease under IFRS (capital lease under U.S. GAAP)	Recognizes leased asset and lease liability	Reports depreciation expense on leased asset	Reduction of lease liability is a financing cash outflow.
		Reports interest expense on lease liability	Interest portion of lease payment is either an operating or financing cash outflow under **IFRS** and an operating cash outflow under **U.S. GAAP**.

Lessor			
Operating Lease	Retains asset on balance sheet	Reports rent income	Rent payments received are an operating cash inflow.
		Reports depreciation expense on leased asset	
Finance Lease[a]			
When present value of lease payments equals the carrying amount of the leased asset (called a direct financing lease in **U.S. GAAP**)	Removes asset from balance sheet Recognizes lease receivable	Reports interest revenue on lease receivable	Interest portion of lease payment received is either an operating or investing cash inflow under **IFRS** and an operating cash inflow under **U.S. GAAP**. Receipt of lease principal is an investing cash inflow.[b]
When present value of lease payments exceeds the carrying amount of the leased asset (called a sales-type lease in **U.S. GAAP**)	Removes asset Recognizes lease receivable	Reports profit on sale Reports interest revenue on lease receivable	Interest portion of lease payment received is either an operating or investing cash inflow under **IFRS** and an operating cash inflow under **U.S. GAAP**. Receipt of lease principal is an investing cash inflow.[b]

[a] **U.S. GAAP** distinguishes between a direct financing lease and a sales-type lease, but **IFRS** does not. The accounting is the same for **IFRS** and **U.S. GAAP** despite this additional classification under **U.S. GAAP**.

[b] If providing leases is part of a company's normal business activity, the cash flows related to the leases are classified as operating cash.

1 - Exhibit 2, Volume 3, CFA Program Curriculum 2014

LESSON 3: PENSIONS AND OTHER POST-EMPLOYMENT BENEFITS AND EVALUATING SOLVENCY

LOS 32j: Compare the presentation and disclosure of defined contribution and defined benefit pension plans. Vol 3, pp 548–551

Companies may offer a variety of benefits to their employees following their retirement. Examples of these benefits include pension plans, health care plans, and medical insurance. In this LOS, our focus is on pension plans. There are two main types of pension plans:

Defined-contribution plans are pension plans in which the company is required to contribute a certain (agreed-upon or defined) amount of funds into the plan. However, the company makes no commitment regarding the future value of plan assets. Further, investment decisions are left to employees, who bear all the investment risk. Since the company's annual contribution is defined and limited to the required contribution (i.e., the company has no further liability once the contribution has been made) accounting for defined-contribution plans is relatively straightforward.

- On the *income statement*, the company recognizes the amount it is required to contribute into the plan as pension expense for the period.
- On the *balance sheet*, the company records a decrease in cash. If the agreed-upon amount is not deposited into the plan during a particular period, the outstanding amount is recognized as a liability.
- On the *cash flow statement*, the outflow is treated as an operating cash flow.

Under a defined-benefit plan, the company promises to pay future benefits to the employee during retirement. For example, a company could promise its employees an annual pension payment each year after her retirement until her death. The annual payment may be based on a formula that considers the final salary at retirement and the number of years of service provided by the employee to the company.

To illustrate, consider a company that determines an employee's annual pension benefit as $0.02 \times$ Final salary at retirement $\times$ Number of years of service. A retiree who served the company for 20 years and had a final salary at retirement of $200,000 would, under the terms of this defined-benefit plan, be entitled to an annual pension payment of $0.02 \times \$200,000 \times 20 = \$80,000$ each year during her retirement until her death.

The company estimates the total amount of benefits that it expects to pay out to an employee during her retirement and then allocates the present value of these payments (this present values is known as pension obligation) over the employee's employment as a part of pension expense. A number of assumptions are made to determine the pension obligation, including:

- Expected salary at date of retirement.
- Number of years the employee is expected to live after retirement.
- The discount rate (typically assumed to be the high-quality corporate bond yield).

An important point that you must understand at this stage is that for each additional year of service provided by an employee (as the number of years of service increases) the annual retirement pension payment owed by the company to the employee would increase, resulting in an increase in the pension obligation (the present value of total payments expected to be made to a retiree).

Defined-benefit pension plans are typically funded through a separate legal entity (usually a pension trust fund). The company makes payments into the fund and invests these assets with a view to accumulating sufficient assets in the plan to meet payment obligations to retirees.

On the *balance sheet,* a company may record a net pension asset or a net pension liability.

- If the fair value of plan assets is greater than the pension obligation (the present value of estimated payments to retirees) the plan has a surplus, so the company's balance sheet will reflect a net pension asset.
- If the fair value of plan assets is lower than the pension obligation the plan has a deficit, so the company's balance sheet will reflect a net pension liability.

On the *income statement,* the change in net pension liability or asset is recognized either in profit and loss or in other comprehensive income.

Under **IFRS**, the change in net pension asset or liability each period (pension expense) has three general components:

- Employee service costs: The service cost during a period for an employee refers to the present value of the increase in pension benefit earned by the employee as a result of providing one more year of service to the company. Service costs also include past service costs (which reflect changes in the value of the pension obligation due to employees' service in past periods when a plan is initiated or when plan amendments are made). Employee service costs are recognized as pension expense in profit and loss.

- Net interest expense or income: This is calculated as the net pension liability or asset at the beginning of a period multiplied by the discount rate used to estimate the pension obligation (present value of expected pension payments). Net interest expense or income is also recognized as pension expense in profit and loss.

- Remeasurements: Remeasurements include (1) actuarial gains and losses and (2) the actual return on plan assets less any return included in net interest expense or income.

  - Actuarial gains and losses arise when changes are made in any of the assumptions used to estimate the company's pension obligation (e.g., mortality rates, life expectancy, rate of compensation increase, and retirement age).
  - The actual return on plan assets (which are invested in a wide variety of asset classes including equity instruments) typically differs from the amount included in net interest expense or income (which is usually calculated based on just the high-quality corporate bond yield).

  Finally, note that remeasurements are not amortized into profit and loss over time; instead they are recognized in other comprehensive income.

Under **U.S. GAAP**, the change in the net pension asset or liability each period (pension expense) has five general components:

- Employee service costs for the period: These are recognized in profit and loss in the period incurred.

- Interest expense accrued on the beginning pension obligation: Interest costs are added to pension expense because the company does not pay out service costs earned by the employee over the year until her retirement. The company owes these benefits to the employee, so interest accrues on the amount of benefits outstanding. Interest expense is also recognized in profit and loss for the period.

- Expected return on plan assets: This reduces the amount of pension expense recognized in profit and loss for the period.

- Past service costs: These are recognized in other comprehensive income in the period during which they are incurred, and are subsequently amortized into pension expense over the future service period of employees covered by the plan.

- Actuarial gains and losses: These are also recognized in other comprehensive income in the period in which they occur and amortized into pension expense over time.

> Effectively, **U.S. GAAP** allows companies to "smooth" the effects of past service costs and actuarial gains and losses on pension expense.

Note that pension expense is not directly reported on the income statement:
- For employees directly related to the production process, pension expense is added to inventory and expensed through cost of goods sold (COGS).
- For employees not directly related to the production process, pension expense is included in selling, general & administrative (SG&A).

However, detailed pension plan-related disclosures are included in the notes to the financial statements (see Example 3-1).

Example 3-1: Pension Obligations

Jupiter Inc. reported the following disclosures related to retirement pension obligations in its 2011 annual report. The company follows **IFRS**.

($ in Millions)	2011	2010
Retirement obligations	2,980	2,510
Plan assets	1,055	985

1. Determine the pension-related amount that would be reported on Jupiter's balance sheet for the year 2011.
2. Indicate the amount of pension expense that would be recognized in 2011. Also describe how these expenses would be reported under the updated standards.

Solution

1.

	2011 $	2010 $
Retirement Obligations	2,980	2,510
Plan Assets	(1,055)	(985)
Deficit/ (surplus)	1,925	1,525

The positive funded status of $1,925 for 2011 indicates that the company's pension plan is underfunded (retirement obligations exceed the value of assets that have been reserved for them). This is the amount that would be reported as a liability in Jupiter's 2011 balance sheet.

2. Total pension expense reported in 2011 would amount to $400 million, which equals the change in the pension deficit over the year.

Since the company follows **IFRS**, pension cost would be reported as follows:
- Service costs and net interest expense (on the beginning pension deficit) would be reported in profit and loss.
- Remeasurements would be reported in other comprehensive income.

LOS 32k: Calculate and interpret leverage and coverage ratios.
Vol 3, pp 551–553

Evaluating Solvency Ratios

Solvency refers to the ability of a company to satisfy its long-term debt obligation (both principal and interest payments). Ratio analysis is frequently used to evaluate a company's solvency levels relative to its competitors. The two main types of solvency ratios used are leverage ratios and coverage ratios.

Leverage ratios are derived from balance sheet numbers and measure the extent to which a company uses debt rather than equity to finance its assets. Higher leverage ratios indicate weaker solvency.

Coverage ratios focus more on income statement and cash flow numbers to measure the company's ability to service its debt. Higher coverage ratios indicate stronger solvency.

Table 3-1 summarizes the two types of solvency ratios. See Example 3-2.

Table 3-1: Definitions of Commonly Used Solvency Ratios

Solvency Ratios	Description	Numerator	Denominator
Leverage Ratios			
Debt-to-assets ratio	Expresses the percentage of total assets financed by debt	Total debt	Total assets
Debt-to-capital ratio	Measures the percentage of a company's total capital (debt + equity) financed by debt.	Total debt	Total debt + Total shareholders' equity
Debt-to-equity ratio	Measures the amount of debt financing relative to equity financing	Total debt	Total shareholders' equity
Financial leverage ratio	Measures the amount of total assets supported by one money unit of equity	Average total assets	Average shareholders' equity
Coverage Ratios			
Interest coverage ratio	Measures the number of times a company's EBIT could cover its interest payments	EBIT	Interest payments
Fixed charge coverage ratio	Measures the number of times a company's earnings (before interest, taxes and lease payments) can cover the company's interest and lease payments	EBIT + Lease payments	Interest payments + Lease payments

Example 3-2: Evaluating Solvency Ratios

Given below are the solvency ratios for Mercury Inc. and Jupiter Inc. for 2008 and 2009:

Ratio	Mercury Inc.		Jupiter Inc.	
	2008	2009	2008	2009
Debt to assets	10.5%	9.4%	12.4%	4.9%
Debt to capital	13.6%	14.9%	25.8%	8.3%
Debt to equity	17.3%	18.5%	32.5%	9.8%
Interest coverage ratio	32.4	15.4	17.7	74.5

Use the information given in the table to answer the following questions:

1. A. Comment on the changes in the leverage ratios from year to year for both companies.
   B. Comment on the leverage ratios of Mercury relative to Jupiter's.

2. A. Comment on the changes in the interest coverage ratio from year to year for both companies.
   B. Comment on the interest coverage ratio of Mercury Inc. compared to Jupiter Inc.

Solution

1. A. As shown in the table, Mercury's leverage ratios have remained fairly stable. On the other hand, Jupiter's leverage ratios have declined considerably from 2008 to 2009, which suggests that the company's solvency position is improving. The decrease in the company's leverage ratios may have resulted from a decrease in the company's debt and/or an increase in its equity.

   B. In 2008, Mercury's leverage ratios were lower than those of Jupiter. However, the situation completely changed in 2009. This is because the capital structure of Mercury remained fairly constant over the 2 years, while Jupiter was able to bring down the proportion of debt in its capital structure significantly.

2. A. Mercury's interest coverage ratio decreased in 2009. This may be the result of a decrease in the company's operating earnings and/or an increase in its interest expense. On the other hand, Jupiter's interest coverage ratio increased in 2009, which may have been caused by an increase in the company's operating earnings and/or a decrease in its interest expense. Given that Jupiter's leverage ratios have declined significantly, it is more plausible that the increase in its interest coverage ratio is due to a decrease in its interest expense.

   B. Based on the numbers for 2009, Jupiter has a greater ability to cover its interest payment obligations (based on its higher interest coverage ratio) compared to Mercury. However, the (relatively high) interest coverage ratios of both companies continue to suggest that they are comfortably placed to cover interest payments.

STUDY SESSION 10: FINANCIAL REPORTING QUALITY AND FINANCIAL STATEMENT ANALYSIS

READING 33: FINANCIAL REPORTING QUALITY

LESSON 1: CONCEPTUAL OVERVIEW AND QUALITY SPECTRUM OF FINANCIAL REPORTS

LOS 33a: Distinguish between financial reporting quality and quality of reported results (including quality of earnings, cash flow, and balance sheet items). Vol 6, pp 565–567

CONCEPTUAL OVERVIEW

In this Reading, we will talk about two interrelated attributes relating to the quality of a company's financial statements: (1) financial reporting quality and (2) earnings quality.

- Financial reporting quality refers to the usefulness of information contained in the financial reports, including disclosures in notes.
  - High-quality reporting provides information that is useful in investment decision making in that it is relevant and faithfully represents the company's performance and position.
- Earnings quality (or quality of reported results) pertains to the earnings and cash generated by the company's core economic activities and its resulting financial condition.
  - High-quality earnings (1) come from activities that the company will be able to sustain in the future and (2) provide an adequate return on the company's investment.
  - Note that the term, **earnings** quality, encompasses quality of earnings, cash flow, and balance sheet items.

These two attributes are interrelated because earnings quality cannot be evaluated until there is some assurance regarding the quality of financial reporting. If financial reporting quality is low, the information provided is not useful in evaluating company performance or to make investment decisions. Figure 1-1 illustrates this interrelationship and its implications.

Figure 1-1: Relationship between Financial Reporting Quality and Earnings Quality

		Financial Reporting Quality	
		Low	**High**
Earnings (Results) Quality	High	LOW financial reporting quality impedes assessment of earnings quality and impedes valuation.	HIGH financial reporting quality enables assessment. HIGH earnings quality increases company value.
	Low		HIGH financial reporting quality enables assessment. LOW earnings quality decreases company value.

LOS 33b: Describe a spectrum for assessing financial reporting quality.
Vol 6, pp 568–578

LOS 33c: Distinguish between conservative and aggressive accounting.
Vol 6, pp 568–583

QUALITY SPECTRUM OF FINANCIAL REPORTS

The two measures of quality can be combined such that the overall quality of financial reports from a user perspective can be thought of as spanning a continuum from the highest to the lowest (see Figure 1-2).

Figure 1-2: Quality Spectrum of Financial Reports

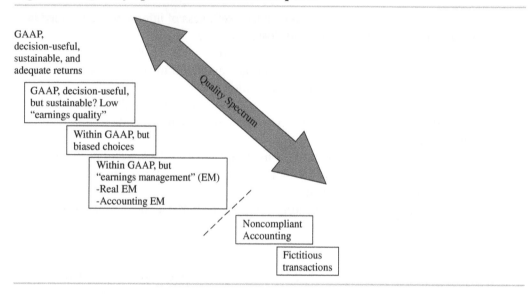

We now describe each of the levels shown in the quality spectrum.

GAAP, Decision-Useful, Sustainable, and Adequate Returns

These are high-quality reports that provide useful information about high-quality earnings.

High-quality financial reports:

- Conform to the accounting standards acceptable in the company's jurisdiction.
- Adhere to all the characteristics of decision-useful information, such as those defined in the *Conceptual Framework*. The fundamental characteristics of useful information are relevance and faithful representation.
  - Relevant information is material and important for decision-making.
  - Faithful representation of information is complete, neutral, and free from error.
- They also meet the enhancing characteristics of useful information as defined by the *Conceptual Framework*.
  - These characteristics include comparability, verifiability, timeliness, and understandability.

> The concept of neutrality is one that we will be discussing in more detail later in the Reading.

High-quality earnings indicate an adequate return on investments. Further, earnings must be derived from activities that the company will likely be able to sustain in the future. Sustainable earnings that provide a high return on investment increase company value.

- An adequate level of return means a return that exceeds the cost of investment and also meets (or even exceeds) the expected return.
- Sustainable activities and sustainable earnings are those that are expected to recur in the future.

GAAP, Decision-Useful, but Sustainable?

This level refers to a situation where high-quality reporting provides useful information, but the information reflects earnings that are not sustainable (low earnings quality). In other words, reporting is of high quality, but the economic reality being depicted is not of high quality. Earnings may be unsustainable because:

- The company cannot expect to earn the same level of return on investment in the future (i.e., earnings are unsustainable).
- Earnings, though sustainable, will not generate a return on investment sufficient to sustain the company (i.e, the company is not earning enough).

Within GAAP, but Biased Accounting Choices

Biased choices result in financial reports that do not faithfully represent the company's true economic situation.

- Management can make aggressive or conservative accounting choices, both of which go against the concept of neutrality, as *unbiased* financial reporting is the ideal. Investors may prefer conservative choices (as they result in positive surprises, which are easier to accept), but biased reporting (conservative or aggressive) adversely affects a user's ability to evaluate a company.
  - Aggressive choices increase a company's reported financial performance and financial position in the current period. These choices can (1) increase reported revenues, (2) increase reported earnings, (3) increase reported operating cash flow, (4) decrease reported expenses, and/or (5) decrease reported debt in the current period.
    - Note that aggressive accounting choices in the current period may lead to depressed reported financial performance and financial position in later periods, thereby creating a sustainability issue.
  - Conservative choices decrease a company's reported financial performance and financial position in the current period. These choices can (1) decrease reported revenues, (2) decrease reported earnings, (3) decrease reported operating cash flow, (4) increase reported expenses, and/or (5) increase reported debt in the current period.
    - Note that conservative accounting choices in the current period may lead to improved reported financial performance and financial position in later periods. Therefore, they do not give rise to a sustainability issue.
- Another source of bias is understatement of earnings volatility (or earnings smoothing). This can result from employing conservative assumptions to understate performance when the company is actually doing well and then using aggressive assumptions when the company is not doing as well.
- Aside from biases in determining reported amounts, biases can also creep into the way information is presented. A company may choose to present information

> Presentation choices are discussed in detail later in the Reading.

in a manner that obscures unfavorable information and/or highlights favorable information.

  ○ For example, emphasizing non-GAAP financial measures like pro forma earnings or non-GAAP operating profit to turn attention away from unfavorable financial results would be an aggressive presentation choice.

Poor reporting quality often comes with poor earnings quality, as aggressive accounting assumptions may be employed to obscure poor performance. However, it is also possible for poor reporting quality to come with high-quality earnings if:

* The company is unable to produce high-quality reports due to inadequate internal controls.
* The company employs conservative accounting assumptions to make current performance look worse. A company may engage in such behavior to (1) avoid political attention or (2) keep some "hidden reserves," which it can tap into to improve future profitability.

Note that as we go down the spectrum the concepts of reporting quality and earnings quality become less distinguishable; it is necessary to have some degree of reporting quality in order to assess earnings quality.

Within GAAP, but "Earnings Management"

Earnings management can be defined as "making intentional choices or taking deliberate action to influence reported earnings and their interpretation." The difference between making biased choices and earnings management is essentially *intent*. There are two ways that earnings can be managed:

* They can be managed by taking real actions.
  ○ For example, a company may defer R&D expenses until the next year to improve reported performance in the current year.
* They can be managed through accounting choices.
  ○ For example, a company may change certain accounting estimates such as estimated product returns, bad debts expense, or asset impairment to manipulate reported performance.

Note that it is typically very difficult to determine intent, so there is a very fine line between earnings management and biased accounting choices.

Departures from GAAP—Noncompliant Accounting

Financial information that deviates from GAAP is obviously of low quality. Further, such financial information cannot be used to assess earnings quality, as comparisons with other entities or earlier periods cannot be made.

* Examples of noncompliant accounting were found in the PPI (where currency losses suffered in the normal course of operations were reported directly through equity instead of through the P&L) and WorldCom (where a significant amount of operating expenses were capitalized to overstate profits) scandals.

Departures from GAAP—Fictitious Transactions

There have been instances of companies using fictitious transactions to (1) fraudulently obtain investments by inflating company performance, or (2) obscure fraudulent misappropriation of company assets.

* Examples of such fraud can be found in the Equity Funding Corp (where fictitious revenues and even fictitious policyholders were created) and Parmalat (where fictitious bank balances were reported) scandals.

Differentiate between Conservative and Aggressive Accounting

When it comes to financial reporting, the ideal situation would be if financial reporting were **unbiased** (i.e., neither conservative nor aggressive). The common perception is that investors may prefer or are perceived to prefer conservative accounting because positive surprises are more acceptable than negative surprises, while management may prefer or is perceived to prefer aggressive accounting as it improves reported financial performance in the current period. However, when it comes to establishing expectations about the future, financial reporting that is relevant and faithfully representative is most useful.

Conservatism in Accounting Standards

The *Conceptual Framework* supports the neutrality of information (i.e., an unbiased selection and presentation of financial information). Conservatism directly conflicts with the concept of neutrality as it leads to biased estimates of assets, liabilities, and earnings. Despite efforts to encourage neutrality in financial reporting, some conservatively biased standards remain.

An example can be found in the oil-and-gas exploration industry, where recognition of revenues generally requires a higher level of verification than recognition of expenses. In this industry, the "good news" event is the discovery of new oil and gas reserves, which can be tapped into in future years to generate profits. Unfortunately, however, one would not learn about this fact from simply looking at a company's financials because accounting standards dictate that revenue can only be recognized once the resources have been extracted, a customer has been identified, and the product has been shipped. As a result, recognition of revenues from new oil and gas reserves is deferred until several years after their initial discovery. Further, accounting standards also require extraction costs to be expensed rather than capitalized, which leads to reduced profits in periods between discovery and first sales from new reserves despite the fact that these reserves possess saleable value.

The previous example illustrates how conservatism in accounting standards (which leads to a delay in recognition of profits until they are highly verifiable) can impair the relevance of financial statements. Note that many jurisdictions, in order to mitigate this issue, now require extensive disclosures from such companies.

Finally, note that different sets of accounting standards may have different degrees of conservatism embedded in them. For example, when it comes to long-lived assets, IFRS recognizes impairment when the recoverable amount (fair value) is less than the carrying amount, while U.S. GAAP recognizes impairment if the sum of undiscounted future cash flows from the asset is less than the carrying amount. If the recoverable amount were less than the sum of undiscounted cash flows, an impairment charge would be more likely under IFRS, making it relatively more conservative. Note that IFRS does allow reversals of impairment charges, while U.S. GAAP does not.

Other examples of conservatism in accounting standards include research costs, litigation costs, insurance recoverables, and commodity inventories.

Benefits of Conservatism

- Given asymmetrical information, conservatism may protect contracting parties with less information and higher risk.
  - For example, shareholders enjoy limited liability so bond investors have limited recourse to individual shareholders to recover losses from default. Financial statements prepared with conservative assumptions may leave room for a "cushion" to protect bond holders.
- Conservatism reduces the possibility of litigation. A company is highly unlikely to be sued if it understated good news/overstated bad news.
- Conservatism protects politicians and lawmakers, as it reduces the possibility that companies under their supervision have overstated earnings or assets.
- In many jurisdictions, companies can lower the present value of their tax payments by employing conservative accounting policies.

Bias in the Application of Accounting Standards

The application of any accounting standard (regardless of whether it is inherently neutral) requires significant amounts of judgment. In order to characterize the application of an accounting standard as conservative or aggressive, we must look at *intent* (rather than at a definition). Intent can be inferred from a careful analysis of disclosures, facts, and circumstances. Examples of biased accounting disguised as conservatism include:

- Big bath behavior: This refers to the strategy of manipulating a company's income statement to make poor results look even worse. The big bath is often implemented in a bad year with a view to inflating subsequent period earnings. New management teams sometimes use the big bath so that poor current performance can be blamed on previous management, while they take credit for the impressive growth that follows in subsequent periods.
- Cookie jar reserve accounting: This refers to the practice of creating a liability when a company incurs an expense that cannot be directly linked to a specific accounting period. Companies may recognize such expenses in periods during which profits are high, as they can afford to take the hit to income, with a view to reducing the liability (the reserve) in future periods during which the company may struggle. The practice results in smoothing of income over time.

LESSON 2: CONTEXT FOR ASSESSING FINANCIAL REPORTING QUALITY

LOS 33d: Describe motivations that might cause management to issue financial reports that are not high quality. Vol 6, pp 583–584

CONTEXT FOR ASSESSING FINANCIAL REPORTING QUALITY

In assessing financial reporting quality, it is important to consider (1) whether a company's management may be motivated to issue financial reports that are not of high quality, and (2) whether the reporting environment is conducive to misreporting.

Motivations

Management may issue financial reports that are not of high quality:

- To mask poor performance, such as loss of market share or lower profitability than other companies in the industry.
- To meet or beat analysts' forecasts or management's own forecasts. Exceeding forecasts typically increases the company's stock price (at least for the short term) and can increase management compensation if it is linked to company and/or stock price performance. Motivations to meet earnings expectations can be classified as:
  - Equity market effects, which refer to management trying to build credibility with market participants and to positively impact the company's stock price.
  - Trade effects, which refer to management trying to improve the company's reputation with customers and suppliers. Trade effects are particularly important for small companies.
- To address managers' concerns regarding their careers. Managers may be concerned that working for a company that is struggling would affect their future career opportunities adversely. Surveys of managers that have exercised accounting discretion to achieve desirable earnings goals have actually found that managers tend to be more concerned about career implications of reported results than with incentive compensation implications.
- To avoid debt covenant violations. Managers of highly leveraged unprofitable companies can be motivated to inflate earnings to get around debt covenant violations.

LOS 33e: Describe conditions that are conducive to issuing low-quality, or even fraudulent, financial reports. Vol 6, pp 584

Conditions Conducive to Issuing Low-Quality Financial Reports

Generally speaking, the following three conditions exist when low-quality financial reports are issued:

- Opportunity: Poor internal controls, an ineffective board of directors, or accounting standards that allow divergent choices and/or provide minimal consequences for inappropriate choices can give rise to opportunities for management to issue low-quality financial reports.
- Motivation: Motivation to issue low-quality financial reports can come from personal reasons (e.g., increasing bonus payments) or corporate reasons (e.g., alleviating concerns about being able to raise funds in the future).
- Rationalization: This is important because individuals need to justify their choices to themselves.

LOS 33f: Describe mechanisms that discipline financial reporting quality and the potential limitations of those mechanisms. Vol 6, pp 584–590

Mechanisms that Discipline Financial Reporting Quality

Markets: Companies compete for capital, and the cost of capital is directly related to the level of perceived risk (including the risk that a company's financial statements will be misleading). In the absence of any other conflicting incentives, companies should aim to provide high-quality financial reports to minimize their long-term cost of capital.

Regulatory authorities: Market regulators establish and enforce rules. They directly affect financial reporting quality through:

- Registration requirements: Companies that plan to issue securities must register them with market regulators before offering them to the public. Registration documents must include current financial statements, relevant information about the risks and prospects of the issuing company, and information regarding the securities being offered.
- Disclosure requirements: Publicly traded companies are required to make periodic financial reports (with management comments) available to the public.
- Auditing requirements: Financial statements must be accompanied by an audit opinion certifying that presented financials conform to relevant accounting standards.
- Management commentaries: Financial reports issued by publicly traded companies must include statements by management including a review of the company's business and description of principal risks and uncertainties facing the company.
- Responsibility statements: Person(s) responsible for the company's filings are required to explicitly acknowledge responsibility and to attest to the correctness of financial reports.
- Regulatory review of filings: Regulators usually undertake a review process to ensure that companies have followed all rules.
- Enforcement mechanisms: Regulators are granted various powers to enforce securities market rules. Examples of these powers include assessing fines, suspending or permanently barring companies, and bringing criminal prosecution against companies.

Auditors

While public companies are required to have their financial statements audited by an independent auditor, private companies also obtain audit opinions regarding their financial statements, either voluntarily or to meet requirements imposed by providers of capital.

Limitations of audit opinions:

- An audit opinion is based on information prepared by the company, so if a company deliberately intends to deceive its auditor, a review of provided information might not uncover misstatements.
- An audit is based on a sample of information, and the sample might not reveal any misstatements.
- An "expectations gap" may exist between the auditor's actual role and what the public perceives the auditor's role to be. Typically, the aim of an audit is not to look for fraud; it is to verify that financial reports are fairly presented.
- Audit fees are often established through a competitive process, and the company being audited bears the cost of the audit (audit fees). As a result, the auditing company may show leniency toward the company being audited, particularly if it provides additional services to the company.

Parties that have a contractual agreement with a company have an incentive to monitor the company's performance and to ensure that financial reports are of high quality. For example, consider the following provisions:

- Loan agreements contain covenants that, if violated, can result in a technical default of the borrower.
- Certain investment contracts contain provisions that enable the investor to recover all or part of its investment if certain financial triggers occur.

Such provisions can motivate borrowers/investees to manipulate reported results to avoid unfavorable repercussions, and this possibility for misreporting in turn motivates lenders/investors to monitor financial reports and ensure that they are of high quality.

LESSON 3: DETECTION OF FINANCIAL REPORTING QUALITY ISSUES

LOS 33g: Describe presentation choices, including non-GAAP measures that could be used to influence an analyst's opinion. **Vol 6, pp 590–595**

DETECTION OF FINANCIAL REPORTING QUALITY ISSUES

Presentation Choices

During the technology boom of the 1990s and the internet bubble of the early 2000s there were companies that were trading at extremely high P/E ratios, and the earnings they were generating could not justify their (extremely high) stock prices. As a result, many market participants tried to justify these valuations based on new metrics such as "eyeballs captured" or the "stickiness" of websites. Further, various versions of "pro forma earnings" or "non-GAAP earnings measures" were commonly reported during those times.

Pro forma reporting was also employed by several established companies in the early 1990s. For example, IBM reported massive restructuring charges in 1991 ($3.7 billion), 1992 ($11.6 billion), and 1993 ($8.9 billion) as it moved its focus from mainframe computers to personal computers; Sears incurred restructuring charges worth $2.7 billion in 1993; and AT&T reported restructuring charges of $7.7 billion in 1995. Further, restructuring charges were quite the norm during those times. Companies were keen to avoid giving the impression that they were struggling, so under the pretext of assisting investors in evaluating operating performance, they would conveniently exclude restructuring charges in pro forma measures of financial performance.

Reporting of pro forma earnings was also facilitated by the accounting principles that applied for reporting business combinations. Before 2001, there were two methods for accounting for acquisitions: (1) the pooling-of-interests method, which is no longer permitted, and (2) the purchase method.

- While it was fairly difficult to qualify for using the pooling-of-interests method, it was greatly desired because it did not result in goodwill amortization charges going forward.
- On the other hand, the purchase method entailed significant goodwill amortization charges (potentially over a 40-year period), resulting in lower earnings over an extended period.

Companies that were making acquisitions aggressively and using the purchase method felt that they were at a reporting disadvantage compared with companies that were able to apply pooling-of-interests accounting. Therefore, these companies began to present earnings excluding amortization of intangible assets and goodwill.

EBITDA (earnings before interest, taxes, depreciation, and amortization) has been widely used by investors to make comparisons across companies on a consistent basis, as it eliminates the impact of the different accounting methods that companies may use for depreciation, amortization of intangible assets, and restructuring charges. As a result of the popularity of this measure, companies have come up with their own definitions of EBITDA (sometimes referring to it as adjusted EBITDA) by conveniently excluding more items from net income. Some of the items that tend to be excluded to manipulate reported performance are:

- Rental payments for operating leases, resulting in EBITDAR (earnings before interest, taxes, depreciation, amortization, and rentals).
- Equity-based compensation. Exclusion of this (normal operating expense) is usually justified on the grounds that it is a noncash expense.
- Acquisition-related charges.
- Impairment charges for goodwill or other intangible assets.
- Impairment charges for long-lived assets.
- Litigation costs.
- Loss/gain on debt extinguishments.

There is a general concern that companies may use non-GAAP measures to distract users from GAAP measures. U.S. GAAP and IFRS have both moved to pacify these concerns. For example, under U.S. GAAP, if a company uses a non-GAAP financial measure in an SEC filing, it must (1) display the most directly comparable GAAP measure with equal prominence, (2) provide a reconciliation of the non-GAAP measure and the equivalent GAAP measure, and (3) explain why it believes that the non-GAAP financial measure provides useful information regarding the company's financial condition and operations. IFRS places similar requirements on companies. Example 3-1 describes a case of misuse and misreporting of non-GAAP measures.

Example 3-1: Misuse and Misreporting of Non-GAAP Measures

Groupon is an online discount merchant. In the company's initial S-1 registration statement in 2011, its CEO said that the company did not measure itself "in conventional ways." He described Groupon's adjusted consolidated segment operating income (adjusted CSOI) measures (see Exhibit 3-1). The company also provided a reconciliation of CSOI to the most comparable U.S. GAAP measure (see Exhibit 3-2).

In its review, the SEC took the position that online marketing expenses were a recurring cost of business. Groupon responded that the marketing costs were similar to acquisition costs, not recurring costs, and that it would ramp down marketing just as fast as it ramped it up, reducing the customer acquisition part of its marketing expenses over time.

Eventually, and after much negative publicity, Groupon changed its non-GAAP measure (see Exhibit 3-3).

Exhibit 3-1: Groupon's "Non-GAAP Financial Measures"

Disclosures from June S-1 Filing

Adjusted CSOI is operating income of our two segments, North America and International, adjusted for online marketing expense, acquisition-related costs and stock-based compensation expense. Online marketing expense primarily represents the cost to acquire new subscribers and is dictated by the amount of growth we wish to pursue. Acquisition-related costs are **nonrecurring noncash items** related to certain of our acquisitions. Stock-based compensation expense is a **noncash item**. We consider Adjusted CSOI to be an important measure of the performance of our business as it **excludes expenses that are noncash or otherwise not indicative of future operating expenses**. We believe it is important to view Adjusted CSOI as a complement to our entire consolidated statements of operations.

Our use of Adjusted CSOI has limitations as an analytical tool, **and you should not consider this measure in isolation or as a substitute for analysis of our results as reported under GAAP**. Some of these limitations are:

- Adjusted CSOI does not reflect the significant cash investments that we currently are making to acquire new subscribers.
- Adjusted CSOI does not reflect the potentially dilutive impact of issuing equity-based compensation to our management team and employees or in connection with acquisitions.
- Adjusted CSOI does not reflect any interest expense or the cash requirements necessary to service interest or principal payments on any indebtedness that we may incur.
- Adjusted CSOI does not reflect any foreign exchange gains and losses.
- Adjusted CSOI does not reflect any tax payments that we might make, which would represent a reduction in cash available to us.
- Adjusted CSOI does not reflect changes in, or cash requirements for, our working capital needs.
- Other companies, including companies in our industry, may calculate Adjusted CSOI differently or may use other financial measures to evaluate their profitability, which reduces the usefulness of it as a comparative measure.

Because of these limitations, **Adjusted CSOI should not be considered as a measure of discretionary cash available to us to invest in the growth of our business**. When evaluating our performance, you should consider Adjusted CSOI alongside other financial performance measures, including various cash flow metrics, net loss and our other GAAP results.

Exhibit 3-2: Groupon's "Adjusted CSOI"

Excerpt from June S-1 Filing

The following is a reconciliation of CSOI to the most comparable U.S. GAAP measure, "loss from operations," for the years ended December 31, 2008, 2009, and 2010 and the three months ended March 31, 2010 and 2011:

(in $'000)	Year Ended December 31			Three Months Ended March 31	
	2008	2009	2010	2010	2011
Loss (income from operations)	(1,632)	(1,077)	(420,344)	8,571	(117,148)
Adjustments:					
Online marketing	162	4,446	241,546		179,903
Stock-based compensation	24	115	36,168		18,864
Acquisition-related	—	—	203,183		—
Total adjustments	**186**	**4,561**	**480,897**		**198,767**
Adjusted CSOI	**(1,446)**	**3,484**	60,533		81,619

Exhibit 3-3: Groupon's CSOI

Excerpt from Revised S-1 Filing

The following is a reconciliation of CSOI to the most comparable U.S. GAAP measure, "loss from operations," for the years ended December 31, 2008, 2009, and 2010 and the nine months ended September 30, 2010 and 2011:

(in $'000)	Year Ended December 31			Nine Months Ended September 30	
	2008	2009	2010	2010	2011
Loss (income from operations)	(1,632)	(1,077)	(420,344)	84,215	(218,414)
Adjustments:					
Stock-based compensation	24	115	36,168	8,739	60,922
Acquisition-related	—	—	203,183	37,844	(4,793)
Total adjustments	**24**	**115**	**239,351**	**46,583**	**56,129**
Adjusted CSOI	**(1,608)**	**(962)**	(180,993)	**(37,632)**	**(162,285)**

Answer the following questions:

1. What cautions did Groupon include along with its description of the "Adjusted CSOI" metric?
2. Groupon excludes "online marketing" from "Adjusted CSOI." How does the exclusion of this expense compare with the SEC's limits on non-GAAP performance measures?
3. In the first quarter of 2011, what was the effect of excluding online marketing expenses on the calculation of "Adjusted CSOI"?
4. For 2010, how did results under the revised non-GAAP metric compare with the originally reported metric?

Solution:

1. Groupon warned that the "adjusted CSOI" metric should not be used in isolation, it should not be used as a substitute for GAAP results in conducting analysis, and it should not be used as a measure of discretionary cash available to the company to invest in growth.
2. The SEC asserts that online marketing expenses were a recurring cost of business (they appear in every period reported and are likely to be incurred going forward). Exclusion of this item from reported adjusted CSOI goes against SEC requirements.
3. The exclusion of online marketing expenses amounting to $179,903 resulted in adjusted CSOI being inflated. In fact, the amount was significant enough to swing the company from a loss to a profit and it enabled the company to show results that 35% higher for the quarter (adjusted CSOI = $81,619) compared to the whole of 2010 (adjusted CSOI = $60,553).
4. Groupon's revised CSOI for 2010 shows a negative CSOI of $180,993 compared to a positive adjusted CSOI of $60,553. Online marketing expenses are included in the revised measure, in line with SEC requirements.

LOS 33h: Describe accounting methods (choices and estimates) that could be used to manage earnings, cash flow, and balance sheet items.
Vol 6, pp 596–613

Accounting Choices and Estimates

In the text that follows, we highlight areas where accounting choices and estimates have an impact on how various accounting elements (assets, liabilities, owners' equity, revenues, and expenses) are recognized, measured, and reported. In the LOS that follows, we provide guidance regarding what investors and analysts must do to find warning signs.

Revenue Recognition

- Does the company recognize revenue upon shipment (referred to as FOB shipping point) or upon delivery (referred to as FOB destination) of goods? Under the former, revenue (and associated profit) is recognized upon dispatch of goods, while under the latter, revenue (and associated profit) is recognized later when goods reach the customer.
  - Sometimes management may be pushing shipments out the door (known as channel stuffing) under FOB shipping point arrangements. A company may engage in such a practice to maximize revenue recognized in the current accounting period. The company can push sales toward the end of the accounting period by inducing customers to buy more through unusual discounts, threatening to increase prices in the near term, or even shipping goods that were not actually ordered in the hope that customers would keep them (at worst, customers would return them, but those returns would not be recognized until the next period).
    - If the ratio of accounts receivable to revenues is abnormally high relative to the company's history or its peers, there is a chance that channel stuffing has occurred.
  - At other times, for shipments toward the end of the reporting period, management may set shipping terms as FOB destination. Management may

engage in this practice if there was an overabundance of orders during the current period, and it does not want investors/analysts to get too optimistic.

- A company can reduce its allowance for sales returns as a proportion of sales to reduce expenses and increase profits. A downward revision in the noncollection rate can easily be justified on grounds such as improvement in the economic prospects of clients. The point is that whatever the justification, it would be difficult to prove whether it is right or wrong until significant time has passed. Since proof of reliability of estimates is not available at the time an estimate is made/changed, managers have a readily available means of manipulating earnings at their discretion.
    - Analysts should examine whether the company's actual collection experience has tended to be different from historical provisioning in order to assess the accuracy of the company's provisioning policies.
- If a company participates in "bill-and-hold" transactions (where a customer purchases goods but requests that the goods remain with the seller until a later date), it is possible that it is recognizing fictitious sales by reclassifying end-of-period inventory as "sold but held" through minimal effort and fake documentation (i.e., simply reclassifying inventory as "bill-and-hold" sales).
- If the company uses rebates as part of its marketing approach, changes in estimates of rebate fulfillment can be used to manipulate reported revenues and profitability (similar to allowance for sales returns).
- If the company separates its revenue arrangements into multiple deliverables of goods or services, investors should look out for any changes in the allocation of revenue across the deliverables.
    - For example, consider a company that sells hardware devices and includes a free two-year service contract in the selling price. The company allocates a portion of revenues to the hardware device (which is recognized immediately upon sale) and a portion to the service contract (which it recognizes over the two-year period following the sale). In order to inflate reported revenue and profits, the company could allocate a higher (than historical) percentage of revenue to hardware.
    - This area provides management with great revenue recognition flexibility, while providing very little visibility to investors. In order to pacify any concerns regarding financial reporting manipulation, investors should ask the following questions:
        - Does the company adequately disclose how revenue is allocated across deliverables and how revenue is recognized on each one?
        - If a certain portion of revenue is recognized over time (as in the previous example) do the financial statements show deferred revenues?
        - Are there unusual trends in revenues and receivables, especially relating to cash conversion?

Depreciation Policies Regarding Long-Lived Assets

- Companies can use changes in depreciation estimates (useful life and salvage value) and depreciation methods to manipulate reported earnings and profits. As was the case with estimates relating to sales returns, choices and estimates relating to depreciation are not proven right or wrong until far into the future, while they can be manipulated to have an immediate impact on earnings.
- If the company has recorded significant asset write-downs in the recent past, it may suggest that the company's policies relating to asset lives need to be examined.

Capitalization Policies Relating to Intangibles

- In classifying a payment made, management must determine whether the payment will benefit the company only in the current period (making it an expense) or whether it will benefit the company in future periods (in which case it should be capitalized as an asset). Management may try to capitalize costs that ought to be recorded as expenses to increase reported income (as was the case with WorldCom).
- In accounting for an acquisition, the purchase price must be allocated to different assets acquired based on their fair values. These fair values are not always objectively verifiable. Management may use low fair-value estimates in order to depress future depreciation expense and inflate future profitability. Further, any excess of the purchase price over the fair value of assets acquired must be classified as goodwill, which is neither depreciated nor amortized in future periods. A higher allocation to goodwill will improve reported financial performance going forward.
- Goodwill reporting brings further avenues for manipulation. Since it is neither depreciated nor amortized, companies must determine whether goodwill (i.e., the excess of the purchase price over the fair value of assets) is recoverable. If it is not, goodwill must be written-down. In order to determine the fair value of goodwill, forecasts of future financial performance must be made, and these projections may be biased upward to avoid a goodwill write-down.
- Analysts should also examine how the company's capitalization policies compare with the competition and determine whether its amortization policies are reasonable.

Inventory Cost Methods

As we learned in the Reading on inventories, the inventory cost flow assumption chosen by management affects the income statement and the balance sheet. In a period of rising prices and stable or increasing inventory quantities:

- LIFO COGS is greater than FIFO COGS, which results in greater profitability under FIFO.
- FIFO EI is greater than LIFO EI, which results in greater liquidity/solvency under FIFO.
- Note that regardless of the trend in prices:
  - FIFO provides a more current picture of ending inventory value, so the balance sheet is more relevant under FIFO.
  - LIFO captures replacement costs more accurately in COGS, so the income statement is more relevant under LIFO.
- Analysts should determine how a company's inventory methods compare with others in its industry.
- If the company uses reserves for obsolescence in its inventory valuation, unusual fluctuations in this reserve might suggest that the company is manipulating them to attain a desired level of earnings.
- If a company uses LIFO in an inflationary environment, it can temporarily increase reported profits through LIFO liquidation (where sales exceed purchases over the period, enabling the company to dip into old units of stock carried at old, lower prices, thereby deflating COGS).

Deferred Tax Assets and Valuation Accounts

As we learned in the Reading on taxes, a company that incurs losses can carry those losses forward to reduce taxable income in the future, thereby reducing its tax liability in the future. In order to recognize these deferred tax assets, there must be an expectation that the company will generate enough taxable income in the future. Otherwise the value of these tax assets must be reduced through a contra asset account known as the valuation allowance.

- Analysts must evaluate whether the company's estimate of the valuation allowance is reasonable given its current operating environment and future prospects. Specifically they should:
    - Determine whether there are contradictions between the management commentary and the allowance level, or the tax note and the allowance level. For example, there cannot be an optimistic management commentary and a fully reserved tax asset (zero tax asset net of the valuation allowance), or vice versa.
    - Look for changes in the tax asset valuation account. It may be 100% reserved at first, and then management may become more "optimistic" whenever an earnings boost is needed. Recall that an increase in deferred tax assets (lowering the valuation allowance) decreases income tax expense and increases net income.

Warranty Reserves

Analysts should examine whether these reserves have been manipulated to meet earnings targets. Further, the trend in actual costs relative to amounts allocated to reserves should be assessed, as it can offer insight into the quality of products sold.

Related Party Transactions

If the company engages in extensive dealings with *nonpublic* companies that are under management control, the nonpublic companies could be used to absorb losses (e.g., through supply arrangements that are unfavorable to the nonpublic company) in order to improve the public company's reported performance.

Choices that Affect the Cash Flow Statement

Many investors scrutinize the operating section of the cash flow statement in detail, as they believe that operating cash flow serves as a reality check on earnings; significant earnings that can be attributed to accrual accounting and are unsupported by actual cash generation may indicate earnings manipulation. Even though the operating section of the cash flow statement is more insulated from management manipulation than the income statement, it can still be managed in the following ways:

Stretching out payables: Management may try to delay payments to creditors until after the balance sheet date so that the increase in accounts payable over the period (source of cash) results in an increase in cash generated from operations. In order to detect this issue, analysts could:

- Examine changes in working capital to look for unusual patterns that may indicate manipulation of cash provided from operations.

- Compare the company's cash generation with the cash operating performance of its competitors.
- Compare the relationship between cash generated from operations and net income. Analysts should be concerned if cash generated from operations is less than net income, as it may suggest that accounting estimates are being used to inflate net income.

Misclassifying cash flows: A company may misclassify uses of operating cash flow into the investing or financing section of the cash flow statement to inflate cash generated from operating activities.

Taking advantage of flexibility in cash flow statement reporting:

- In certain areas where investors may not even be aware that choices exist (e.g., amortization of discount/premium on capitalized interest), accounting standards offer companies the flexibility to manage cash generated from operations to a certain extent.
- Certain jurisdictions offer significant flexibility in classification of certain cash flows. For example, under IFRS:
  - Interest paid can be classified as operating or financing cash flow.
  - Interest and dividends received may be classified as operating or investing cash flow.
  - Dividends paid may be classified as operating or financing cash flow.

LOS 33i: Describe accounting warning signs and methods for detecting manipulation of information in financial reports. Vol 6, pp 613–618

WARNING SIGNS

Warning Signs Related to Revenue

Analysts should:

- Determine whether company policies make it easy to prematurely recognize revenue by allowing use of FOB shipping point shipping terms and bill-and-hold arrangements.
- Determine whether a significant portion of revenues comes from barter transactions (which are difficult to value properly).
- Evaluate the impact of estimates relating to the company's rebate programs on revenue recognition.
- Look for sufficient clarity regarding revenue recognition practices relating to each item or service delivered under multiple-deliverable arrangements of goods and services.
- Determine whether the company's revenue growth is in line with its competitors, its industry, and the overall economy.
- Determine whether receivables are increasing as a percentage of sales. This may suggest channel-stuffing activities or even recognition of fictitious sales.
- Determine whether there are any unusual changes in the trend in receivables turnover and seek an explanation for any changes.

- Compare the company's receivables turnover (or DSO) with competitors, and look out for suggestions that revenues have been recognized prematurely or that the provision for doubtful accounts is insufficient.
- Examine asset turnover.
  - If post-acquisition revenue generation is weak, management may try to play with estimates to increase reported revenue in order to be able to justify their strategic choices.
  - If asset turnover is trending lower, or if it lags the asset turnover of competitors, it may signal future asset write-downs by the company.

Warning Signs Related to Inventories

Analysts should:

- Compare growth in inventories with competitors and industry benchmarks.
  - If inventory levels are increasing with no accompanying increase in sales it could suggest (1) poor inventory management or (2) inventory obsolescence. In case of the latter, current profitability and inventory value would be overstated.
- Compute the inventory turnover ratio.
  - Declining inventory turnover could also suggest inventory obsolescence.
- Check for inflated profits through LIFO liquidations (only applicable for firms using LIFO).

Warning Signs Related to Capitalization Policies and Deferred Costs

Analysts should examine the company's accounting policy notes for its capitalization policy for long-term assets (including interest costs) and for its handling of other deferred costs, and compare those policies with industry practice. If the company is the only one capitalizing certain costs while other industry participants expense them, a red flag is raised.

Warning Signs Related to the Relationship between Cash Flow and Income

If a company's net income is persistently higher than cash provided by operations, it raises the possibility that aggressive accrual accounting policies have been used to shift current expenses to later periods. Analysts may construct a time series of cash generated by operations divided by net income. If the ratio is consistently below 1.0, or has declined consistently, there may be problems in the company's accrual accounts.

Other Potential Warning Signs

Depreciation methods and useful lives: As discussed earlier, the choice of depreciation methods, useful lives, and salvage values of long-lived assets can have a significant impact on reported profitability. Analysts should compare a company's policies with those of its competitors to determine whether they are significantly different.

Fourth-quarter surprises: Analysts should suspect possible earnings management if a company's earnings routinely disappoint in the first three quarters of the reporting period and then spring a positive surprise in the fourth quarter, if the business is not seasonal.

Presence of related-party transactions: Related-party transactions are often an issue when company founders are still involved in its day-to-day running, and have their own wealth and reputations tied to the company's performance. For example, they may (through another company of their own) purchase unsellable inventory from the company in order to avoid write-downs.

Nonoperating income and one-time sales included in revenue: A company may engage in such behavior to cover weak revenue growth, or to boost reported revenue growth. If undetected, analysts would overestimate the sustainability of company revenues.

Classification of an expense as nonrecurring: This would inflate reported operating profits. If the same "special items" are classified as nonrecurring by the company year after year, analysts would be better off focusing on net income rather than operating profit.

Gross/operating margins out of line with competitors or industry: While this could signal superior management performance, it may also indicate the presence of accounting manipulation. The point is that it is a sign that further analysis is required.

Younger companies with an unblemished record of meeting growth projections: While it is completely possible for a young company with popular products to generate impressive returns for a period of time, analysts should keep in mind that as the industry matures, the company may be tempted to extend its record of rapid growth in sales and profitability by using aggressive estimates, drawing down cookie jar reserves, selling assets for accounting gains, or window-dressing financial statements.

Management has adopted a minimalist approach to disclosure: Analysts should be concerned when large companies only have one reportable segment, or when management commentary is similar from period to period. While a plausible explanation for providing minimal guidance could be protecting investor interests by keeping information from competitors, this may not necessarily be the case.

Management fixation on earnings reports: Analysts should be wary of companies whose management is obsessed with reported earnings, as this may be to the detriment of real drivers of value. Fixation with earnings could be indicated by:

- Aggressive use of non-GAAP measures of performance, special items, or nonrecurring charges.
- Decentralized operations where management compensation is heavily tied to reported earnings or non-GAAP performance measures.

Other factors that analysts should consider include:

The company's culture: Management with a highly competitive mentality would serve investor interest well when it comes to conducting business (as long as it does not take actions that are illegal or unethical), but analysts should assess whether such a min-dset also exists when it comes to preparing financial statements. A predisposition to manage earnings is more likely to exist when:

- The CEO also serves as the board chair.
- The audit committee of the board lacks financial reporting sophistication and is subservient to the CEO.
- When the CEO is not penalized (and instead may even be rewarded) for exercising financial reporting discretion to artificially smoothen earnings.

Restructuring and/or impairment charges: At times, it has been observed that a company's stock price rises upon recognition of a "big bath" charge against current income. The rationale is that management has identified and parted with underperforming portions of the company, and has shifted its attention to more profitable activities. Analysts, however, should appreciate that the restructuring charge suggests that expenses reported over prior years were probably understated (even if no financial statement manipulation occurred) and therefore make appropriate (downward) adjustments to prior years' earnings.

Management has a merger and acquisition orientation: Consider Tyco International Ltd., a company that acquired 700 companies in the period 1996–2002. The SEC found that Tyco was consistently fraudulently understating assets acquired in order to lower future depreciation and amortization charges, and overstating liabilities assumed. The point is that a growth-at-any-cost strategy can create issues when it comes to operational and financial controls.

Note that these warning signs are **signals**, not declarations of accounting manipulation. They should be evaluated cohesively, not on an isolated basis. If an analyst finds several warning signs, the particular investment should be viewed with skepticism and perhaps discarded in favor of other alternatives.

LESSON 1: EVALUATING PAST FINANCIAL PERFORMANCE AND PROJECTING FUTURE PERFORMANCE

LOS 34a: Evaluate a company's past financial performance and explain how a company's strategy is reflected in past financial performance. Vol 3, pp 629–637

An analysis of a company's past performance should address *what* happened (how well the company performed over the period) and also *why* it happened (the reasons behind its performance). Analysis should focus on:

- Important changes that have occurred in corporate measures of profitability, efficiency, liquidity, and solvency and the reasons behind these changes.
- Comparisons of the company's financial ratios with others from the same industry and the reasons behind any differences.
- Examination of performance aspects that are critical for a company to successfully compete in the industry and an evaluation of the company's performance on these fronts relative to its competitors'.
- The company's business model and strategy and how they influence its operating performance.

A company's strategy is usually reflected in its financial statements. Some examples of different strategies across companies and how we might expect their financials to differ are given below:

Low cost airlines like Southwest® focus on generating profits through high volumes with low margins. Others, like Silverjet® (an exclusively business class airline) cater to high-end customers only. While Silverjet's sales volume (in units) would be significantly lower than Southwest's, Silverjet's gross margin should be higher as it offers a premium service.

McDonald's® initially concentrated on building its business within U.S. borders. Over recent years, it has focused more on increasing sales outside the United States. This strategy is reflected in McDonald's financial statements, in the form of a higher sensitivity of total profits to changes in the value of the dollar. For example, foreign-exchange gains helped boost McDonald's profitability in early 2008 (when the dollar depreciated against most currencies) as a significant portion of revenues came from its international (non-U.S.) operations.

The bigger, well-known pharmaceutical companies in the developed world (e.g., Glaxo Smith Kline® and Sanofi Aventis®) devote significant amounts of money to R&D to come up with vaccinations and medications to tackle various illnesses more effectively. They invest so much in R&D because they are able to obtain patents for their products, which protect them from competition from imitators and allows them to set prices high enough to generate profits. Other companies (e.g., Dr. Reddy's Laboratories®) focus on simply producing generic drugs whose patent-protection periods have expired. The ASP (average selling price) of Dr. Reddy's products is lower than that of its Western counterparts, but it relies on high volumes to generate profits.

In the year 2004, Motorola® revamped its cellular phone business and came out with a revolutionary thin cell phone called the Razr®. Motorola's heavy investment in R&D in previous years paid off as it saw sales not only rise due to the increase in the size of the cell phone market, but also because of a significant increase in its individual market share. In subsequent years, Motorola rolled out a greater quantity of lower-priced phones, which reduced its ASP, but continued to fuel an increasing market share, especially in more cost-conscious emerging markets. The high sales volume of lower-priced handsets hurt gross profit margins, but did help sales and profit growth.

In the year 1994, Apple Inc. identified itself in its prospectus as "one of the world's leading personal computer technology companies." Over time however, the company expanded its product line beyond just personal computers to include other technology products as well. This shift in the company's strategy was evident in Apple's financial statements.

- In 2005, the iPod became Apple's best-selling product, accounting for a third of revenues.
- In 2007, Apple launched the iPhone, and by 2009 the iPhone accounted for 30% of revenues.
- In 2008, with the launch of the iTunes App Store, Apple became the world's largest music distributor.

With the introduction of these revolutionary products:
- The company's gross margins increased from 33% of sales in 2007 to 40% of sales in 2009. Operating profit margins also improved, but to a lesser extent due to the significant advertising expenses (SG&A) required to support differentiation.
- Apple was now not only comparable with other computer manufacturers, but also with mobile phone manufacturers and companies developing competing software and systems for mobile internet devices.
- By the end of 2009 Apple had accumulated nearly $40 billion in the bank (cash and marketable securities). With this "war chest" Apple could undertake large acquisitions or return cash to shareholders in the form of dividends or share repurchases.

LOS 34b: Forecast a company's future net income and cash flow.
Vol 3, pp 637–647

Projections of a company's future financial performance are used to determine the value of the company and to evaluate its creditworthiness.

The top-down approach that is typically used to forecast sales involves the following steps:

- Attain forecasts for the economy's expected GDP growth rate.
- Use regression models to determine the historical relationship between the economy's growth rate and the industry's growth rate.
- Undertake market share analysis to evaluate whether the firm being analyzed is expected to gain, lose, or retain market share over the forecasting horizon.

Once a forecast for sales has been established, income and cash flow can be estimated by using the following methods:

Estimate gross or operating profit margins over the forecasting horizon and apply them to revenue forecasts. Net profit margins are affected by leverage ratios and tax rates, so historical data provides a more reliable measure for gross profit margins. This model tends to be simpler and works well for mature companies that operate in nonvolatile markets. Analysts should still examine the underlying data to identify items that are not likely to occur again in the future (e.g., restructuring charges, sales of business segments and assets, and results of discontinued operations), and remove these transitory items from margin estimates that will be used to make projections.

Make separate forecasts for individual expense items, aggregate them, and subtract the total from sales to calculate net income. This is a very subjective exercise, as each expense item must be projected based on some relationship with sales or another relevant variable. Even more complex models are used for firms with volatile earnings (e.g., oil companies whose earnings have fluctuated significantly with oil prices over the last few years), and those with no significant performance histories (start-ups in new industries characterized by rapid technological change).

To forecast cash flows, analysts must make assumptions about future sources and uses of cash. An example of a typically employed assumption is that noncash working capital as a percentage of sales remains constant. The most important things that an analyst must consider when forecasting cash flows are:

- Required increases in working capital.
- Capital expenditures on new fixed assets.
- Repayment and issuance of debt.
- Repurchase and issuance of stock (equity).

Exhibit 1-1 leads us through a forecasting model that employs fairly straightforward ssumptions.

Exhibit 1-1: Income and Cash Flow Projections

Assumptions

First-year sales	$100
Annual sales growth	20%
COGS as a percentage of sales	30%
Operating expenses as a percentage of sales	55%
Tax rate	30%
Noncash working capital as a percentage of sales	70%
Annual investment in fixed capital as a percentage of sales	5%
Beginning noncash working capital	$75
Beginning cash	$10

	Yr 1	Yr 2	Yr 3	Yr 4	Yr 5
Sales (20% rise every year)	100	120	144	172.8	207.4
Cost of goods sold (30% of sales)	30	36	43.2	51.84	62.21
Operating expenses (55% of sales)	55	66	79.2	95.04	114
Pretax income	15	18	21.6	25.92	31.1
Taxes (30% of pretax income)	4.5	5.4	6.48	7.776	9.331
Net income	10.5	12.6	15.12	18.14	21.77

> $5 can be disinvested from working capital, as the company started with $75 and only requires $70 for the first year of operations.

	Yr 1	Yr 2	Yr 3	Yr 4	Yr 5
Net income	10.5	12.6	15.12	18.14	21.77
Less: Investment in noncash working capital	−5	−14	16.8	20.16	24.19
Less: Envestment in fixed capital	5	6	7.2	8.64	10.37
Change in cash	10.5	−7.4	−8.88	−10.66	−12.79
Beginning cash	10	20.5	13.1	422	−6.436
Ending cash	20.5	13.1	4.22	−6.436	−19.22

> $14 must be invested in working capital in Year 2.

	Yr 1	Yr 2	Yr 3	Yr 4	Yr 5
Cash	20.5	13.1	4.22	−6.436	−19.22
Noncash working capital (70% of sales)	70	84	100.8	121	145.2
Current assets	90.5	97.1	105.02	114.5	125.9

In practice, forecasting includes an analysis of the risks inherent in the forecasts. For the example in Exhibit 1-1, the analyst must assess the impact on income and cash flow if the actual realized values of certain variables significantly differ from the assumptions used in the model.

LESSON 2: ASSESSING CREDIT RISK AND SCREENING FOR POTENTIAL EQUITY INVESTMENTS

LOS 34c: Describe the role of financial statement analysis in assessing the credit quality of a potential debt investment. Vol 3, pp 647–650

Credit risk is the risk of loss from a counterparty or debtor's failure to make a promised payment.

Credit analysis involves evaluation of the 4 "C's" of a company.

- Character refers to the quality of management.
- Capacity refers to the ability of the issuer to fulfill its obligations.
- Collateral refers to the assets pledged to secure a loan.
- Covenants are limitations and restrictions on the activities of issuers.

Financial statements are used to calculate several types of ratios that are used to evaluate the credit risk of a company. The four general categories of items considered are:

Scale and diversification of the business: Larger companies enjoy significant leverage in negotiations with suppliers and lenders. Those with more product lines and a wider geographical reach offer more diversification and have lower credit risk.

Operational efficiency: Firms that earn a higher return on their assets and have better operating and EBITDA margins have lower credit risk.

Stability and sustainability of profit margins: Consistently high profit margins indicate a higher probability of repayment and reflect low credit risk.

Degree of financial leverage: Comfortable levels of cash flow compared to interest payment requirements indicate that a firm is adequately cushioned and should be able to meet debt-servicing requirements comfortably. High ratios of free cash flow to total debt and to interest expense indicate low credit risk.

Example 2-1: Peer Comparison Ratios

Consider the following information regarding two companies operating in the same industry:

	Rex Autos	Roadways Inc.
EBITDA/Average assets	9.2%	6.7%
Debt/EBITDA	3.4	4.1
Retained cash flow to debt	15.8%	7.3%
Free cash flow to net debt	8.2%	1.4%

Which company is likely to be given a higher credit rating?

Solution

Based on the given information, Rex Autos is likely to be given a higher credit rating. This is because it has:
- A higher level of EBITDA relative to average assets.
- Lower level of debt relative to EBITDA.
- Higher retained cash flow relative to debt.
- Higher free cash flow relative to net debt.

> Before calculating these ratios and drawing conclusions, analysts should also evaluate the impact of off-balance sheet debt on the company's leverage. This is discussed later in the reading.

LOS 34d: Describe the use of financial statement analysis in screening for potential equity investments. Vol 3, pp 650–654

Screening is the process of filtering a set of potential investments into a smaller set (that exhibits certain desirable characteristics) by applying a set of criteria. These criteria include financial ratios and other characteristics such as market capitalization and membership of popular indices.

Security selection may be based on top-down analysis or bottom-up analysis.

- Top-down analysis involves identifying attractive geographical and industry segments, and then choosing the most attractive investments from them.
- Bottom-up analysis involves selecting specific investments within a specific investment universe.

Example 2-2 illustrates the use of financial ratios to screen for equity investments.

Example 2-2: Stock Screens

The table below illustrates a simple stock screen:

	Stocks Meeting Criterion	
	Number	**Percent of Total**
P/E < 13	11	22%
Net income/Sales > 0	9	18%
Total debt/Assets < 0.4	18	36%
Dividend yield > 0.4%	12	24%
Meeting all 4 criteria simultaneously	3	6%

Notice the following:
- Certain screens serve as checks on other screens.
  - The first criterion (P/E < 13) aims to select stocks that are relatively cheaply valued.
  - The second (Net income/Sales > 0) and third (Total debt/Assets < 0.4) criteria serve as checks on the results from applying the first criterion.
    - The requirement for net income to be positive serves as a check on profitability. Companies with negative earnings would have a negative P/E ratio, and would therefore find their way through the first screen.
    - The limit on financial leverage serves as a check on financial risk.

- Criteria are often not independent. This results in more stocks passing the set of screens than if the criteria were independent. In this example:
  - If the criteria were completely independent, the number of stocks meeting all 4 criteria would be $(0.22 \times 0.18 \times 0.36 \times 0.24) \times 50 = 0.17$
  - However, the actual number of stocks that meet all 4 criteria is 3.
  - To understand the lack of independence, note that dividend-paying capacity (criterion 4) is linked to the ability to generate positive earnings (criterion 2).

- Analysts must recognize that the application of certain screens can lead to the results of screens being concentrated within certain sectors. In this example, the criterion 3 (limit on financial leverage) will probably result in banking stocks being excluded from the filtered subset.

Growth investors invest in those companies that are expected to see higher earnings growth in the future. A growth investor would set earnings growth and/or momentum screens like a high price-to-cash flow ratio and sales growth exceeding 20% over the last three years.

Value investors try to pay a low price relative to a company's net asset value or earning prowess. A value investor might set screens like a higher-than-average return on equity (ROE) and a lower- than-average P/E ratio to shortlist equity investments that suit her style. Use of screens involving financial ratios is most common among value investors.

Market-oriented investors are an intermediate group of investors who cannot be categorized as growth or value investors.

Analysts evaluate how a portfolio based on particular screens would have performed historically through the process of back-testing. This method applies the portfolio selection rules to historical data and calculates returns that would have been realized had particular screens been used. Back-testing has its limitations in that it suffers from various biases (e.g., survivorship bias, look-ahead bias, and data-snooping bias).

When applying a set of screens to filter investements, analysts must also bear in mind that:
- Inputs to ratios are derived from financial statements. Companies within the analyst's investment universe may differ with respect to (1) the set of standards they subscribe to (**IFRS** vs. **U.S. GAAP**), (2) specific accounting methods permitted within a particular set of standards, or (3) the estimates used in applying a particular accounting method.
- Back-testing may not provide accurate predictions of future performance.
- Implementation decisions (e.g., frequency and timing of portfolio re-evaluation that affect taxes and transaction costs) can dramatically influence returns.

LESSON 3: ANALYST ADJUSTMENTS TO REPORTED FINANCIALS

LOS 34e: Explain appropriate analyst adjustments to a company's financial statements to facilitate comparison with another company. Vol 3, pp 654–669

Analysts often need to make adjustments to a company's financial statements to facilitate comparisons with other companies that use different accounting methods or estimate key accounting inputs differently. Some of these adjustments are described below:

Adjustments related to investments: Investments in securities issued by other companies can be classified under different categories. Unrealized gains and losses on securities classified as "financial assets measured at fair value through other comprehensive income" ("available-for-sale" under **U.S. GAAP**) are not recorded on the income statement. Changes in their values are reflected in other comprehensive income as a part of equity on the balance sheet. Changes in the value of "financial assets measured at fair value through profit or loss" ("trading" under **U.S. GAAP**) are recorded on the income statement and have an impact on reported profits. If an analyst is comparing two firms with significant differences in classification of investments, adjustments for the different financial statement impact of the two classifications would be necessary.

Adjustments related to inventory: A last in, first out (LIFO) company's financial statements must be adjusted to first in, first out (FIFO) terms before comparisons with FIFO companies can be undertaken. Important accounts affected by conversion from LIFO to FIFO are net income, retained earnings, inventory, cost of goods sold (COGS), and deferred taxes.

U.S. GAAP requires firms that use the LIFO inventory cost flow assumption to disclose the beginning and ending balances for the LIFO reserve in the footnotes to the financial statements. The LIFO reserve equals the difference between the value of inventory under LIFO and its value under FIFO. In periods of *rising* prices and stable inventory levels, LIFO EI is *lower* than FIFO EI. Therefore,

$$EI_{FIFO} = EI_{LIFO} + LR$$

where
LR = LIFO Reserve

$$COGS_{FIFO} = COGS_{LIFO} - (\text{Change in LR during the year})$$

Since $COGS_{FIFO}$ is lower than $COGS_{LIFO}$ during periods of rising prices, FIFO gross profits and net income before taxes are greater than their values under LIFO by an amount equal to the change in LIFO reserve. However, net income after tax under FIFO will be greater than LIFO net income after tax by:

$$\text{Change in LIFO Reserve} \times (1 - \text{Tax rate})$$

The year-end balance of the LIFO reserve represents the cumulative difference in COGS between the FIFO and LIFO cost flow assumptions over the years. Cumulative $COGS_{FIFO}$ will be less than cumulative $COGS_{LIFO}$, and consequently, cumulative FIFO gross profits will be *higher*. However, the entire LIFO reserve will not be added to retained earnings when converting from LIFO to FIFO. The LIFO reserve will be divided between retained earnings (increase in equity) and taxes that have been avoided and delayed by recording lower profits under LIFO (increase in deferred tax liabilities).

When converting from LIFO to FIFO assuming rising prices:

Equity (retained earnings) increase by:

> Before calculating these ratios and drawing conclusions, analysts should also evaluate the impact of off-balance sheet debt on the company's leverage. This is discussed later in the reading.

$$\text{LIFO Reserve} \times (1 - \text{Tax rate})$$

Liabilities (deferred taxes) increase by:

$$\text{LIFO Reserve} \times (\text{Tax rate})$$

Recall the following adjustment to inventory on the balance sheet, which would also make the balance sheet balance:

Current assets (inventory) increase by:

$$\text{LIFO Reserve}$$

Example 3-1: LIFO to FIFO Conversion and Analysis

ABC Company uses the LIFO cost flow assumption to value inventory. An analyst wants to convert ABC's financial statements to FIFO to facilitate comparisons with a FIFO company in the same industry. ABC faces a tax rate of 30%. Inventory levels have been stable and prices have gradually risen over the year.

ABC Company
Balance Sheet

	2009 $	2008 $
Gross fixed assets	3,730	1,910
Accumulated depreciation	(1,450)	(1,060)
Net fixed assets	**2,280**	**850**
Long-term investments	**2,500**	**2,500**
Cash	410	160
Receivables	1,900	1,200
Inventory	1,000	1,950
Total current assets	**3,310**	**3,310**
Total Assets	**8,090**	**6,660**
Payables	250	1,890
Short-term debt	130	100
Deferred taxes	600	1,000
Current portion of long-term debt	440	210
Current liabilities	**1,420**	**3,200**
Long-term debt	**1,760**	**830**
Common stock	1,500	1,250
Retained earnings	3,410	1,380
Common Shareholders' Equity	**4,910**	**2,630**
Total Liabilities and Shareholders' Equity	**8,090**	**6,660**
Notes:		
LIFO Reserve	270	225

Income Statement

	2009
	$
Sales	30,650
COGS	(26,000)
Gross profit	**4,650**
Operating expenses	(1,350)
Operating profit	**3,300**
Interest expense	(400)
EBT	2,900
Taxes	870
Net income	2,030

Questions

1. What would ABC's 2009 ending inventory be on a FIFO basis?
2. How much would ABC's COGS for 2009 be on a FIFO basis?
3. What would ABC's net profit be had it used FIFO?
4. What is the cumulative amount of tax savings that ABC has generated by using LIFO instead of FIFO?
5. What amounts would be added to ABC's deferred tax liabilities and retained earnings to convert them to FIFO?
6. Comment on how the following ratios would change if FIFO were used in preparing ABC's account.
   a. Inventory turnover.
   b. Number of days of inventory.
   c. Gross profit margin.
   d. Current ratio.
   e. Debt-to-equity ratio.

Solution

1. $EI_{FIFO} = EI_{LIFO} + LIFO\ reserve$
   $EI_{FIFO} = \$1,000 + \$270 = \$1,270$

2. $COGS_{FIFO} = COGS_{LIFO} - (LR_{ending} - LR_{beginning})$
   $COGS_{FIFO} = \$26,000 - (\$270 - \$225) = \$25,955$

3. FIFO net income = LIFO net income + Change in LIFO reserve × (1 − Tax rate)
   FIFO net income = $\$2,030 + [(\$270 - \$225) \times (1 - 30\%)] = \$2,061.50$

4. Cumulative amount of tax savings from using LIFO = LIFO reserve × (Tax rate)
   Cumulative tax savings = $\$270 \times 30\% = \$81$

   If the company had used FIFO, the additional potential tax liability would amount to $81, which should be apportioned over several years in the future.

5. The cumulative tax savings calculated in part 4 above would be added to deferred tax liabilities. By using LIFO, the company showed higher COGS and consequently lower profits than it would have reported had it used FIFO.

Retained earnings$_{FIFO}$ = Retained earnings$_{LIFO}$ + LIFO reserve × (1 − Tax rate)
Retained earnings$_{FIFO}$ = $3,410 + $270 × (1 − 0.3) = $3,599

6. a. The inventory turnover ratio would be lower under FIFO because when prices are rising, costs of goods sold is lower and ending inventory higher under FIFO as compared to LIFO.
   b. The number of days of inventory would be higher under FIFO because the inventory turnover ratio is lower under FIFO in a period of rising prices.
   c. The gross profit margin would be higher under FIFO because COGS is lower.
   d. The current ratio would be higher under FIFO primarily because ending inventory is carried at a higher cost under FIFO when prices are rising.
   e. The debt-to-equity ratio would be lower under FIFO because retained earnings are higher.

Adjustments related to property, plant, and equipment: A company that uses accelerated depreciation methods and shorter estimated life assumptions for long-lived assets will report lower net income than a firm that employs longer useful life assumptions and uses straight-line depreciation. Depreciation and net fixed asset values must be assessed and necessary adjustments made to bring sets of financial statements on the same footing before making comparisons.

The footnotes to the financial statements provide useful information about a company's long-lived assets and depreciation methods. This information can be used to estimate the average remaining useful life of a company's assets.

Recall that gross fixed assets (historical cost) minus accumulated depreciation equals net fixed assets (book value).

Gross fixed assets = Accumulated depreciation + Net fixed assets

Below, we divide both sides of this equation by annual depreciation expense and assume straight-line depreciation and zero salvage values for all fixed assets.

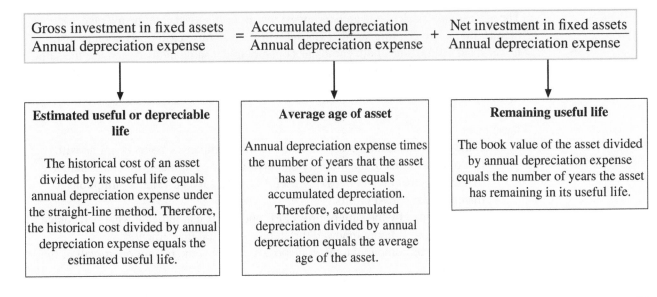

$$\frac{\text{Gross investment in fixed assets}}{\text{Annual depreciation expense}} = \frac{\text{Accumulated depreciation}}{\text{Annual depreciation expense}} + \frac{\text{Net investment in fixed assets}}{\text{Annual depreciation expense}}$$

Estimated useful or depreciable life	Average age of asset	Remaining useful life
The historical cost of an asset divided by its useful life equals annual depreciation expense under the straight-line method. Therefore, the historical cost divided by annual depreciation expense equals the estimated useful life.	Annual depreciation expense times the number of years that the asset has been in use equals accumulated depreciation. Therefore, accumulated depreciation divided by annual depreciation equals the average age of the asset.	The book value of the asset divided by annual depreciation expense equals the number of years the asset has remaining in its useful life.

The calculations of estimated useful life, average age, and remaining useful life are important because:

- They help identify older, obsolete assets that might make the firm's operations less efficient.
- They help forecast future cash flows from investing activities and identify major capital expenditures that the company might need to raise cash for in the future.

In reality, these estimates are difficult to make with great accuracy. Fixed asset disclosures are often quite general, with assets that have different salvage values, depreciation methods, and useful lives often grouped together. However, these estimates are helpful in identifying areas that require further investigation.

Example 3-2: Analysis of Fixed Asset Disclosures

Harton Inc. and Benset Inc. operate in the same industry. An analyst gathers the following information from their fixed asset disclosures.

Harton Inc. (2007)
- Gross fixed assets = $500,000
- Accumulated depreciation = $200,000
- Depreciation expense = $100,000

Benset Inc. (2007)
- Gross fixed assets = $750,000
- Accumulated depreciation = $600,000
- Depreciation expense = $150,000

Calculate the average age, average depreciable life, and remaining useful life of the companies' fixed assets. What conclusions can be drawn from these estimates?

Solution

	Harton	Benset
Average age	200,000/100,000 = 2 years	600,000/150,000 = 4 years
Average depreciable life	500,000/100,000 = 5 years	750,000/150,000 = 5 years
Remaining useful life	300,000/100,000 = 3 years	150,000/150,000 = 1 year

The age estimates calculated above suggest that Benset's assets are, on average, older than Harton's. We can forecast that Benset will need to raise cash fairly soon to invest in newer fixed assets. Since both companies operate in the same industry and use the same depreciation method, we would expect the average depreciable lives of their assets to be similar.

Please note:

- If the calculated average depreciable life of a company's assets is in line with that of other firms in the industry that use similar equipment, we can conclude that management is not tweaking useful life and salvage value assumptions to manipulate reported profits.
- Capex divided by the sum of gross PPE and capex can indicate what percentage of the asset base is being renewed through new capital investment.
- Capex can be compared to asset disposals to gain some insight on growth of the asset base.

Adjustments related to goodwill: Goodwill is recognized when the price paid for the target company in an acquisition exceeds the fair value of the target's net assets. When a company that grows via acquisitions (and recognizes goodwill on acquired companies) is compared to a firm that grows internally, the former will have higher reported assets and a greater book value even if the real economic values of the two companies are identical. Analysts must remove the inflating effect of goodwill on book value and rely on the price-to-tangible book value ratio to make comparisons.

Example 3-3: Ratio Comparisons for Goodwill

The following information relates to two companies, Alpha and Beta:

	Alpha ($m)	Beta ($m)
Total market capitalization	70	110
Shareholders' equity	75	120
Goodwill	30	20
Other intangible assets	55	60

Based on the above information:

1. Calculate the P/B ratio for both companies.
2. Calculate the P/B ratio adjusted for goodwill for both companies.
3. Calculate the price/tangible book value ratio for both companies.
4. Given that the industry average P/B multiple is 3.49 and the average price/tangible book value ratio is 4.23, comment on the ratios for the two companies.

> Tangible book value equals book value reduced by all intangible assets (including goodwill).

Solution

1. Alpha's P/B ratio = 70/75 = 0.93
   Beta's P/B ratio = 110/120 = 0.92

2. Alpha's P/B ratio adjusted for goodwill = 70/(75 − 30) = 1.56
   Beta's P/B ratio adjusted for goodwill = 110/(120 − 20) = 1.1

3. Alpha's Price/Tangible book value ratio = 70/(75 − 30 − 55) = Not meaningful (negative)
   Beta's Price/Tangible book value ratio = 110/(120 − 20 − 60) = 2.75

4. Based on the P/B ratios, both companies appear to be selling at a significant discount to the industry average P/B multiple.

   Looking at the P/B ratios adjusted for goodwill, Beta appears to be selling for a lower price relative to book value than Alpha.

   Although Beta's price/tangible book value ratio is mathematically higher than that of Alpha, it is still lower than the industry average of 4.23. Alpha has a negative tangible book value, which makes its price/tangible book value ratio meaningless. Based solely on this information, Alpha appears to be relatively expensive compared to Beta.

Adjustments related to off-balance sheet financing: If classified as an operating lease, the lease is treated as a rental contract (with rent expense recorded on the income statement and no asset or liability recognized on the balance sheet). In contrast, if classified as a capital lease, the lessee records the asset and associated liability on its balance sheet. When a lease confers all the risks and benefits of ownership on the lessee but is still accounted for as an operating lease by the lessee, the arrangement gives rise to off-balance sheet financing. As the following example illustrates, off-balance sheet financing arrangements improve reported solvency ratios.

Example 3-4: Analysis of Lease Disclosures

ABC Company has significant future commitments under finance and operating leases. Presented below is selected financial statement information:

	Year	Capital $	Operating $
	2009	1,500	4,500
	2010	1,500	4,000
	2011	1,500	4,250
	2012	1,500	5,000
	2013	1,500	5,250
	2014	1,850	4,750
	2015	1,850	4,800
	2016	1,850	4,800
	2017	2,000	3,500
	2018	2,000	3,200
Minimum future lease payments		17,050	44,050
Less: Total interest amount		7,116.34	
Present value of minimum lease payments		9,933.66	

1. Calculate the implicit rate used to calculate present value of minimum lease payments.
2. Why is this implicit rate important in evaluating the company's leases?
3. If operating leases were to be classified as capital leases, what additional amount would be recognized on the balance sheet under lease obligations?
4. What would be the effect on the debt-to-equity ratio of treating all leases as finance leases?

Solution

1. The rate implicit in the lease is the discount rate that equates the present value of future lease payments to the given present value ($9,933.66). It is equivalent to the internal rate of return (IRR) of the cash flow stream. In this example, the rate equals 10.5%.

2. The rate implicit in the lease is important because it is used to determine the present value of lease obligations (liability), the value of the leased asset on the balance sheet, interest expense, and the lease amortization schedule. Companies may use higher implicit rates to report lower debt levels. The validity of the rate used by the company can be evaluated by comparing it to the rates used by comparable firms and considering recent market conditions.

3. If the operating leases were treated as finance leases, the present value of lease payments would be recognized as an asset and a liability. The present value of operating lease obligations equals $26,798 (using the 10.5% implicit rate).

4. Debt levels rise when operating leases are recognized on the balance sheet. Therefore, the debt-to-equity ratio rises (worsens).

Note that another way to estimate the PV of operating lease payments that do not appear on the balance sheet is to assume that the ratio of discounted to undiscounted operating lease payments is the same as the ratio of discounted to undiscounted capital lease payments. In this example, the ratio of discounted to undiscounted capital lease payments is 58.26% (= 9,934/17,050). Therefore, the PV of future operating lease payments can be estimated as 58.26% of 44,050, which equals $25,664.

Aside from the balance sheet adjustments described above, analysts must also perform the following adjustments to the income statement when reclassifying an operating lease as a capital lease:

- Rent expense (recognized under an operating lease) must be eliminated. Typically, rent expense when performing this adjustment is estimated as the average of two years of rent expense.
- Interest expense is added. Interest expense is estimated as the interest rate times the present value of operating lease payments.
- Depreciation is added. Depreciation is estimated on a straight-line basis for the number of years of future lease payments.

Example 3-4: Effect on Coverage Ratio for Operating Lease Adjustments

Consider the following information:

	Alpha Inc.	Beta Inc.
EBIT before adjustment	1,540	1,235
Reported interest expense	210	150
Operating lease payments:		
For the year 2010	100	30
For the year 2011	80	20
Present value of lease obligations	440	115
Number of lease payments remaining	8	8
Average interest rate on debt	7%	11%

Based on the given information, calculate the interest coverage ratios for both companies before and after adjusting for operating leases.

Solution

Interest coverage ratio = EBIT / Interest expense

Interest coverage ratios before adjusting for the operating leases are calculated as:

Alpha's interest coverage ratio = 1,540 / 210 = 7.33
Beta's interest coverage ratio = 1,235 / 150 = 8.23

Adjusting the income statement to reflect financial performance under a capital lease requires us to assume that the asset acquired under the lease was purchased (with borrowed funds) rather than rented. Under this assumption:

- There will be no rent expense (so we will need to add it back to EBIT).
- Depreciation expense will have to be charged against the asset (so we will need to deduct it from EBIT).
- Interest expense will have to be charged on the liability (so we will need to add it to reported interest expense).

These adjustments are made in the following table:

	Alpha Inc.	Beta Inc.
EBIT before adjustment	1,540	1,235
Add back: Rent expense[1]	90	25
Less: Depreciation expense[2]	55	14.38
EBIT after adjustment	1,575	1,245.63
Interest expense before adjustment	210	150
Assumed cost of interest on lease obligation[3]	30.80	12.65
Interest expense after adjustment	240.80	162.65

[1] Alpha's rent expense = [(100 + 80) / 2] = 90
[2] Alpha's depreciation expense = 440 / 8 = 55
[3] Alpha's assumed cost of interest on lease obligation = 440 × 7% = 30.80

Interest coverage ratios after adjusting for the operating leases are calculated as:

Alpha's interest coverage ratio = 1,575 / 240.8 = 6.54
Beta's interest coverage ratio = 1,245 / 162.65 = 7.65

Notice that the interest coverage ratios for both companies have declined. These adjusted coverage ratios reflect the increased obligations associated with the operating leases.